D0328827

THE MEASURE OF MANAGEMENT

designing organizations for human effectiveness

ELIOT D. CHAPPLE

President of the E. D. Chapple Company, Inc.

LEONARD R. SAYLES

Professor of Management, Graduate School of Business, Columbia University

NEW YORK THE MACMILLAN COMPANY

First Printing

Library of Congress catalog card number: 60-6654

The Macmillan Company, New York
Brett-Macmillan Ltd., Galt, Ontario

Printed in the United States of America

PREFACE

We have tried to write a book about organizations and their management practices which would be useful to the executive as well as to the student and scholar. Although business is the focus of our interest, we hope that persons interested in the operations of government agencies, hospitals, and educational institutions will also find the conclusions relevant. Since every executive has to come to grips with the problems of organizing and maintaining an on-going "business," this is not a volume exclusively for the industrial relations or organization specialist. Executives in marketing or engineering and in production or research must solve almost identical problems concerning the management of their human resources.

With the growing interest in management as a profession have come attempts to develop a science of management. Unfortunately, these efforts most frequently concentrate on purely technical decision-making (e.g., operations research) or treat human problems of organization primarily as psychological issues. Only limited attempts have been made to solve organization problems through the use of measurement. In the future we believe that the criterion of effective management will be its ability to achieve the same degree of sophistication in this area that it has achieved in such fields as finance and engineering.

Controversies have raged within the social sciences over how organizations ought to be studied. In this book we have based our approach on the results of a number of years of research in the field of human interaction. The advantage of using this method is that it allows us to make unambiguous (operational, observational) statements about the behavior of people in time and space.*

Only recently, perhaps as a result of growing disillusionment with and

* Related research has been done by George Strauss, at Buffalo; Melville Dalton, at California; Peter Blau, at Chicago; Conrad Arensberg, at Columbia; William Whyte and Frank Miller, at Cornell; George Homans, Paul Lawrence, and Abraham Zaleznik, at Harvard; Margaret Chandler, at Illinois; George Saslow and Joseph Matarazzo, at Oregon; Charles Walker and Robert Guest, at Yale; and F. L. W. Richardson.

many rebuttals to the "human relations movement," executives have become aware that a great deal of what they have been accepting as scientific fact is not based on unequivocal research. Both privately and in print, strong doubts have been expressed about many of the assertions of "leadership" studies, certain aspects of psychological testing, and the "principles" of organization.

By measurement, we mean something other than what has come to be common usage in the social sciences. In default of facing the realistic fact that the advance of knowledge in the physical sciences has been due to the kinds of measurements of length, duration, temperature, with which we are all familiar and which by definition require that every unit is interchangeable, many behavioral scientists talk about measurement and the operational approach when these are clearly inapplicable.

Management itself has expended a great deal of ingenuity in developing morale surveys, performance and job rating scales, psychological tests, and the like. They of course have important uses, but we do not believe that they provide an adequate basis for executive action because they do not describe in unambiguous, operational terms how people will act in given situations.

Thus one of our objectives has been to develop a consistent and generally applicable system of measurement so that the executive can describe the personality of a fellow manager, elements in the organization structure, and the work-flow pattern of his department "in the same language." Since nearly every organization problem requiring solution is a composite of individual, structural, and technical factors, any future science of management must develop such common variables.

This volume is a product of the continuing research interest of the Graduate School of Business in the field of human behavior in organizations. The authors are appreciative of the support given this project by the Faculty Research Fund of the Graduate School of Business of Columbia University. Through their personal interest and encouragement, Dean Courtney C. Brown and Associate Dean Clarence Walton played important roles in this project.

ELIOT D. CHAPPLE
LEONARD R. SAYLES
Morningside Heights

CONTENTS

Preface iii

INTRODUCTION

I Organization Behavior: Knowns and Unknowns 1

PART 1: BUILDING THE ORGANIZATION AND MEASURING ITS PERFORMANCE

II Work Flow as the Basis for Organization Design 18
III Production Standards for Managerial Jobs 46
IV The Development and Use of Organization Controls 60
V Technological Determinants of Work-Group Behavior 79

PART 2: THE INDIVIDUAL, HIS PERSONALITY AND HIS JOB

VI The Man, the Job, and the Organization 98
VII How Managers Can Evaluate Personality 114
VIII The Impact of the Organization on Employee Health 142

PART 3: MANAGING INSTABILITY AND CHANGE

IX Morale: The Measure of Organizational Health 152
X Union-Management Relations and Productivity 170
XI Alternative Approaches to Organizational Change 189

CONCLUSION

XII New Responsibilities for Executives 207

Index 215

CHAPTER I

ORGANIZATION BEHAVIOR: KNOWNS and UNKNOWNS

This book considers how management can better utilize the human resources of the organization. There are many descriptive words used for this area of study: administration, organization, and human relations, to name a few. For the reader who has delved into this field before, recounting these terms may stimulate the reaction: "another one?"

Admittedly, the field is not neglected, stemming in large measure from the universality of the problem. Every organization whether family, business, government, or social must solve the problem of relationships among people. As in the assessment of the adequacy of someone's cooking, all are experts, or at least avid commentators.

Because management has been given such widespread attention, one might assume many of the major questions have been answered so the administrator is able to use tested and established principles and generalizations to handle organizational problems. In this respect, the authors agree with Robert D. Calkins, President of Brookings Institution, who remarked, "It is rather astonishing that we know so little about administration in view of the very extensive literature on the subject and its prevalence and importance in nearly all aspects of modern life." [1]

Whether the problem is deciding if Jones is the man to move into the opening in Department A, if Smith is really doing a good job in the central office, or how many of the new engineers should report directly to Brown, managers are frequently ignorant of how to make the decision and then how to assess its adequacy. In view of the efforts expended, why does this situation exist? To answer this question it is necessary to examine hastily some developments in the interrelated fields concerned with the management of

[1] Robert D. Calkins, "The Decision Process in Administration," *Business Horizons*, vol. 2, no. 3, Fall, 1959, p. 19.

people: production management, organization, human relations, and administration.

Formal Organization Theory

Historically the best work in organization was done by men in the "management movement," as the pioneer industrial engineers were called, but their efforts were impeded because they had no techniques or general principles to apply to the study of organization structure.

Beginning with Frederick Taylor at the end of the last century, industrial engineers have concentrated on studying the jobs of production workers. Time and motion studies were used to simplify the motion paths in each operation and to reduce the amount of time needed. They were also the basis for vast improvements in the technological organization of the work. Industrial engineers annexed the work of the mechanical engineers in technology, a field now known as production management, dealing with the rate of flow, timing and sequence of units of product, management of inventory, and the like. Automatic feeds, high-speed machines, the assembly line, and material handling equipment all are examples of how the flow of work has been rationalized by engineering studies. After establishing standards of productivity for each job, it was possible to develop production scheduling and to bring it to a high degree of efficiency.

The leaders of the management movement also attempted to prescribe for the ills of organization above the level traditionally treated by time and motion study. However, when they found themselves in the administrative area, the tools of their trade were inapplicable. They began to develop the classical theory of organization, made up of rational, logical theorems that have been supplemented by mathematical elaborations in recent years. The preservation of authority was the major objective of most of these organization models. Just as economists sought formulas to preserve competitive pricing and resource allocation with their models of the firm, the industry, and the economy, the organizational theorists sought systems of transmitting orders from the policy maker at the peak of the pyramid to the operator at the bottom. To do this, they specified the limits on spans of control, distinguished staff function from that of the line, and set forth principles such as "authority equal to responsibility" and "one boss per employee." They also prescribed sequences in their effort to substitute reason for impulse: objectives must come before plans, plans before actions, and check-ups after orders.

Organization Charts

The management movement fostered the use of organization charts to define the relations of departments with each other. These were supplemented by job descriptions and standard practice instructions or administrative orders. Some attempt might also be made to indicate what the duties of a department are by a few qualifying terms added to the title. Under the Sales department, for example, there may be such subsidiary functions as "general publicity," "development of new markets," or "advertising." The Engineering department may have as one of its duties "giving advice to customers." Actually, there is overlapping and potential conflict between the two departments in their relationships with customers, and the charts make no attempt to define the limits of these relations. Anyone who has used organization charts knows that the information on them often has little correspondence to the operating realities of the company.

In any sizable company, efforts to show the relations of one department to the others on an organization chart would fail because of the limitations of graphical techniques and the lack of any system to obtain relevant information. The chart would either be covered with a fine network of lines and almost indecipherable or, if all but the direct lines of authority between departments were eliminated, it would be almost useless for anything but decorative purposes.

As a result, most companies supplement the organization chart or replace it with "administrative orders," describing these relationships in words. If these orders lay down general rules for behavior, they suffer because they are not based upon an operating picture of the company but upon what some members of management think it should be. With rare exceptions, the terms are more often wishes than realities. A statement such as "the Sales department will cooperative with the Advertising department, the Service department, and the Order department" merely indicates that there is some sort of relationship between some members of these four departments. However, what it is, when it should take place, and how "cooperate" is defined are left unspecified.

Emergence of Human Relations

The efforts of the production-management-organization specialists in dealing with the human problems of organization left them vulnerable. One of the first groups to take the offensive was the human relations group led by

Elton Mayo and Fritz Roethlisberger at the Harvard Business School. They charged industry with failing to solve its human relations problems because it was overly concerned with purely technical and logical methods of analyzing leadership responsibilities:

> An industrial concern is not only an organization for the promotion of economic purposes; it is also a human organization in which the hopes and aspirations of individuals are trying to find expression. In these terms the leader of an industrial enterprise has two functions to fulfill, an economic function and a social function. First, he has to manufacture and distribute a product at a profit. Second, he has to keep individuals and groups of individuals working effectively together. A great deal of attention has been given [only] to the first function . . . Effective relations between employer and employee largely reside in skills that are personal, empirical, and intuitive—skills which the individual utilizing them cannot make very explicit. Unlike the skills developed in the technological area, they are difficult to communicate. To them science has been little applied.[2]

More recently, the attack was joined by such groups as the Institute for Social Research at the University of Michigan, which claimed that large organizations, following the dictates of scientific management or principles of public administration, were being misled by a machine theory of organization:

> The major criterion of organizational functioning is the efficiency of its operation . . . This machine theory of organization is essentially non-psychological and pays scant attention to the nature of human beings. Error is prevented by recourse to protocol and procedures. Standard operating procedures encourage the assumption that the best method is the following of the rules and regulations. Allied with this is the assumption that most people are essentially alike and that a uniform method will suit all people equally well . . . The machine theory, moreover, is not concerned with human motivation and does not inquire into the relationships between its own principles and procedures and the corresponding motivation and effectiveness of human beings caught up in the system. In fact, it makes the blatantly erroneous assumption that motivation is unrelated to job content, to methods and procedures. It emphasizes standardization, uniformity, and highly limited responsibility.[3]

Almost as a *coup de grâce,* Prof. Chris Argyris argues more pessimistically that a choice must be made between modern corporations and individual mental health because the two are not compatible: "Formal organizational principles make demands of relatively healthy individuals that are

[2] F. J. Roethlisberger, *Management and Morale,* Harvard University Press, Cambridge, Mass., 1946, p. 27.

[3] Daniel Katz and Robert L. Kahn, "Human Organization and Worker Motivation," *Industrial Productivity,* Industrial Relations Research Assn., December, 1951, pp. 152–154.

incongruent with their needs. Frustration, conflict, failure, and short time perspective are predicted as resultants of this *basic incongruency*." [4]

What was the reaction of managers to this onslaught directed at their efforts for efficiency through the logic of scientific management and such military principles as "unity of command"? Not unexpectedly, the steady stream of criticism and dire predictions had its effect.

Aware that the human element did not follow the logical prescriptions of the textbook or the well-thought-through orders from the supervisor, managers tried to soften the bite of authority long before the days of Mayo. At first, this was attempted in a rather naïve fashion. A system totally separate from management was designed to handle the human problems of industry (with the blessing of many experts). Industrial relations departments, counselors, and recreation programs sprang up to service human needs. It was assumed that the two systems could function simultaneously but separately, one part producing the work and the other providing compassion and human responsiveness.

Although there were other sources for the problem, the difficulties first-line supervisors have had in retaining stature and effectiveness in many organizations can be attributed in part to these efforts which made them responsible for the "bad" things (production), while some other group in the organization controlled the "good" things (financial and nonfinancial rewards).

Consequently, newer applications of human relations concentrated on taking the sting out of authority by giving the supervisor some palliatives. While accepting the production system as a firm "given," they advocated supervisory techniques to make engineering decisions more palatable by giving the employee advance knowledge and assurances of his value and job security.

Unquestionably management has moved toward greater concern for the welfare of members of the organization. Although recurring labor shortages after the cessation of immigration, the fear and the actuality of government intervention, and the growth of a strong and widely dispersed union movement must be given substantial credit for improvements in the treatment of employees, enlightened executives now take for granted human relationships as a vital part of management responsibilities. This redefinition of the qualities of a successful business leader is partially a product of the human relations movement.

[4] Chris Argyris, *Personality and Organization*, Harper & Brothers, New York, 1957, p. 74 (italics authors').

The economic position of the subordinate in American industry, whether hourly or managerial, has improved tremendously in recent years. So has his emotional position: fears concerning arbitrary discharge, gross discrimination in company benefits, excessive work loads, and capricious supervision have been eliminated to a significant degree, at least in the larger firms. Adequate redress procedures are provided by both union and company grievance machinery. The situation is still not utopian, but certainly the position of the employee, per se, and the consideration shown his needs, is hardly an underprivileged one.

In an address given at the Columbia University Graduate School of Business, Margaret Mead, the anthropologist, argued with some seriousness that there is no longer a need to worry about the debilitated employee who lacks adequate energies to make his home life a fruitful source of satisfaction. Quite the contrary, it is the "tired father in the office," exhausted from the twin demands of "do-it-yourself" and weekends of "togetherness," who is the problem.

The Present Conflict Surrounding Human Relations

Recently, the surprisingly resurgent forces that stress efficiency and production regrouped and mounted a strong counterattack against the common antagonist: the human relations expert. The basis of this counterreformation is that management cannot ignore responsibilities for profits and work output or does so at great peril. These are the primary goals, and the satisfaction of people in the organization must assume a secondary place. Professor Malcolm McNair of Harvard University has written widely on this theme. One of his clearest statements appeared in *Look* magazine:

> But we have carried this new insight [respecting human relations] so far now that it interferes seriously with getting the world's work done. It encourages people to feel sorry for themselves, to find excuses for failure, to act like children . . . A boss needs to see that an employee does a good, honest day's work. The boss should be able, if necessary, to bring a worker up to that standard without any concern as to whether his childhood was unhappy or whether he is having trouble with his wife.
>
> Many young executives, indoctrinated in human relations, have been so overconcerned with people's problems and excuses that they could not make effective business decisions when they had to. As one business executive admitted to me, "To a very large extent, we in management have become pure, simple, unadulterated hypochondriacs about morale." [5]

Certainly there have been excesses that deserved criticism, and undoubt-

[5] Malcolm P. McNair, "Too Much 'Human Relations'?" *Look*, Oct. 28, 1958, p. 47.

edly these are the stimuli for the most virulent attacks.[6] Some of the most popular writers and lecturers on human relations alternated between impossible extremes. On one hand, the executive was told that management is a complex art and cannot be reduced to a simple formula. Indeed, the successful manager was envisioned as having almost magical qualities enabling him to mold uncooperative, indolent subordinates into a hard-hitting team of high-spirited employees. It was implied that stating these skills explicitly would destroy their potency. Bluntly, an executive either had it or he did not; managerial skill could not be developed.

On the other side of the argument, there were those who also simplified to the point of absurdity. Management was a matter of liking people and getting them to like you. By spending enough time to really get to know his people, an executive could be guaranteed success. Frequently a reservation was added: "Don't get too pushy about productivity; it annoys people."

In the same vein, the emphasis on two-way communications assumed that organizational problems were simply the result of misunderstanding. Jones misinterprets Brown's motives, and Brown does not realize Jones has a different "assumption" or a different "frame of reference."

Given this overly simple definition of the problem, management could appropriately ask why human relations difficulties did not disappear. A ready answer is that human beings are recalcitrant and not easily changed. As a logical extension of the "inadequate understanding" point of view, there was a mushrooming of quasi-therapeutic cures for insensitive, uncommunicative people. These took such numerous forms as group therapy, sensitization training, or nondirective counseling—a whole arsenal of techniques to change the personality. Unfortunately, such a change is expensive and arduous, and the results are usually poor.

Furthermore, the critics of human relations argue that many of these programs open a Pandora's box of ethical questions regarding the use of psychological techniques to persuade, convert, or dissuade employees. The critics declare that most of the programs aimed at improving the leadership qualities of the manager and upgrading his "intuitive" skills in handling communication problems are really efforts to make him more adept at manipulation. Peter Drucker, who is among those fearing this development, states:

> In many cases human relations has been used, or is intended to be used, to manipulate, to adjust people to what the boss thinks is reality, to make them con-

[6] Cf. Malcolm P. McNair, "What Price Human Relations?" *Harvard Business Review*, March, 1957; Ronald Schoen, "Human Relations: Book or Bogle?" *Harvard Business Review*, Nov., 1957; and Robert N. McMurray, "The Case for Benevolent Autocracy," *Harvard Business Review*, Jan., 1958.

form to a pattern that seems logical from the top down, to make them accept unquestioningly what we tell them. Frankly, sometimes I think it is better not to tell employees anything rather than to say, "We tell them everything, but they must accept it, and it is our job to make them accept it." Then why tell them? While the criticism may be ill-informed and carping, and very often purely snide, it has a fundamental validity to it. Our excuse that manipulation doesn't work is not acceptable. The intention is vicious.[7]

Some critics have gone so far as to predict a new feudalism with serflike employees under a leadership spell that binds them to the plant and reduces their participation in a pluralistic society and its trade unions.[8]

The Need for a Middle Road

The preceding text described the prolonged struggle among groups with diametrically opposed points of view toward the problems of organization and administration. They have given "either-or" solutions, almost a Dr. Jekyll and Mr. Hyde approach to the task of management. Persons traditionally interested in production management and formal organization (distinguished in many books from the more "humane" counterpart, informal organization) bear the onus of being concerned with goods, services, and their costs rather than people. The part of Dr. Jekyll is played by the opposition, which concentrates on leniency, morale, and communications. The employee occupies a sort of no man's land in between both groups. Few real skirmishes take place, however, because both sides use different language and are concerned with different variables.

To further complicate matters, there is an arbitrary dividing line within the scientific management field itself. In both present and traditional practice, the design of organizational structure for business is essentially divorced from the design and management of the production process. Two separate professional and academic fields, management and industrial engineering, are involved. The two areas are often taught in separate university departments, making the estrangement more pronounced.

In the schools of business and among executives, organization design starts from the *top* and is concerned with levels of authority, relations of line and staff departments, classification of functions, and problems of decentralization—questions primarily involving middle and upper management. The field of industrial engineering, in both engineering schools and companies, deals

[7] Peter F. Drucker, "Human Relations: How Far Do We Have to Go?" *Management Record,* March, 1959.

[8] Cf. Clark Kerr and Lloyd H. Fisher, "Plant Sociology: The Elite and the Aborigines," *Common Frontiers of the Social Sciences* (ed. Mirra Komarovsky), The Free Press, Glencoe, Ill., 1957, pp. 281–309.

with the factors affecting the flow of work, product design, layout, equipment routing, scheduling, and controls affecting cost, quality, and quantity in addition to its traditional concern with time and motion study and work simplification. These involve the *bottom* of the management pyramid or the level of operating work.

The subject matter of these two fields is not integrated systematically even though production is carried on and managed through the organizational structure. Management frequently sets up the organization structure and makes decisions that change it without giving explicit consideration to the basic work flows the structure is designed to control. The converse is equally true.

As a consequence, each specialty runs the risk of becoming sterile by leaving out the essential factors for which both exist. In the realities of a specific business enterprise, innumerable compromises are made between "proper" organizational design and "proper" engineering practice.

In effect, there are no objective criteria by which to make or evaluate decisions on organizational design, including production management. Although there are rules of thumb that represent the accumulated experience and wisdom of people who necessarily are clinicians, they do not allow predicting with any accuracy the precise effects of a new process, technique, procedure, or the method of controlling the relationships of the individuals involved. Conversely, it is impossible to predict with relative certainty how the use of specific organizational structures will affect the operation of a given production system.

It is a commonplace to say that the organization exists solely to accomplish the job for which it is set up, yet the implications of such a statement have hardly been realized. A comparative study of both simple and complex organizations in American and other cultures clearly suggests that work flow and the administration processes by which it is controlled are fundamental in shaping the realities of the organization viewed as a system of relationships.[9] In this view, which represents the authors' theoretical position, organization is the resultant of the layout, techniques, processes, and controls, or technology in its broadest sense, of the formal structure of authority as represented in charts and manuals of standard operating practice, and of the individual personalities within it.

Thus, the distinction between formal and informal organization, to which so much attention is paid in the literature, is largely an arbitrary one stemming from the academic and professional division of the total organization.

[9] Cf. Eliot D. Chapple and Carleton S. Coon, *Principles of Anthropology,* Holt, Rinehart, and Winston, Inc., New York, 1942.

The data cited in discussions of informal organization from the time of the Western Electric studies to the present have been derived largely from the pattern of relationships produced by the technological constraints of the production system. The conflict that is supposed to exist merely represents the separation of production management and organization into independent fields. It is necessary to enlarge the scope of organization to include all the factors that control the relationships of individuals in the enterprise.

This volume seeks to demonstrate that the job of the manager cannot be divided into compartments. The human relations expert mistakenly considers technology and organization structure as "givens" or areas to be determined by the engineer or organization specialist on the basis of another rule book. Similarly, those interested in technical efficiency, costs, and profits are in error when they imply that people can be taken for granted and that management first of all ought to worry about getting the work out. Organizations can operate only through the coordinated activities of people. In the light of this approach, the fears about the ascendance of the organization man take on a different cast.

The Organization Man: A Real Problem?

Recently a new variation of the old theme that business destroys, or at least eats away, those who come within its grasp has gained popular appeal. The eating-away process used to refer to ethics and morality: caught up in the profit-making system, men who might otherwise have dedicated their lives to unselfish service sought instead a tinnier Holy Grail, the dollar.

Although, as generalizations about an entire system, these condemnations embodied exaggerations, they did sensitize the community to excesses. Quite possibly their harsh repetition is partially responsible for the growing sense of business responsibility and protection against willful discharge and sweatshop servitude.

If this is so, there may be virtue in the new accusation that life in the business organization induces excessive conformity and dependence. Two of the most extensive works on this new critique of business are: William H. Whyte, Jr., *The Organization Man,* and, with a very different point of view, Chris Argyris, *Personality and Organization.*[10]

According to the critics, this new trend is not a matter of converting people into money-grubbing robots or fearful wage slaves, but rather contemporary

[10] William H. Whyte, Jr., *The Organization Man,* Simon and Schuster, Inc., New York, 1956.
Chris Argyris, *Personality and Organization,* Harper & Brothers, New York, 1957.

organizations threaten the psyche. Employees and managers in the large companies are losing their sense of independence and their daring. Instead of devoting themselves to individualistic programs of self-improvement, they are dedicated to the seductive goal of being accepted and liked by the boss and colleagues. These are the organization men.

The fear of losing acceptance is becoming the dominating motive, replacing the more positive goal of conquering new frontiers, the critics argue. They maintain that conforming to the group and kowtowing to the boss absorb energies that might be devoted to constructive improvement of personality, the firm, and the community. The result they predict is a slow but sure destruction of national character.

Perhaps the ready acceptance of these fears is a hallmark of the steady progress in humanizing working conditions and the position of the subordinate. Instead of the callous, overdemanding boss who gets what he wants regardless of the human cost, people are apparently now troubled by his diametric opposite, the group thinker with more concern for social cohesion than profit. Surely the full circle has been made. Less than two decades ago Mayo's concern about the lack of administrators who could remove the sense of individual isolation (or "anomie," the concept he drew from Durkheim) was the accepted tenet of faith.

As more adherents join the band wagon, one is reminded of the extremes of progressive education and child rearing. Not long ago, the school and the home were the villains. Both at the hearth and the blackboard the young were being repressed, their individualism squashed long before it could flower.

The reasoning was much the same: humans flourish best in an unrestricted environment where they are free to do as they please. Fixity of structure, the proponents insisted, must produce rigidity of mind. Like the organization-is-an-inhibitor school of thought, the extremists believed that discipline and controls or externally imposed goals hurt the individual who both desires and needs complete freedom.

Parenthetically, it is worth asking why the concept of an organization man had such wide and immediate appeal? It is a perfect self-rationalization for persons whose success has not measured up to their ambitions. It is reassuring to believe that group thinking and conformity have won over the decision-makers in the large corporations so the distinctive individual cannot get ahead. Some people who use this ready-made excuse confuse the use of such phrases as "teamwork" and "participation" by companies with an actual description of what management expects. Platitudinous company statements concerning objectives, values, or goals may have little resemblance to the types of activities in which it engages. The organization both needs and rewards such distinctive and unique personality characteristics as energy, initiative, and ability to tolerate unfriendly responses. Companies may talk about a good team man, but the uncommon men are the ones who will get ahead and eventually reach the top level positions.

Opposite Findings from Research

Students of human behavior may be amused by this trend in the critique of business because there are no studies that show man in a state of complete independence. In the most primitive societies and throughout history, man has sought and flourished in tribes, clans, communities, and associations. In fact, if half a dozen people are placed in a room with a common task, it can be predicted that they will quickly evolve common behavior routines and even a self-imposed organizational structure.[11] The organization will include leadership to initiate instructions, and the group will penalize deviations from approved standards of behavior. Conformity will be expected and dependence will be readily forthcoming. The street-corner gang, like the office clique, demands conformity in thought and action with an impunity that often makes the routines and demands of the organization mild by comparison.

Men apparently neither want nor have experienced this postulated state of complete autonomy. People have always demanded structure in their lives. With few exceptions, men depend on human relationships, some fixity of structure, routine, and habit to survive psychologically. Although many would hesitate to admit it, most persons flee from a vacuum-like absence of structured relationships. Students of business organization know that a basic problem of management is to find enough people with leadership characteristics to take initiative and operate in a relatively unstructured situation.

Thus, the demand from subordinates for situations in which they can be dependent is frequently the problem, not the overbearing authority. Companies trying to decentralize frequently discover that unwillingness to accept responsibility or to take initiative and the desire to have each decision approved by the boss block successful delegation.

What about the emotional needs of the men on the work level? Extreme divisions of labor and autocratic, dominating supervisors are purported to rob the individual of any real sense of accomplishment and job satisfaction.

Put in different terms, this might also prove to be a misplaced concern.

[11] Cf. William F. Whyte, *Leadership and Group Participation*, New York State School of Industrial and Labor Relations, Bull. 24, Cornell University, Ithaca, N. Y., 1953. Whyte provides a shattering criticism of the traditional group dynamics emphasis on the values to be derived from "leaderless groups."

Many workers voluntarily choose the simplest, most routine, and most subdivided task. Although job enlargement appeals to some, for many it is a threat to the more idyllic assurance of untroubled working hours that are free for daydreaming, conversation, and planning to "beat the rate." Employees do not always seek additional responsibility and decreased dependence.

Successful Organization Requires Patterns

The fate of the individual in the large organization has become a popular subject for contemporary fiction, sermons, and the social sciences. Unfortunately, the eagerness with which the term "organization man" was adopted resulted in substantial confusion. The essence of organization and organizational behavior involves routines. Of necessity, the organization must be a predictable system of human relationships where rhythm and repetition are vital components. This may shock persons who think managers are constantly improvising new activities. Chester Barnard once commented that during a year as President of the New Jersey Bell Telephone Company he had to make only *one* decision that was, in fact, a real choice among alternatives. Although his statement may well be exaggerated, the preponderant elements of organizational behavior consist of such matters as Joe's knowing that he must check Bill's activities two or three times a week, be available if Al gets into trouble, and spend at least an hour a day with his boss to work through plans for the following day. As will be shown in chapters to follow, the combination of work-flow imperatives and personality needs provide the raw material for these predictable and repeated patterns of interaction.

It must be remembered that in speaking of an organization some degree of permanence is implied, that is, the need for predictable repetition, self-maintenance, assured continuity, and regulated activity. The regular routine business of an organization must function properly before individuals can apply, or are likely to be permitted to apply, all their rational, creative talents to the challenge of new problems. Imagination and intellectual vigor cannot prosper if individual energies are fully utilized in handling recurring crises. According to Calkins:

> If administrators are asked to nominate the aspects of the task that are most time-consuming and frustrating to the exercise of their responsibilities, they will agree that they are preoccupied with distractions; with inconsequential little things that push themselves ahead of important issues; with the tyranny of the telephone; with the relentless flitting from one issue to another; with the ceaseless procession of interviews and ceremonials; with the pressure of circumstance and deadlines;

and with the absence of time to collect one's wits, much less to think or reflect. Only a superb or a hard-boiled administrator can cut through this daily morass to concentrate on the important responsibilities that he cannot shirk.[12]

Among the most crucial problems of any organization are the development of predictable routines. Frayed tempers, suppressed or open hostility, and individual frustration resulting from ineffective organization all destroy individual competence.

In other fields in which organization plays a part, the need for predictable routines is taken for granted. Sports are a good illustration. Baseball and football teams are common examples of organizations where the interrelation of the work routines or the plays is dependent upon the adjustment of the players to each other and to the coaches. Complicated plays and split-second coordination cannot be executed unless the individuals in the organization are well adjusted to one another. The coach must see that this is accomplished, select plays that are best fitted to the capacities of his material, and fit together players who can supplement each other's abilities. To develop a smooth-working organization, he must handle personalities skillfully so good teamwork becomes almost second nature. Both experts and fans discuss learnedly whether coach A is getting the most out of his material, whether catcher B can handle his pitchers, or whether star C is wrecking the morale of the team.

Business organizations are like teams but vastly more complicated. The same factors of plays and personalities combine to make an organization, and the day-to-day adjustments determine whether the company has effective coordination or constantly suffers from personnel dissatisfaction, labor disputes, and inefficiency.[13]

Does this necessarily create organization men? Members of outstanding instrumental groups like the Budapest String Quartet have developed almost perfect coordination; they can count on each other for completely predictable behavior. It is doubtful that this has destroyed their individuality. Off the job, in terms of the full development of their personalities and interests, they live different lives. Sometimes great athletic teams have consisted of people who disliked one another intensely and showed this dislike in their personal lives, for instance, in baseball, "Tinker to Evers to Chance." Nevertheless, they learned the skills and routines essential for the successful conduct of their organizational affairs.

[12] Calkins, *op. cit.*, p. 20.

[13] The authors are not indulging in the old stereotype of the company president exhorting his coworkers with, "We're all on the same team, boys," but rather the development and synchronization of a complex set of plays (organization) by which the company operates.

Probably a great deal of the excitement about conformity stems from the absence of knowledge concerning what is required for effective organizational activity. Because people do not know how to assess Jones's contribution to effective management, they evolve irrational fetishes and taboos. Clothing styles, diplomas, tone of voice, automobile, wife, home location, and even testing programs designed to exclude all but the safe pedestrian types are all manifestations of imperfect knowledge on how to evaluate an executive or a new employee. They are not the inevitable products of life in a large organization.[14]

The authors believe the nonsensical elements will disappear as more understanding about methods to improve the mastery of organizational behavior is developed. Fitting personalities together to evolve coordination and sound structure does not necessarily require fixed patterns of thought or of family and community life.

Businessmen must learn to deal with the real problem areas, not those that are easiest to sell during a period when terms like conformity are so popular. The human relations problems of business will not be solved by extreme, sweeping assertions and accusations. It has always been good sport to beat at the sources of institutional power, including business, but sermons must not be confused with science.

The Modern Manager versus the Business Buccaneer

In opposition to the organization man, the old-style business buccaneer is having a renaissance. Even the robber baron has had a resurrection. After all, weren't these the true nonconformists who did not allow codes, public disapproval, or inhibition to stand in the way of their single-minded profit objectives? The contemporary manager, concerned with public and industrial relations and an organizational structure to maximize human effectiveness, casts only a timid shadow by contrast. Or so the critics say.

Actually, it is strange that the contemporary manager is being maligned for his greatest challenge and potential accomplishment. The maintenance of effective human relationships in large-scale organizations is one of the marvels of this age. The administrative skills required to direct and control

[14] The authors readily concede that there are large-scale, contemporary problems here. Mass communications, for example, raise serious questions about opportunities for individual expression. Living with authority, of course, has never been easy. Philosophers undoubtedly will continue to struggle with the problem of freedom versus authority; the balance is always a tenuous one. Life in the presence of other human beings involving cooperative endeavors and government necessitates authority. We must always live with an uneasy balance between the inevitable personal restrictions and our ambivalent needs for both dependence and freedom. But, the problem neither began nor will it end with the corporation.

large numbers of people with different backgrounds and interests and to coordinate their effort toward predetermined objectives pale the achievements of the old business buccaneers. They dealt with a few, simple variables primarily in the market place and their apparent courage and daring was more a product of the simplicity of their problem than extraordinary skills. The diverse and complex responsibilities of modern business are much more of a challenge to human abilities than merely securing maximum personal profits.

Criteria for Good Management

Although the successful manager in the contemporary organization should be complimented, there is still something lacking. In most cases, no one knows why these executives are successful, and the reasons they themselves give are often after-the-fact rationalizations bearing little resemblance to what they really do. A systematic way to provide all managers with techniques for the organization and administration of their enterprises beyond the intuitive skills of successful businessmen is needed. The most vital part of this job, the authors believe, is the development of quantitative criteria upon which to base administrative decisions for the human problems of the organization, i.e., some method of obtaining information about an organization upon which to base managerial decisions. These are essential because management in any reasonably large organization cannot hope to have the same kind of intimate association with its employees that a coach has with his players.

Subjective methods were abandoned long ago in the fields of production and finance. Before a new machine is purchased, the engineers make a careful analysis of its performance, limitations, advantages, operating costs, and its proper place in the total production system. After installation, records are kept of its actual performance, cost, and output. Excellent methods have also been developed to maintain control over the quality of the finished product. Unfortunately, the same thing is not true of organization devices.

No similar analysis is undertaken or believed possible in planning the relations of the people in a newly automated department or fitting a man into the supervisory hierarchy. With few exceptions, management usually hopes people can be persuaded to do anything. Moreover, there is little realization that an objective analysis of a departmental situation is not a one-time process. The amount of teamwork displayed by any organization constantly varies. Although a manager may be satisfied with the teamwork one day, the next day or two months later the organization may not have the same efficiency.

A manager with problems wants techniques and systems that enable him to analyze the facts and predict the outcome of several possible courses of action. Put another way, he wants to know what facts he needs, how they can be obtained, what predictions can be made from them, and how the merits of the predictions can be tested, after he puts his decision into effect. Each one of these steps involves measurement or quantitative assessments rather than descriptive statements. Knowing he has a leadership or a morale problem or that people are not working together effectively does not provide an executive with much useful information. These questions are more to the point: what behavior on the part of supervision, as related to a specific work process, is resulting in certain types of breakdowns? At what point in the work flow? When? Where? How often? For how long? These questions indicate some of the variables that must have quantitative definition if the executive is to learn the dimensions of his problem. Then, he needs some verifiable theories to make predictions on where changes should be introduced and to assess whether the changes actually remedy the problem. But the method of accomplishing these in the process of building an effective organization is the subject matter of the remainder of the book.

Conclusion

This chapter has endeavored to explain the lack of clear, objective criteria for management decision-making on organizational matters by reviewing the struggle between the human relationists and the efficiency experts. Their battle of words has raised this spurious dilemma although productive efficiency and human satisfaction can both be achieved.

The chapters to follow will stress:

1. Management as a profession can be more science than art; intuitive skills can be replaced by learnable techniques of administration.
2. Measurements, providing criteria for management action, are basic to all organization and administration decisions, and human behavior in the organization is quantifiable.
3. The organization of work—technology, methods, and systems—must be undertaken as a preliminary to, and by principles consistent with, the development of the total organization structure and techniques of administration.
4. Hierarchical organizations are not inconsistent with individual satisfaction and development, nor are organization routines and controls necessarily stifling and debilitating to the personality.
5. Human satisfaction and productive efficiency are compatible objectives for a company or any organization.

CHAPTER II

WORK FLOW as the BASIS for ORGANIZATION DESIGN

In a business of any size, decisions that affect its organizational design are made almost daily. Constant changes in technology, markets, and financial conditions impel management to make decisions to keep the company on its course. The personalities of top management also shape the design; as its members come and go, changes are made to suit their private philosophies and their attitudes toward "proper" organization, although such changes are usually rationalized as fitting the demands of internal conflict or external forces.

For guides to decisions on organizational design, a manager has available the writings of experts in the "management movement" or he can call on a present-day consultant. Taken as generalizations from experience, the rules, doctrines, and principles of organization are thought-provoking. They represent the accumulated experience and wisdom of clinicians. Interpreted in the light of a specific problem, they often can help find the way to a solution. Yet, as in the comparable case of clinical medicine, they do not, in fact cannot, provide the precise criteria for diagnosis and therapy.

The medical axiom "Nature is the great healer" applies to organizations as well as to human beings. Far too many triumphs of clinicians stem from the persistence or inertia of the system. Thus, organizations often show extraordinary resistance to poorly considered attempts to change them. Surveys are made, often costing many hundreds of thousands of dollars; new charts and new manuals of procedure are prepared; and orders are issued to put the recommendations into action. Then, frequently within a few months, the enterprise sloughs off its new organizational skin, and only a few of the new titles remain. The expensive reports and manuals are put in an unused file, and the rest is abandoned.

Many organizations, both private and governmental, are reorganized almost yearly and usually by a different set of experts, each with their personal remedies for presumed organizational illness. The human damage is often great. People are fired, resign, or are moved from one end of the country to the other and back again. Yet, the organization holds together. The old habits are soon reestablished if they were ever put aside even temporarily. Employees with such ill-starred companies, which are often in a financially successful market position, soon develop the uneasy caution of the inhabitants of the Great Plains in the tornado season. At the barest tremor of the barometer or the first trace of blackness in the sky, they dive headfirst into the inactive safety of whatever organizational storm cellar they can find.

Toward a Science of Organization

Certainly there is no lack of clinical experience, but what is needed is a science of organization. To do the job, the criteria for decision on which the practitioner can call, as the physician relies on the laboratory to substantiate or overrule his clinical judgment, must be developed. Fortunately, most of the essentials are already at hand, the tools of measurement and accurate observation.

In the approach to be taken to organizational structure, two elements will appear. The technology or flow of work is the major criterion for designing the structure. This contrasts sharply with a well-established tradition of planning the organization from the top down. Secondly, any tendency to group people and activities together simply because they have or involve similar or purportedly similar functional responsibilities is avoided.

Traditionally, the scientific approach in studying any human group considers the environment and the technology developed to adapt to the environment. Each individual operation involves an implement or machine using some sort of power, a sequence of actions to accomplish the task, and possibly the interaction of several people in some kind of team activity. In this sense, the term "implement" can be applied to any object, a sheet of paper, a loom, an accounting machine, or a bulldozer. The products of business, or of any organization for that matter, result from interrelated techniques, some of which are essential and others secondary.

If an entire technique or series of techniques can be performed by a single individual, such as a silver craftsman who sells his wares himself, no organization results. But, if a division of labor occurs, some interaction between technicians must take place, and organization on the work level results. On the production level, a relatively large number of techniques may be linked together to make up the work flow through the plant, with a single owner-manager providing the entire management. If there is only a small number of employees and few demands on his time for other activities (for example, if he subcontracts for a larger corporation on a regular basis), the owner may have a foreman in the shop even though the operation does not require one. The ensuing growth of such enterprises usually comes about rather simply with the owner taking a partner who is often a relative. Then, the management begins to specialize, typically with one man selling and the other overseeing production.

Designing the Structure from the Bottom up

Regardless of the type of business organization—a small retail shop, the trader or merchant acting as intermediary between buyers and sellers, or a bank—a similar elaboration of organization takes place. The division of labor on the work level may involve sales people, clerks recording transactions, or cashiers; as the division of labor proliferates, so does management. The development of specialized managers or of a management division of labor is clearly secondary in the evolution of business to the growth of specialization on the work-flow level. This sequence is of critical importance in designing the organization.

Yet, in many writings about modern business organizations, the prime and determining influence of technological process is lost sight of. In their writings, the designers of the organization, who are perhaps under the spell of a two-dimensional chart, start at the top. Beginning with the directors and the president, they work down, level by level, discussing the functions of the various divisions, considering the relationships of "staff" or "service" departments to the "line," weighing the importance of the "span of control," and defining their graphic representations by referring to the nature of executive authority and responsibility. They may casually mention the first-line supervisor, but what he supervises is usually incidental to their recommendations.

The Tradition of Functional Concentration

Most decisions on "proper" organizational structure are based primarily on similarities of activities or functions. Traditionally, organizations are divided into such major functions as sales, production, finance, and personnel. Each may have subsidiary functions such as engineering, training, market research, inventory control, etc., that, in many companies, compete for equal standing with the others. It is usually recognized, of course, that a common location, product, customer, or specialization may vary the design, but within each divisional setup functional considerations predominate.

If a new function or activity is identified or grows in importance, the question always is, "Who will take it over?" For instance, should sales engineering be assigned to the sales division or engineering? It is an important adjunct in making the sale and helping the sales force bring in business. On the other hand, is it wise to divorce the sales engineers from first-hand involvement in engineering activities? What about sales training, another constant source of conflict? The sales division is sure personnel does not understand what it takes to make a salesman, but the personnel division does have a training department with broad responsibility for the entire corporation. Personnel has the specialized skills and specialists to do the training that salesmen are supposed to be incapable of doing well.

The endless arguments about proper placement of organizational activities are usually only temporarily settled. Because only verbal criteria exist, no one can define a function accurately, and no one wins a conclusive victory. In the meantime, the organization may acquire a cover of charts which, like a turtle's shell, conceal what goes on inside the animal.

Organization Based on Actual Work Flow

Clearly, a different approach to the problem of organizational design is needed. The structure built for members of management can be ignored for the moment to go back to the bottom where the work is done.

This requires looking at the way the technology separates out a series of jobs that must be accomplished if the product is to result. We may manufacture something, buy it for resale, or hire it, as in the case of money, but whatever the business—manufacturing, retailing, banking, or service—we follow certain techniques. There is a beginning, when the process starts, something is done, and the process ends. Put another way, something comes in the door, something is done to it, and it moves on its way out another door to the customer.

In the cases to follow, which are drawn from the authors' field studies, the problems created when the work-flow sequence is not used as a criterion of organizational design, as well as the techniques of analyzing the work process and identifying the work-flow sequences will be examined. By using a comparative point of view, we shall describe a method to isolate some general principles of organization.

CASE 1—*The Sales-Credit Controversy*

In this case, the general sales manager of a manufacturing company was engaged in a major battle with both the credit manager and the treasurer, who was the credit manager's boss. Such conflicts are not rare. Salesmen usually believe the credit department tries to prevent them from making sales, and credit personnel often think the salesmen will sell to anyone, no matter how bad the risk, to get their commissions. This case illustrates the nature of the problem and why management structure and work flow are too often incongruous.

Although interpreted by management as a clash of personalities, the argument between the sales manager and the credit manager stemmed from much more mundane sources. To understand it, it is necessary to look at the actual work flow through their departments and observe the way the work was organizationally split up. The key implement was the salesman's order, which he mailed in to the home office after filling out what the customer required and extending the dollar figures. Figure 2–1*a* illustrates what happened to the order and how the people who handled it were divided between the various functional divisions.

When the office opened in the morning, the mail was sorted in the mail room. Orders were separated and taken immediately by a mail boy to the sales office which occupied one section of the large, open general office of the company, a one-floor layout. There, the clerks checked over the orders to see if there were any special problems of handling shipments or questions raised by the salesmen that might require correspondence. Any order presenting a problem was given to a sales correspondent who wrote to the customer or the salesman, if necessary.

When the sales department completed its work, the order was sent to what was called an order-editing department. This was under the jurisdiction of the factory manager because he superintended warehousing. The orders were checked to see that they were correct, the prices up-to-date, the arithmetic accurate, and the goods in stock at the warehouse nearest to the customer. A copy of the order was sent to another warehouse if the closest one did not have stock. If inventory records showed no stock available, the order editor made out a back-order form to be mailed to the customer.

Then one of the editors would take a batch of orders to the credit department, where credit analysts (clerks) checked the credit ratings to be sure each customer's credit was within the limits set by management. They ascertained whether it was permissible to sell on any other terms than C.O.D. and whether the volume of the order was within the limits of his credit rating. If there was a credit problem, i.e., a deviation, the order was given to a credit correspondent who wrote the customer, with a copy for the salesman, telling him his order could not be accepted and stating the terms,

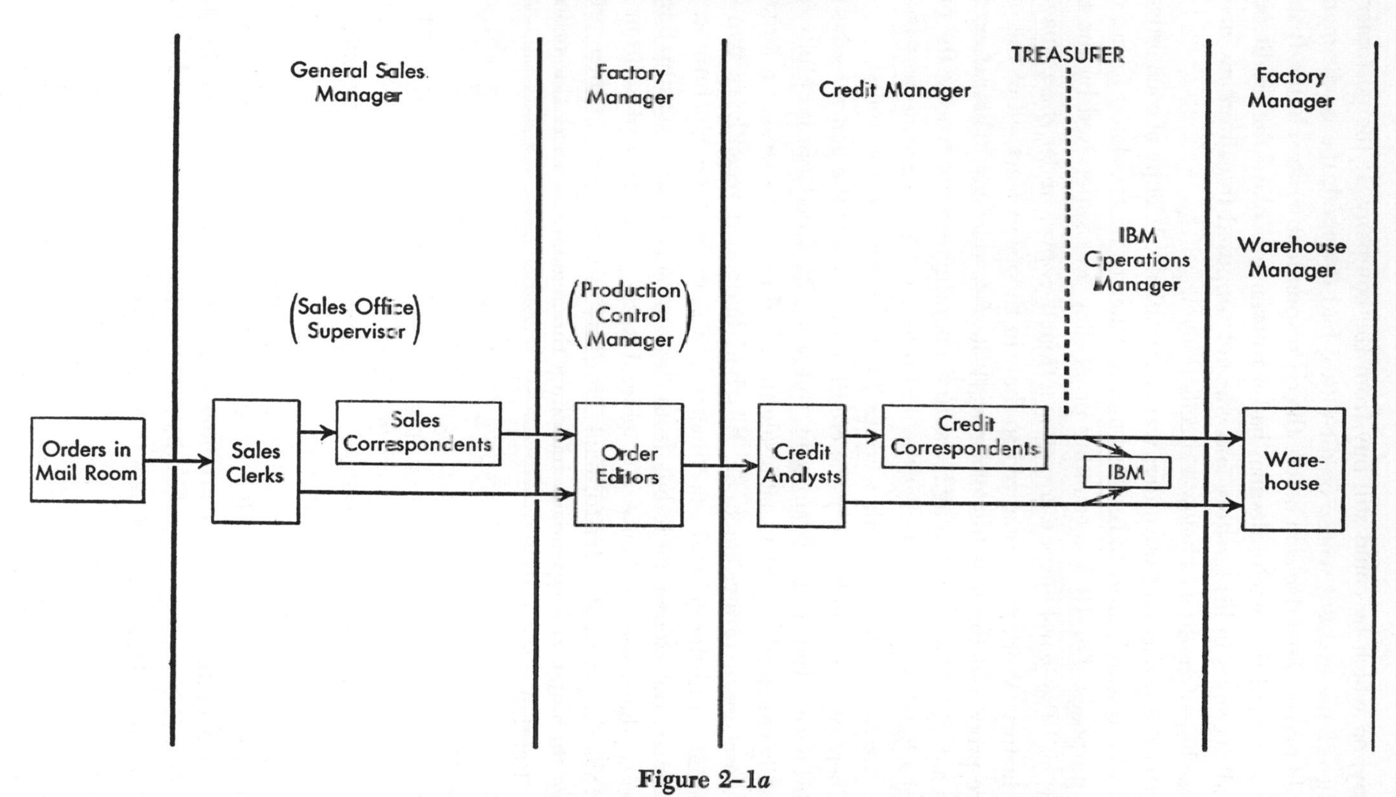
Executive Vice-President
General Sales Manager
Factory Manager
Credit Manager
TREASURER
Factory Manager
(Sales Office Supervisor)
(Production Control Manager)
IBM Operations Manager
Warehouse Manager
Orders in Mail Room
Sales Clerks
Sales Correspondents
Order Editors
Credit Analysts
Credit Correspondents
IBM
Ware-house

Figure 2–1a

if any, on which he could still buy from the company. If the customer was a big-volume account whose credit rating had dropped, the credit manager would make a final decision before the correspondent wrote a letter. It should be mentioned that each salesman had a reference book of the credit ratings for all accounts in his territory and was not supposed to call on any account whose line of credit was below a specified level.

After this processing, the orders were assembled, one copy of each order was sent to the warehouses to be filled and another to be tabulated for accounting purposes. The IBM accounting processing was supervised by the treasurer, and the warehouses were, as mentioned above, under the manager of the factory. Work was organized so that, in theory at least, all of the orders were processed through this office work flow in one day. Thereafter, there was a definite break in timing because accounting did not receive the orders until a batch was completed at the end of each day. The same was true for the warehouses where goods were pulled for shipment and billed.

There was tension between the credit manager and the general sales manager because the credit department, following its procedure faithfully, occasionally canceled an order that a salesman had made, sometimes a large one. Because credit ratings fluctuate, this had happened recently to two large accounts, and the general sales manager was understandably furious. Both customers threatened not to buy from the company again. The situation was more embarrassing because the general sales manager had written each customer a personal letter to thank him for his confidence in their product after the sales correspondent handling the accounts called the orders to his attention.

Reorganization

Now let us look at a series of improvements in the organization. The first and most obvious change in the work flow of handling orders was to reverse the position of the sales and the credit departments. If credit could not be extended, there was no point in checking the accuracy of an order or carrying out the "sales" functions involved. Moreover, this change would prevent recurrences of the kind of embarrassment the general sales manager had undergone. The rearrangement was also more efficient because it eliminated the processing of orders that ultimately would be thrown out. However, it did not deal with more basic issues.[1]

[1] The reader may consider the illogical arrangement of having the credit checked after sales correspondents and order editors worked on an order as an obvious mistake that anyone should have recognized. However, because it was not recognized for many years in a relatively alert company, it reflects the strong attraction of organizing by functional specialty. All the sales activities were put together and handled first, with salesmen con-

As the organization chart (Figure 2–1*a*) indicates, three separate divisional heads, reporting to the executive vice-president, were involved in the movement of a piece of paper and its carbons from one clerical position to another in the general office. Not only were three separate divisions writing to the customer (sales, credit, and the order editor if he issued a back order) but also there was no assurance that there would be any coordination in what each said. Credit correspondents were accused by sales of being too brusque with customers and they, in turn, accused sales of promising too much.

Many other practical problems of management arose. The policy of the company was to clear the orders in a single day. Tight scheduling was sometimes necessary to get the work completed because volume fluctuates. Absenteeism, inadequate performance, or the assignment of other work to the people in a department would upset the even flow of work. If there was disagreement because one department was holding up another, the only recourse when the immediate supervisors could not agree was to settle the dispute on the level of the executive vice-president. Thus, in heated disagreements between the general sales manager and the credit manager, the executive vice-president had to listen not only to complaints about customer relations, but also to all the petty grievances each had about the performance or management of the other.

The difficulty was created when the work flow was divided into separate pieces on the basis of functional similarities. The solution was to put it back together as a single flow under a single supervisor. He would control the entire flow of an order from the time the paper arrived in the mail room until it left the general office to go to the tabulating department or the warehouse as well as credits, payments, and invoices after the billing was completed. He was responsible for individual performance and could move people around to fit the needs of fluctuating volume. He did not have to argue with other divisions on the management of the process. See Figure 2–1*b*.

There was still the problem of functional responsibilities. Sales wanted and deserved some voice in the quality of letters sent to customers. Credit, too, had some legitimate concerns, primarily that company policies regarding credit be followed and any cases not under these policies be referred to higher authority. Both departments outlined standards and procedures that could be carried out by the new department. In this way, representatives of

---

tacting their own departments. Then, and only then, was it time for the next function to begin, in this case, that of the credit department. Unfortunately, the logic of functional organization is rarely challenged in practice.

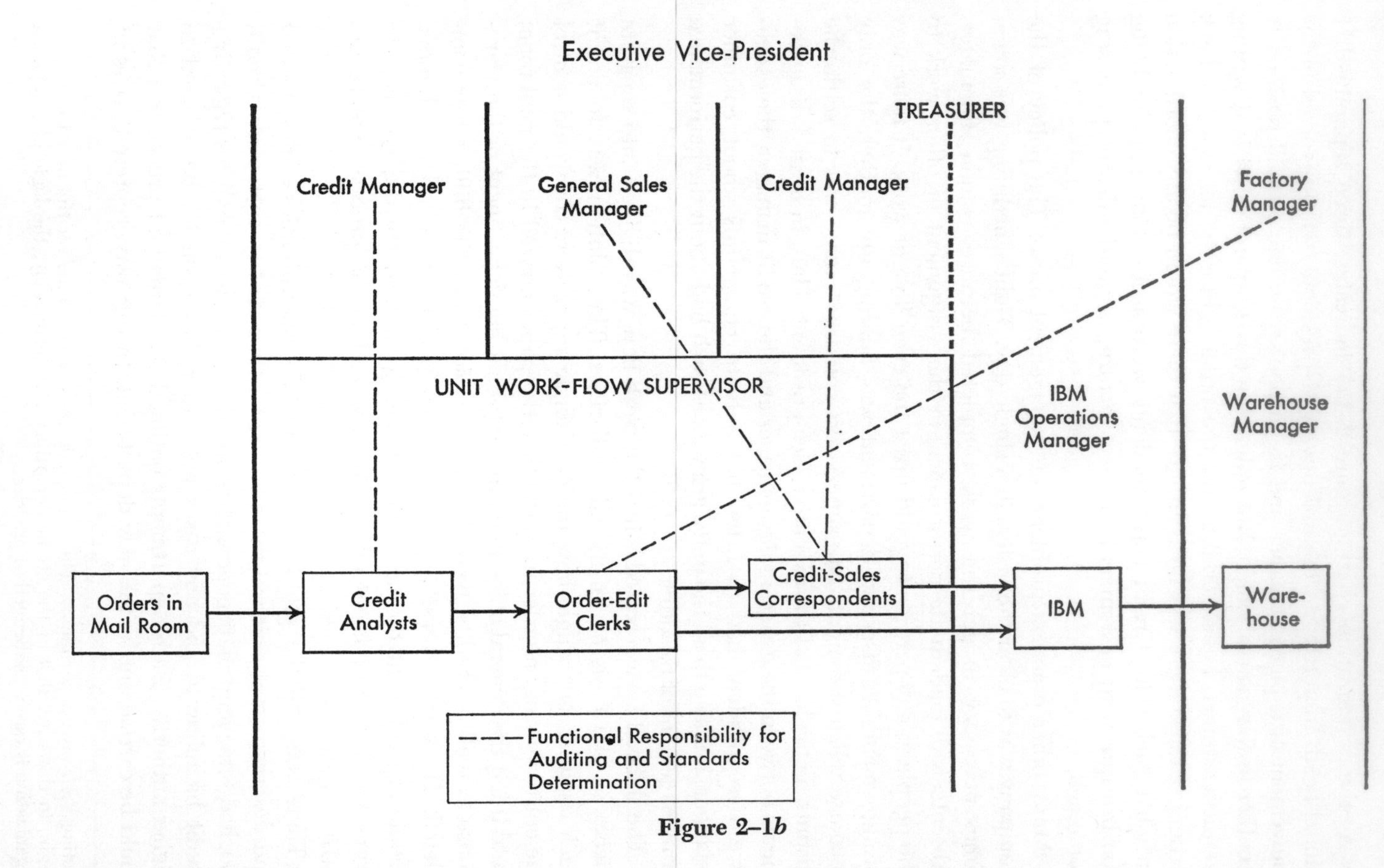
Executive Vice-President
TREASURER
Credit Manager
General Sales Manager
Credit Manager
Factory Manager
UNIT WORK-FLOW SUPERVISOR
IBM Operations Manager
Warehouse Manager
Orders in Mail Room
Credit Analysts
Order-Edit Clerks
Credit-Sales Correspondents
IBM
Ware-house
Functional Responsibility for Auditing and Standards Determination

Figure 2–1*b*

sales or credit would only come into the picture when an exceptional situation required higher-level attention. These procedures also included a periodic auditing program so the sales department could satisfy itself that the correspondents' letters to customers were not antagonistic. The credit department checked that this new work unit only made routine credit decisions and all exceptions needing the credit manager's decision actually got to him. As a result, only one correspondent, a credit-sales-order editing specialist, wrote to each customer although several did identical work. In turn, the correspondent was supervised, together with the clericals handling the proceduralized work flow of the order, by one individual. Credit, sales, and factory set the standards of action for which this single supervisor was responsible.

CASE 2—*Integrating Inspection, Material Handling, and Machine Maintenance*

The case just described has many counterparts in manufacturing organizations. Because work flow is more easily associated with traditional production processes, a typical assembly operation has been chosen. Some of the parts are produced directly from raw materials purchased by the company, and others are purchased from subcontractors. Both types of components are combined into subassemblies and final assemblies. Figure 2–2*a* illustrates the flow of work and the organizational segmentation. The existence of material-handling units between each production unit is typical. They report to the production planning department whose manager reports to the vice-president in charge of manufacturing, rather than to the general superintendent. The inspection units, again reporting through a separate channel of authority to the same vice-president, are less typical. Mechanical maintenance, which also had its own chain of command, was the third specialization organizationally separated from production.

Inspection may appear to be the greatest justification for a separate structure because production people might ignore, or at least slight, the quality problem. On closer examination, however, it could be observed that two types of inspection were really being carried on. As a regular part of the finishing operation, a cursory visual check was given to all products by one group of inspectors. This check was paced identically with the production process itself as another step after finishing. There was also a quality-control procedure handled by other inspectors who followed routine sampling methods, quite distinct from the 100 per cent inspection process.

The first group of inspectors was the source of frequent holdups that seriously aggravated the relationship of production and inspection personnel. In retrospect, the obvious basis for the friction over the complete inspection

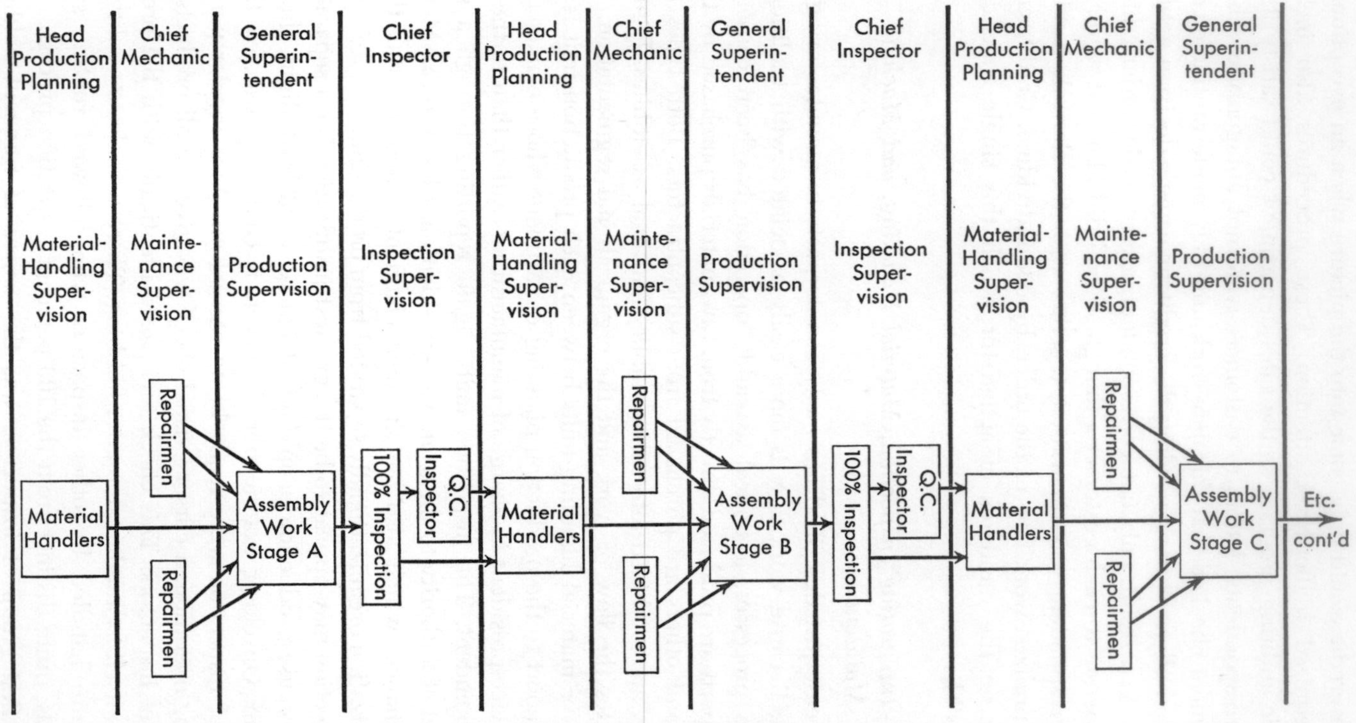
Vice-President – Manufacturing
Head Production Planning
Chief Mechanic
General Superintendent
Chief Inspector
Head Production Planning
Chief Mechanic
General Superintendent
Chief Inspector
Head Production Planning
Chief Mechanic
General Superintendent
Material-Handling Supervision
Maintenance Supervision
Production Supervision
Inspection Supervision
Material-Handling Supervision
Maintenance Supervision
Production Supervision
Inspection Supervision
Material-Handling Supervision
Maintenance Supervision
Production Supervision
Material Handlers
Repairmen
Repairmen
Assembly Work Stage A
100% Inspection
Q.C. Inspector
Material Handlers
Repairmen
Repairmen
Assembly Work Stage B
100% Inspection
Q.C. Inspector
Material Handlers
Repairmen
Repairmen
Assembly Work Stage C
Etc. cont'd

Figure 2–2a

stage can be noted. The source of intramanagement feuds is usually not hard to discover. The 100 per cent inspection stage was clearly an integral part of the finishing work flow. Materials passed through all of the stages, including inspection, at the same rate, or at least were supposed to if production schedules were to be maintained. This meant that the "balancing" problem within this work process was always shuttled back and forth between two separate jurisdictions. Quality-control inspection, on the other hand, involved a different sequence of product movement and had no effect on the flow of work.

The remedial steps were obvious. First, 100 per cent inspection was recognized as a necessary part of the production process and transferred to the general foreman so inspection became merely an audit or visual checking within the production framework. Quality-control inspection, which did not interfere with the flow of work since it was done on a sampling basis, remained where it was. This and other organization changes are illustrated in Figure 2–2*b*.

Matters were made worse by the material–handling department, which supplied the lines with parts on the basis of a schedule set up by production planning to whom the supervisor of material handling reported. The master schedule for the month's production was broken down by weeks and operations planned around it. However, day-to-day and even hour-to-hour upsets would interfere. A key machine went down. The production rate of a given unit was greater, or slower, than expected. The crucial parts needed to keep production moving were not available, and foremen, general foremen, and superintendents were constantly calling each other, and the material–handling supervisors and the production planning department to straighten things out. The constant arguments could only be settled by the vice-president in charge of manufacturing.

The source of the difficulty was twofold: the scope of production planning, that is, the inherent conflict between a master schedule and the day-to-day variation that every factory experiences, was not adequately analyzed, and, more important, the inevitable lack of coordination between the several units making up a single continuous work-flow system.

In a reorganization, the material–handling units were transferred to production. Units that tied together work groups of two foremen were to report to the general foremen. If departments under the supervision of general foremen were involved, the material–handling reported to the superintendents who bridged the general foremen. Production planning was also re-examined to differentiate between day-to-day and long-range scheduling operations.

The factory manager acquired two planners whose sole responsibility was

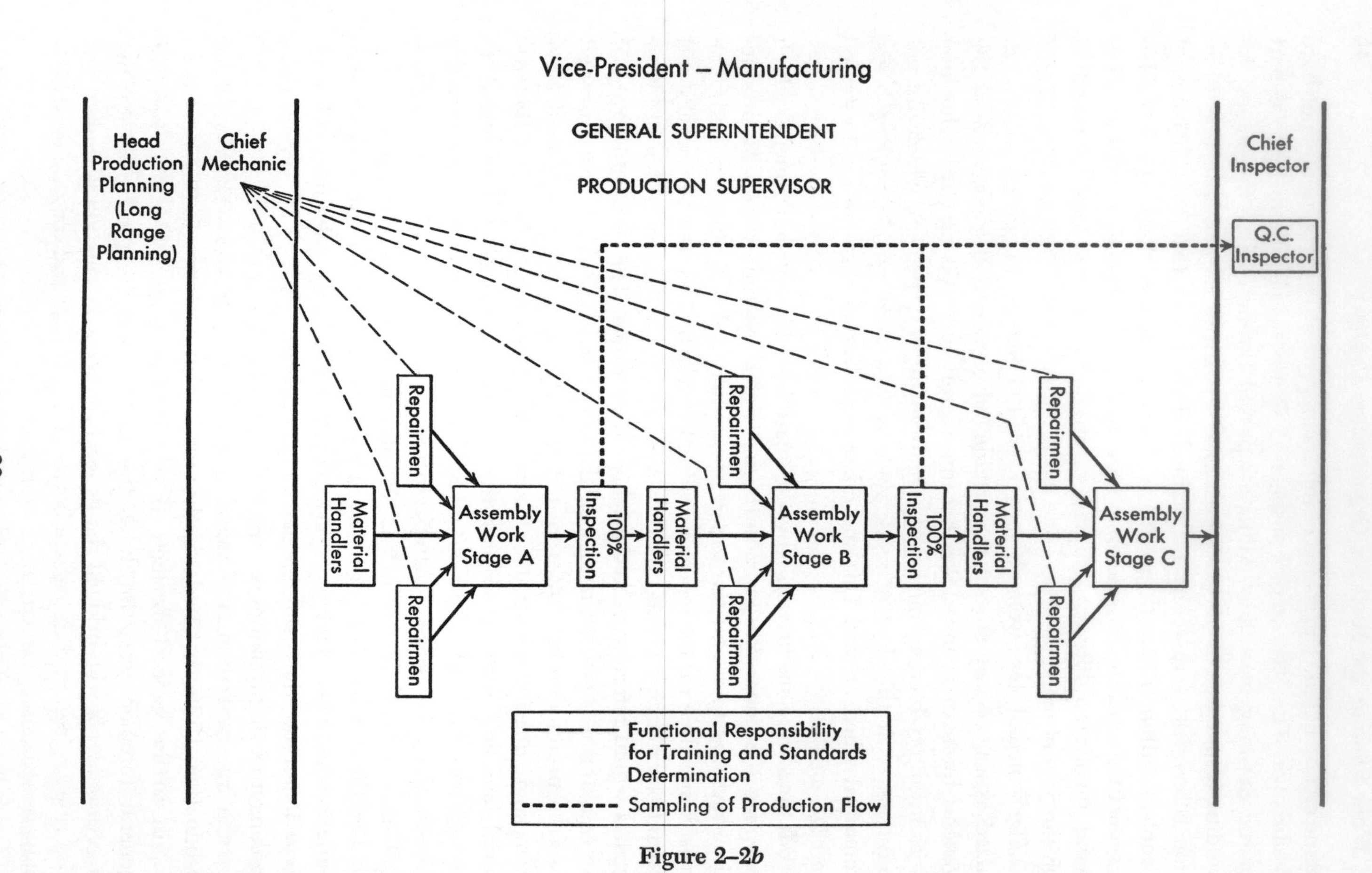
Vice-President – Manufacturing
GENERAL SUPERINTENDENT
PRODUCTION SUPERVISOR
Head Production Planning (Long Range Planning)
Chief Mechanic
Chief Inspector
Q.C. Inspector
Material Handlers
Repairmen
Repairmen
Assembly Work Stage A
100% Inspection
Material Handlers
Repairmen
Repairmen
Assembly Work Stage B
100% Inspection
Material Handlers
Repairmen
Repairmen
Assembly Work Stage C
Functional Responsibility for Training and Standards Determination
Sampling of Production Flow

Figure 2–2b

to control the daily variations and relate them to the long-range schedule, which involved purchasing of parts and raw materials. Thus, control of raw materials, processes, and finished inventories remained unchanged in the organizational structure.

The company was also plagued by a slightly different problem. As the chart in Figure 2–2*a* indicates, the chief mechanic reports to the vice-president in charge of manufacturing, which is traditional functional specialization. The assumption is that placing all the people concerned with mechanical service together in one department leads to more efficient operation and thereby saves money.

But what happened in this case? The floor mechanics, who repaired the machines, worked under their own foremen. The production foreman used a call light to signal for a mechanic when a machine went down. If the mechanic was already working on a machine in another department, the production foreman had to ask the mechanical foreman to take the mechanic off the job he was doing and send him over to the new machine. The mechanics and their foremen usually objected to this even though the whole line might otherwise be held up. The mechanics complained that most of the breakdowns resulted from bad maintenance by the operators and there would be no trouble if the production foremen would make sure their people kept the machines oiled and adjusted. The production foremen countered by saying the mechanics always fixed the wrong machines, had no understanding of production problems, and usually were just stubborn when they insisted on fixing an unimportant machine, i.e., unimportant to the production foreman at the moment. Moreover, the production foremen were constantly arguing among themselves. If all the mechanics were busy in one department and another department needed one, the first-come, first-served principle was not . . . satisfactory to the man with a rush order to get out.[2]

As in the other cases, the heated arguments were complicated by personalities and also had to be settled on the top-management level. No matter how carefully the vice-president tried to get the foremen to agree on a procedure to determine the importance of any machine breakdown and to emphasize preventive maintenance, the foremen usually ended up in his office.

He finally decided the only way to eliminate the stress was to assign mechanics to the general foremen in production and in some instances superintendents. The mechanical department continued to train the me-

[2] Cf. George Strauss, "The Set-Up Man: A Case Study of Organizational Change," *Human Organization,* vol. XIII, no. 2, 1954, pp. 17–25.

chanics in its shops, and set up repair performance standards to make sure each mechanic's work met specifications. Most importantly, however, the assignment of mechanics was controlled by production. As a result, the conflicts ended, and the vice-president was able to devote time to more constructive activities than settling intramanagement rows. In terms of cost, the company was better off than before. Although the original centralization of facilities appeared efficient, no additional mechanics were needed for the reorganization, and it reduced delays in the work flow because of mechanical failure, actually saving money for the company.

So far, the examples of work flow have dealt with the processing of paper or materials through a production line. The final case illustrates how work flow also involves people.

CASE 3—*Handling the Training Function*

The conflict between employment and training is a common problem in many personnel departments. At the simplest level, it is often a matter of scheduling because it is difficult to synchronize recruiting and hiring with the training necessary after the employee is hired. Training activities include both the initial training and indoctrination programs the individual receives before he is sent to a specific department and also on-the-job training that may include a wide range of activities from counseling to sales promotion or educational programs.

Here, the same pattern of functional specialization repeats itself. In this company all training was concentrated organizationally in a single department although the component parts were very different. The initial training program was actually a part of the employment process (Figure 2–3*a*).

Large numbers of applicants applied in person at the employment department where they were given an application form by the receptionist. Those who passed a preliminary interview with a screening interviewer were sent to a systematic employment interview and a clerical stage where all the record forms were filled out. If several departments requisitioned personnel, the newly hired employees were sent to a training class that met the next day. Coordination was necessary if employees were to complete this stage and get on the payroll. When there were delays, some of the newly hired people did not come back because they became discouraged waiting for a class which would qualify them for the job. Furthermore, operating departments became impatient when requisitioned personnel had not been "processed" and were not ready when they were needed.

Within the training department, many pressures competed for the time available. Top management was constantly trying out new programs, some of them on a crash basis, although sometimes an existing program simply

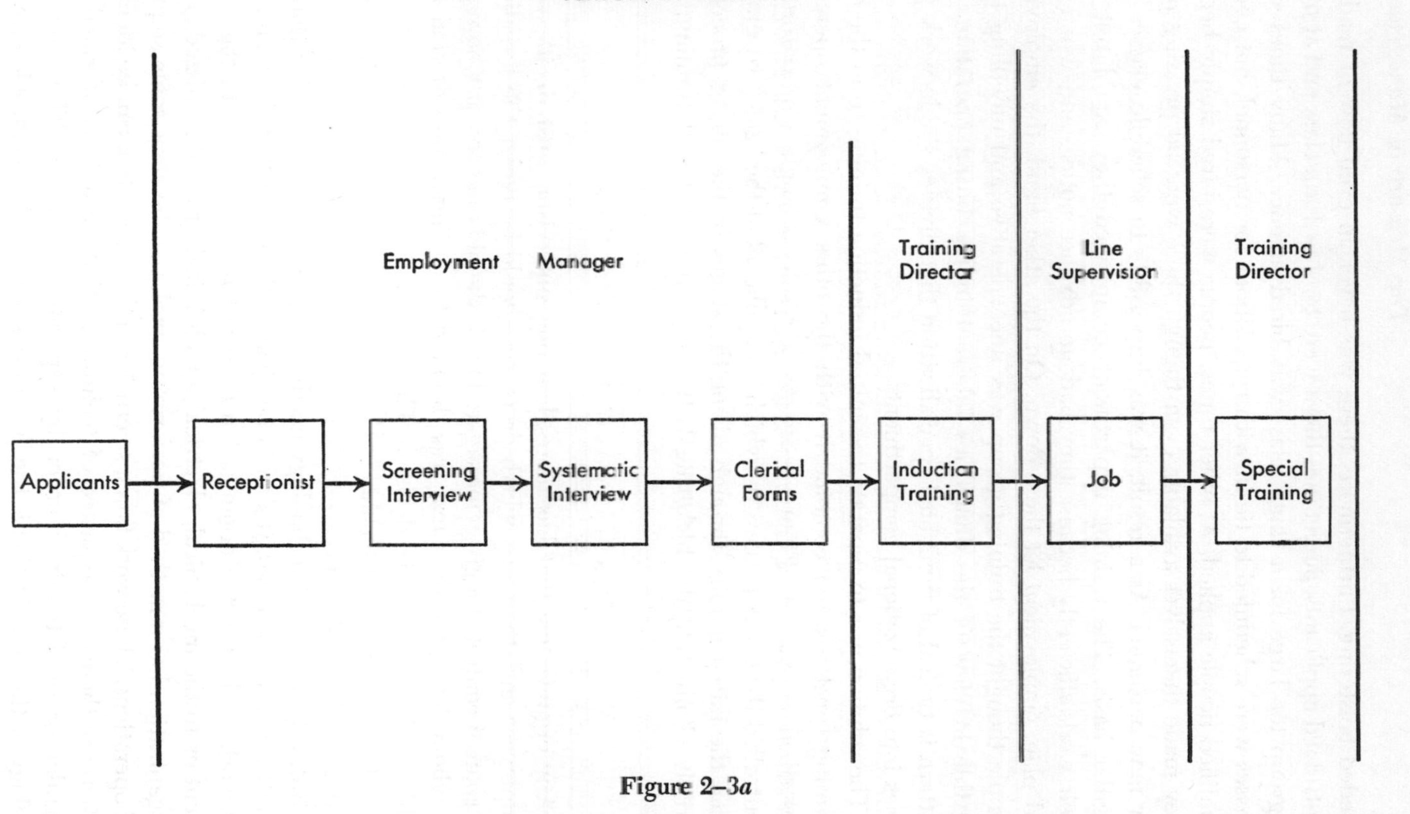
PERSONNEL DIRECTOR
Employment Manager
Training Director
Line Supervision
Training Director
Applicants
Receptionist
Screening Interview
Systematic Interview
Clerical Forms
Induction Training
Job
Special Training

Figure 2–3a

needed bolstering. Furthermore, there was never an even flow of ready-to-be-trained applicants. Sometimes there were too few for a class and at others a group too large for a single class was hired at once. Many times when classes were scheduled to tie in with requisitions for personnel, not enough qualified people applied. At other times, people were hired simply because they made themselves available even though there were no pressing needs for new personnel. As a result, it was impossible to schedule classes on a regular basis. The training department complained they could not plan their work efficiently because they had no advance notice, and when they did plan, employment let them down. On the other hand, the employment people thought the training group was uncooperative and unwilling to be flexible in view of the difficulties inherent in the hiring operation. This pattern is typical of functional specialization that divides single work processes into organizational compartments.

The solution was to separate the initial induction training from the other training functions and combine it with the other employment operations described above. See Figure 2–3*b*. As a result, a single supervisor now controlled the entire process by which an applicant at the "gate" was moved from the initial inquiry through all of the stages of the hiring procedure, largely eliminating the bickering between employment and training.

Identification of Unit Work Flow

Any organization that has more than one supervisor must decide which employees and, therefore, which processes should be under the jurisdiction or span of control of a given manager. This is the old question of who reports to whom. The preceding text was directed to finding some criterion upon which to base this crucial decision. The case studies were presented to illustrate the significance of technology as the critical determinant of this aspect of organizational structure.

But, this concept of technology needs a more careful explanation than the implications of the cases. It should be clear at the outset that the technology or work method of the organization does not refer primarily to the equipment or to the mechanical, electrical, or chemical processes utilized. Every organization has a method of performing work that involves some sequence of operations. These work flows, so crucial in the cases cited, can be identified wherever there is a sequence of techniques that must be performed in a regular or predetermined order by separate individuals. Thus the technology of the organization is the "who does what with whom, when, where, and how often."

These kinds of work flows are not the same as the work-flow analyses of

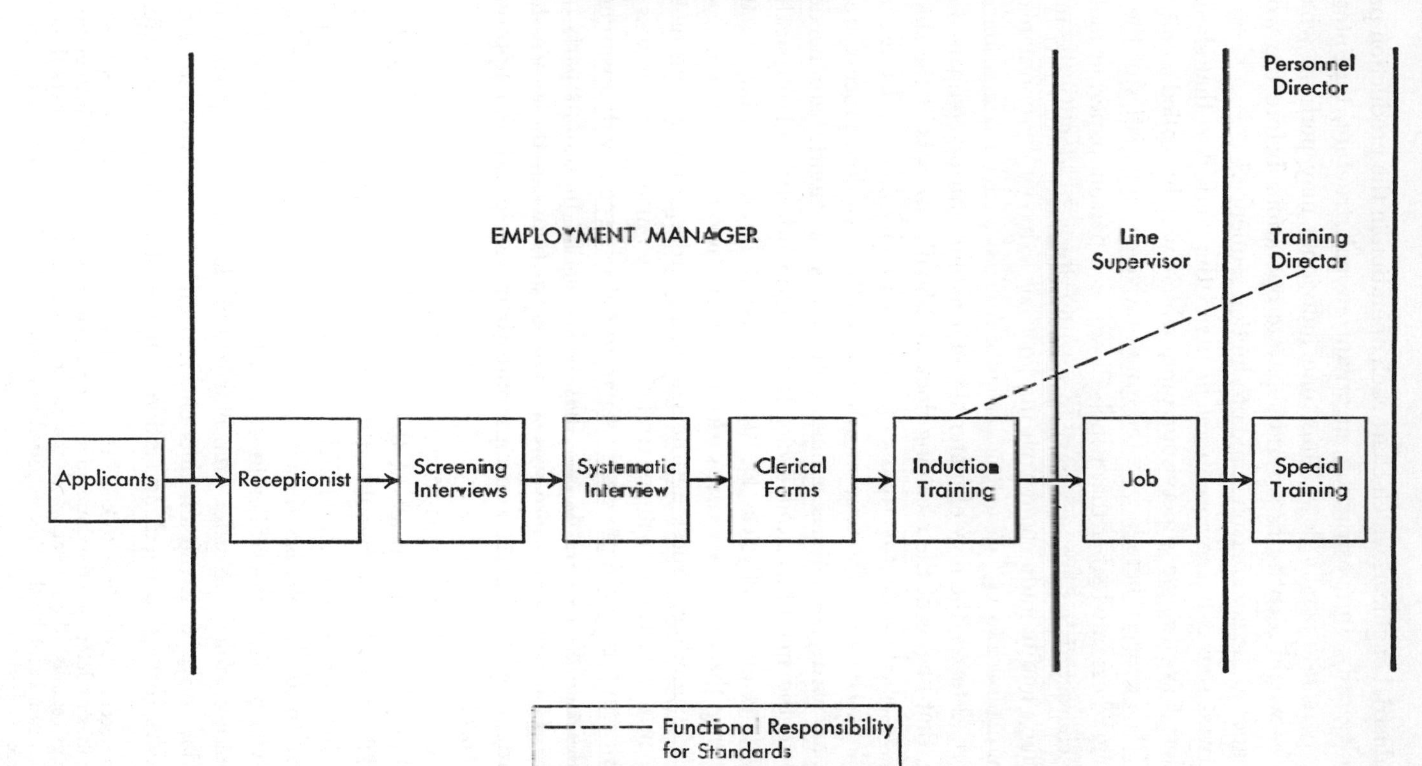
PERSONNEL DIRECTOR
EMPLOYMENT MANAGER
Line Supervisor
Personnel Director
Training Director
Applicants
Receptionist
Screening Interviews
Systematic Interview
Clerical Forms
Induction Training
Job
Special Training
Functional Responsibility for Standards

Figure 2–3b

the industrial engineer, which chart each operation in the production process chronologically. In constructing an organizational structure, the interest is in the person-to-person flow. Thus, one individual may perform what the engineer would identify as several separate operations before the work or paper goes to the next person in the production sequence.[3]

The next step is to separate the elements of the work flow that should be considered as a single supervisory unit, which will be called "unit work flows." The concern here is with the quantitative characteristics of the work flow regardless of whether that which "flows" is a person, paper, or material. These characteristics are necessary to set up criteria to identify the unitary work flows and to understand their implications behaviorally in organization design.

In broad terms, the flow of materials, in a manufacturing company for example, that begins at the receiving dock and finally appears at the shipping door as finished product ready for the customer could be considered a single work flow. However, the time coordinates of the complete process are generally too wide; sometimes a matter of weeks or months are needed to complete the manufacturing cycle. Besides the question of physical contiguity is relevant. Physical location or layout is an important factor in identifying the unit flows that make up an organizational design.

In the example of processing the salesman's order, a controlling factor in the separation of warehousing work flow from the office work flow was location. Although they are physically separate out of necessity, the warehouses could be contiguous. In this case they were located in various parts of the country. Consequently, there was a time lapse between the processing of the orders by the clerical groups and their receipt at the appropriate warehouses.

Yet, even if this time was reduced to a minimum and the location of the warehouse was, so to speak, at the end of the order processing line, the order-filling work flow would still differ quantitatively from the order-processing work flow in its time characteristics. When the day's orders were received in the warehouse, they were sorted according to customer location and given to each order filler in groups having a common shipping route. He then assembled the order from bins or bulk locations and placed it with the order copy (with the amounts checked off) on a conveyer that moved the orders through a checking station, a manifest clerk, a packer, etc. The

[3] It is necessary, of course, to know the total time required by each person to complete his activities to determine the duration of that particular stage in the production sequence. This helps establish the rate at which the paper, material, or a person moves through the line. This rate is set by the time required to complete the slowest or longest step in the sequence.

order-filling work flow did not begin until after the orders for an entire day were processed; the office work flow essentially was done one order at a time. Hence, this procedural difference caused a break in continuous flow similar to the one in geographical location.

If the existing procedural and locational discontinuities can be determined by time criteria, a total work flow can be divided into its unitary parts.[4] Obviously, by changing the technological system, the constituent techniques in a single unit flow can be varied and combined into more inclusive units, through the introduction of a conveyer, for example. Such changes are continually being made in business and require concurrent organizational changes to avoid creating management problems.

Sources of Stress in Organization

A unit work flow becomes segmented and its parts placed under different chains of command largely, although not necessarily entirely, as a result of the emphasis on functional specialization in organizational design. Sales and credit managers were both responsible for the order-processing flow in one company, and chaos resulted. In the second case, material handlers, maintenance employees, and the inspectors all had separate chains of command that conflicted with the management responsible for maintaining production. In the third illustration, the employment and training departments failed to coordinate the induction training procedure with the employment office functions. The true interrelationships among the processes, eventually merged under a single supervisor, had been disguised by artificial functional designations.

However, in one instance the problem was procedural not structural: the sequence within one group had not been thought through in terms of work flow. As a result, orders reached the credit checking clerks after they passed through earlier stages rather than at the beginning of the process which is more efficient.

Let us look more closely at the resulting organizational disturbances. In a situation requiring cooperative endeavors, whether it is a work group, employees and managers, or staff and line officials, each tries to develop a stable pattern of work, of interaction. When these stable patterns are disturbed, individuals experience stress or an uncomfortable feeling of pressure and dissatisfaction. A breakdown in the flow creates opposition as the individuals struggle to restore it. The expected responses from the indi-

[4] With the use of statistical techniques, it is possible to determine the homogeneity of the measurements within any unitary flow and to develop accurate criteria to test for discontinuities.

viduals in the sequence prove inadequate, and new coordination problems arise. Chapter VII will describe more explicitly the impact of these work flow "faults" on different types of personality.

The regularities of actions and interactions disappear when this stress occurs, and erratic variation takes over. The difference is obvious between a smoothly running operation and one with a problem. Under stress, people react emotionally, and, because more than one individual is involved, the reactions usually conflict with each other. (The impact of these situations on different personality types is described in Chapter VI.)

Thus, a vicious circle is established. Something happens in the work situation that causes the relationship of individuals to change or to depart from the normal pattern. This creates a stress, either of opposition or nonresponse, that is further complicated by higher levels of supervision and staff specialists whose unexpected interactions, i.e., outside the usual organization pattern, irritate the disturbed work-flow relations. People get upset; they become angry with each other and, depending on their individual characteristics, react temperamentally. These personality conflicts have direct ramifications in the work process because the emotional reactions change the pattern of contact and interaction. Joe is angry with Bill, so he does not check with him before starting a new experimental run. Consequently, a special test that should have been included in the run is left out, and the whole thing has to be done over. To complete the circle, these emotional disturbances damage the work-flow sequence, which causes additional personality stresses.

Robert Guest of the Yale Technology Project described this accurately when he said:

> Foremen are always getting caught in this familiar vicious circle. Material inspection, say, has failed to spot some faulty pieces. Something goes wrong at a welding operation. The general foreman is on the foreman's neck to "get it straightened out, or else!" The foreman drops everything to spend time on this one item. He cannot pay attention to the man he was breaking in on a new job. He cannot check on the stock bin which the stock man forgot to replenish. He meant to warn an operator about a safety condition. He knew another man was down in the dumps about a personal problem. By the time he has cleared up the original trouble and satisfied the boss, something else has blown up and the general foreman is roaring down the aisle again.[5]

What produced these stresses and where do these changes come from? They are not directly interactional on the worker level. With rare exceptions, the work flow does not require a direct interactional contact between two

[5] Robert H. Guest, "Of Time and the Foreman," *Personnel*, May, 1956, pp. 478–486.

contiguous persons as team operations do. That is, the upsets and bickerings are not caused by people who occupy adjacent positions in the flow process and place pressures on one another. In fact, orders could be put on the next desk or on a conveyer without any real contact. Material or parts in an assembly operation usually move from one operator to the next on a conveyer. But, they may also be brought and taken away by service personnel, just as a mail boy may move orders from one group to the next in the office. In these examples, the flow of work does not cause any direct interpersonal problems,[6] except that the action of one person depends on the action of his predecessor, causing him not to act and thus breaking the sequence. As Guest indicates, however, the initiating sources of stress are primarily fluctuations in the rate at which work flows through the supervisory unit. The critical variable is time. Production schedules require tight coordination; holdups must be avoided. If they occur, production suffers and the relationships of the supervisor to his workers and of the workers among themselves change as a consequence.

The objective of any organizational structure is to minimize the incidence of deviations from the established interaction patterns of the work process. The realistic administrator knows complete stability is a never-to-be-achieved utopia. Equipment will always break down; employees will always be absent; and changes in procedures will be introduced continuously. Work will not always come through on time, or when it does, the quality may be so poor the normal process time must be increased significantly. Rush orders or a flood of work may press upon his unit. Whatever the type of fluctuation, his interaction patterns have to change. He may have to spend more time with individual workers, supervisors in other departments, engineers, mechanics, maintenance men, or various persons in control positions, such as production planners or factory cost controllers, who occupy a place in the paper-work flow of which the line supervisor also is a part. And, as a result, less time is available to maintain other vital contacts.

Even if his unit flow is not complicated by other supervisors who directly affect him, the supervisor will still have coordination and timing problems in his own unit and in his relations with those who give him work and to whom he transmits it. The possibility of stress is much greater if he does not have control over the key individuals who work directly with his segment

[6] This contrasts with the usual conception of work-flow stress. Among the best known studies in this area is William F. Whyte's work in the restaurant industry. Whyte found stress was caused by the direct pressure emanating from interworker contacts. "Lower-status" runners placed pressure and thus disturbed "higher-status" kitchen personnel, and demanding customers upset the waitress who could not tolerate a high frequency of demands. (William F. Whyte, *Human Relations in the Restaurant Industry*, McGraw-Hill Book Company, Inc., New York, 1948, pp. 49–59, 104–128.)

of the flow and cannot get a response from them when he needs it, as in the case of the maintenance mechanics, or if he must constantly gear his segment to the next one, as in the examples of the material handling and inspection.

This is the major point of the discussion. Although the dynamic organization will always experience changes that cause variations in the work-flow system, most of these can be dealt with effectively by the supervisor affected. But, his job becomes almost impossibly difficult if there is no semblance of stability.[7] If the parts of a unit work flow are distributed among several supervisors, the individual manager cannot hope to maintain any stability in internal relationships because erratic changes are introduced by individuals whose behavior he cannot control. Because these other supervisors are meeting different organizational needs, they do not and cannot adjust to the requirements of any single manager. Significant irregularities in the rate of flow and significant changes in the interaction of the individuals concerned indicate the existence of a point of organization stress.

In companies where such problems are common, informal working arrangements usually develop over the course of time. Assuming the individual supervisors get along, i.e., the frequency or intensity of stress is not too great or their personalities are not obviously incompatible, they frequently get together to plan the work and discuss their mutual problems. The objective is for each supervisor to create the least upset to the next group in the line. Unfortunately, it is almost impossible because the segmentation of the work flow makes informal arrangements vulnerable to unexpected changes emanating from higher up.

Higher Level Management Problems

Because people, not lines on a chart, are the major concern, the elimination of points of stress within the work flow should be the first consideration of organization design. This means the traditional functional classification must be abandoned and each job analyzed as a part of one or perhaps, as in the case of an executive, many work flows. Merely recognizing that "informal" organization exists and hoping that management will grant it equal importance to the "formal" structure will not solve the problems.

Studies of the informal organization discuss how people actually relate themselves to each other in the process of getting the work done. Thus, the

[7] The degree to which the use of functional organization introduces stress and instability is cogently analyzed by James Worthy, Sears Roebuck and Co., in his paper, "Some Aspects of Organization Structure in Relation to Pressures on Company Decision-Making," in *Proceedings of Fifth Annual Meeting of the Industrial Relations Research Association* (ed. L. Reed Tripp), IRRA Publ. 10, 1953, pp. 69–79.

pattern of relationships that evolve in completing the job is what some observers consider the uncontrolled or spontaneous aspect of the organization. The authors believe this aspect must be the objective of the consciously contrived organizational structure. The organization must be designed for people not in the hope that people will somehow fit into it.

Accordingly, the first step is to identify the unit work flows and set their boundaries, placing each one under a single supervisor. As stated previously, these work flows consist not only of the people through whom the material, paper, or person flows, but also all the individuals who help maintain the flow, the mechanics, service people, etc. All the factors required to get the work done should be concentrated under a single person with responsibility centered at the lowest managerial point, not at the highest, as in the examples where top management officials were constantly arbitrating interdepartmental disputes.

Span of Second-level Supervision

So far, a series of unit flows, each with its own supervisor, has been constructed. However, each still depends upon the other. Although the stress points within the unit work flows are eliminated by effective organizational design, areas of interdependence between these units necessarily remain. As noted above, the pace of the work generally shifts between unit work flows, there are different rhythms and sequences, and, as a result, the coordination problems are not as great, but there is still an obvious need to coordinate relationships. In the example, the application of quantitative criteria revealed that orders went to the warehouse or tabulating or material from a fabricating unit to assembly with a definable discontinuity. This indicates the need for at least one further level of supervision, a manager over the unit work-flow managers whose responsibility is to see that they are coordinated into a larger system.

Controls

Combining unit work flows into a work-flow system does not depend upon arbitrary assumptions as to the number of individuals such a manager can supervise. These factors are determined by analysis of the controls the manager has available to maintain the system, not by abstract formulas. Worthy pointed out that in the Sears organization a store manager may have thirty to forty department heads reporting to him.[8] This works not merely because the company does not want a manager spending too much time with any single

[8] William F. Whyte, *Modern Methods in Social Research,* prepared for the Office of Naval Research under Contract Nonr-401(2), pp. 25–28.

department head but, more fundamentally, because the department store manager receives daily and weekly reports which are sufficient to tell him whether significant deviations are occurring in the ratio of stock (inventory) to sales, in markdowns, markups, etc. Consequently, he spends time with subordinates only in cases where managers are in trouble or where the reports suggest difficulties. As the theory of administrative controls is developed, similar control procedures can be adopted for any business operation (discussed in Chapter IV).

Many companies find it difficult to organize for effective operation because their reporting systems do not adequately pinpoint responsibility. Most administrative controls are by-products of accounting controls. They were developed for financial record keeping, not management control. Consequently, they are issued by the controller as financial documents and, although completely accurate, they are usually so late as to be matters of ancient history and too general because costs are both prorated and arbitrarily assigned. As such, these reports have little use as operating tools.[9] Thus the number of unit work-flow supervisors reporting to the second management level is a function of the state of development of the organization's controls: the measures which assess how things are going in the production process. Primarily, controls signal troubles at the points where two unit work flows come into contact. These juncture points are the potential stress areas that the second level manager oversees. Improvements in management reporting technology, particularly by the computer, will substantially increase the span of control at this management level.

The use of controls is based on the same criterion utilized in defining each of the unit work flows, the time coordinates of the system. The controls should indicate when the individual unit flows are intermeshing with one another. If they show homogeneity, in the statistical sense, in the interrelationships of the component units, the system is operating as planned. If the sequential movement of goods, paper, or people between units is stabilized, as reported through appropriate controls, the manager can relax. He must go into action when his controls show stressful situations are developing that require attention and action to avoid complete breakdowns in the system.

Assuming some ingenuity is shown in the development of controls, the

[9] There is an increasing concern with what is called "management accounting." However, present practice indicates it has by no means reached its declared goal of defining organizational responsibility within an accounting framework. Too many costs are still allocated and prorated. True managerial accounting cannot be achieved without loosening the bonds placed in the way of organizational change by poor accounting logic.

number of unit supervisors within the flow is of little significance, because each unit is self-sufficient.

Handling the Staff-Line Relationships

What is to be done with specialists such as the chief mechanic, the chief inspector, the production planning manager, the training director, and the credit manager? As pointed out previously, the specialists are responsible for developing standards, the procedures to implement these standards, and auditing results. Although this was mentioned explicitly only in the case of the credit manager, each specialist also plays a part in one or more work flows, as will be discussed in Chapter III. The significance of the specialists' development and auditing is that they have been removed from direct work-flow decision. The chief mechanic, for example, does not directly or through the foremen decide on what machine the mechanic is to work. He is responsible for the standards of mechanical repair, the program of preventive maintenance, and the evaluation of the mechanic's performance.

Thus, the unit work-flow supervisor and the chief mechanic have a dual responsibility for performance: the first, for the mechanic's contribution in maintaining the production flow, and the latter for the quality of his work. Both factors must be considered in evaluation and control. Otherwise, it is easy to overemphasize short-term gains in production at the cost of the long-run impact on the mechanical equipment.

Moreover, this shift in responsibility gives the specialist time to develop programs and to carry out his auditing responsibility. Otherwise, he is too busy with the day-to-day operating decisions to determine the source of the problems. Under the pressure of the immediate situation, his only interest would be to put the fire out; he would have little time to see what caused the problem in the first place.

However, the specialists need to be fitted into the organizational system. Because they are concerned with developing programs to expedite the work flow and eliminate stresses both within and between unit work flows that affect the total work-flow system, the specialists inevitably become the specialized assistants of the work-flow system manager. Their responsibility then is to act for him in their respective areas to improve the operation on the unit work-flow level. It is important to note the word "responsibility." In the usual sense of the word, specialists do not have staff responsibility with advisory or consultative relations to the line, nor do they have the responsibility of line supervisors, one step removed. They are actually *of* the staff of the manager and accountable to him for developing, installing, and auditing the results of programs in terms of the major objective of removing stress.

Conclusion: Work Flow and Organization Design

The type of organization design just described, based on the actual work flow within a technological and procedural framework, requires the complete use of time measurements as its basis. Not only is the delimitation of unit work flows dependent on the possession of quantitative criteria, but improvements of the technological process, in its broadest sense, require the examination of how each individual, whether worker, specialist, or supervisor, spends his time. The effective use of the method by any company depends also upon layout and location, the techniques by which paper, materials, or people are handled, and the controls used to signal real or impending deviations.

For example, if the record system is not or cannot be tied to individual responsibility, it is that much more difficult to locate points of stress and, in the absurd but common case, the supervisor may have to spend his time continually "on the floor" looking and listening because he does not routinely receive adequate information about his operation. The exception principle, one of the oldest in management, is useful in organizational planning only if the systems and procedures make its use possible.

The work-flow theory requires the specification of what each person does, when, where, with whom, how long, and how often. Therefore a type of job analysis or job description, to use a somewhat discredited term, is needed to outline the flows for each individual and to specify in quantitative measurements the duration of the action and interaction required to carry them out. These administrative patterns will be discussed in the next chapter, with the executive in mind, but similar, although much simpler, descriptions are necessary for the workers themselves. Any contact, whether it is a mechanic repairing a machine, a service boy bringing parts, or a set-up man making adjustments for a new run, involves some interaction, and the time involved is not simply a matter of the actual physical action.

Variations introduced by personality must also be considered within the organization design that results from the application of work-flow theory to any particular technological system. The supervisor who fails to act when stress is indicated in his control reports, waiting until someone calls it to his attention, hinders the operation of his unit work flow if it is set up on close time tolerances. Similarly, the manager who cannot spend the time with his staff specialists to see that preventive programs are developed and installed always faces stress within his area. In contrast, a staff specialist may find his development and audit responsibilities uncongenial in terms of his personality and, unconsciously, try to build a segregated work unit for himself, isolated from the people with whose performance he is concerned. The results of all of these are damaging to the work-flow system.

Personality and the reactions of the individual to specific types of stress limit both the construction of an organization to a given design and also its operation under the specifications. Fortunately, the same methods used to assess organization design also apply to the evaluation of individual personality and temperament. (This area will be discussed in Chapters VI and VII.) Through measurements of interaction, it can be determined precisely how an individual adjusts to a given type of organizational position and its potentialities for stress. In this way, it is possible to offset shortcomings either by modifications in the job or by selecting assistants who complement the individual's abilities.

The purpose here has been to suggest criteria upon which to base the design of an organization: the structure must be built from the bottom up and it must be superimposed upon a known technology. In fact, technology, as defined earlier, should be the basis for the distribution and assignment of supervision. Supervisory jobs are largely products of the time coordinates of the production process, regardless of the kind of work the organization does. The significance of this will become more apparent in the next chapter.

CHAPTER III

PRODUCTION STANDARDS for MANAGERIAL JOBS

Every manager faces questions like these with painful regularity: "How can I evaluate the effectiveness of my supervisors? Are there too many or too few supervisors in the Receiving department? What does Jones lack as an executive in this new position?" The answers all require the same type of knowledge: objective, measurable data about the components of a given managerial job. Designing an effective organization structure is only the first step in the groundwork for efficiency and productivity. Next, management must find ways to implement the design decisions with supervisory skill.

THE THREAT OF RISING OVERHEAD

Those testing the competitive health of the economy are preoccupied with the question of productivity. What are the criteria for technological efficiency and how well do the organizations designed to accomplish it perform in the cold light of managerial and economic appraisal? In terms of the costs of doing business, administrative overhead has increased steadily over the last thirty years relative to increases in the productivity of labor.[1]

A study published in *Nation's Business* points out the problem of rising administrative expenses with the conclusion: "The dollar amount of these expenditures (selling, general and administrative expenses) between 1950 and 1957 almost doubled, while sales were increasing by 60%." [2] More spe-

[1] Seymour Melman, "Industrial Productivity in Relation to the Cost of Management," *Productivity Measurement Review*, May, 1956.

[2] The findings were based on a compilation made by *Nation's Business* for manufacturing companies in twenty-three industry classifications, including all manufacturing and processing except the publication of newspapers. The study was based on the operating reports of representative companies that, when combined, conform with industry percentages developed on a quarterly basis during 1952 and 1953 by the Securities and

cifically, during the period from 1950 to 1957, selling and general administrative costs increased at a rate 50 per cent greater than the volume of sales or the cost of the goods sold! Put another way, although the cost of goods sold as a percentage of gross sales remained almost constant during this period, overhead costs increased significantly.

Management has been unduly concerned with the productivity of the individual worker, the hourly-rated employee, while the productivity of the salaried workers—executives, technicians, staff specialists of various sorts, and clerical help—has escaped attention almost entirely. Only clerical workers, if they perform repetitive tasks, have been evaluated in the same way as manual workers. The tools of industrial engineering are only beginning to invade the office.

Yet, the ratio of hourly to salaried workers is changing rapidly, and, as automation spreads, it will add to the rate of change. Looking at the superstructure of large corporations and their governmental counterparts, one is struck by the growth of bureaucracy. Certainly, the popularity of *Parkinson's Law* [3] stems from the reader's own experiences with his not too solemn investigations of organizations.

Moreover, the situation is not unique to the United States, and, contrary to some apologists, the growth of administrative overhead cannot be attributed to a better technological system and higher production efficiency. Actually, as Melman shows, the trend is characteristic of organizations everywhere. In fact, the ratio of administrative personnel for 100 production workers in manufacturing industries is the same (20 to 25) in Russia, Great Britain, and the United States, even though the average product-per-production-worker man-hour is five and a half times greater in the United States than in Russia and three and a half times greater than in Great Britain.[4] Apparently, the determining factor is the number of people to be supervised, not what each produces.

One of the most important observations tucked into *Parkinson's Law* is the executive's abhorrence of a time vacuum.[5] Few executives appear to be wasting time or even think they are. The smallest job can easily be magnified with more detailed (and, of course, more usefully precise) methods, systems, and policy statements. Complexities and nuances can expand the smallest task into a major operation. In the process, of course, both executive and staff time is taken up, and the manager has the sense of satisfaction that

Exchange Commission and the Federal Trade Commission. *Nation's Business*, vol. 47, no. 4, April, 1959, pp. 54–55.

[3] C. Northcote Parkinson, *Parkinson's Law*, Houghton Mifflin Company, Boston, 1957.

[4] Melman, *op. cit.*

[5] Parkinson, *op. cit.*

stems from a feeling of busyness (as distinct from business), time pressure, and a heavy work load.

Companies have no means to assess the relative usefulness of a manager's distribution of time except the growing uneasiness that overhead costs are increasing and constant shortages of time and managerial talent. Other indirect evidence is the fact that there are never enough secretaries or managers to process all of the administrative paper.

What is behind this administrative increase? The executive and other administrative personnel must necessarily be involved in the management of a whole series and sequence of human interactions that are essential to complete the work requirements in their sections of the organization. The sum total of time devoted to these contacts plus the time involved in preparatory and succeeding activities determines the work load of an executive. What are these interactions, how are they obtained, and how can they be utilized to improve managerial efficiency? Can they explain why the superstructure of business seems to grow unendingly?

The Executive Work Flow

It is necessary to begin at the simplest level of observation with the tools available. The first step is to make a study of the sequences of events or motions that constitute the job. Granted, an executive's job is not as repetitive as the machine operator's, who repeats the same motion cycle continuously throughout the day, varied only by differences in the parts to be machined. Yet, every manager is as much a part of a work flow, or more correctly several work flows, as the operator. Pieces of paper come to him from someone, he does something to each (reads it, computes figures from it, or initials it) and sends it on its way to some other person. People come to him, or he goes to them, sometimes as a consequence of receiving a piece of paper but not always. The contacts that take place vary in both the length of time required and in the pattern of the give-and-take within them.

By watching the daily activity of the executive, it is possible to identify the pieces of paper (reports, memos, letters, etc.), their sources, their next destinations, and their patterns and frequency of occurrence in the organizational calendar. A similar analysis can be made of the pattern of his other contacts, with whom, when, and so on. Looked at as sequences, they can be differentiated into a series of work flows that occur at different times, involve a different order of contacts with other executives, and deal with different operations within the company.

A New Type of Job Description

Figure 3–1 is an analysis of a job made in accordance with this procedure. Unlike traditional job descriptions, there is no mention of "general responsibility for," "coordinate," "act in an advisory capacity," or other ambiguous,

Figure 3–1

SUPERINTENDENT'S JOB DESCRIPTION
(In Work-Flow Terms)

1. (*a*) Receives daily inspection reports from the Inspection department. Looks them over, marks each "out of limit" figure, makes comments on margin, and returns to the foremen. (*b*) Where quality is out of limits for two successive days, contacts foremen to try to find out what is causing the poor quality.

2. (*a*) Receives daily machine-load charts from each of his departments. Analyzes to see what machines were down and for how long. (*b*) If he was not notified by the foreman as to the reason on the preceding day, goes to him to find out the cause. (*c*) If he and foreman agree that faulty material caused the down time, gets a sample and takes it to the superintendent of the responsible department to request corrective action. (*d*) If the cause is mechanical, goes to chief mechanic to determine whether the fault is routine maintenance, operating, or machine construction.

3. (*a*) Receives daily production reports from each of his departments, indicating what orders were run the previous day. Checks these off on his schedule sheet to know the current status of his production. (*b*) Where orders are running behind schedule, may request permission from the general superintendent to hold up other orders and then direct his foreman to reallocate the machine loads, or (*c*) may act directly if the over-all production schedule will not be thrown out of weekly balance.

4. (*a*) Receives copies of orders from Production Planning daily. Checks them over to be sure that materials, dies, etc., are on hand and indicates where it is necessary to take special precautions. Sends to the foreman, and if he wishes to see the actual order in production, makes a note on the order for the foreman to notify him when the order is ready to run. (*b*) Foreman calls him when order is ready, and he goes down to department to watch operation.

5. (*a*) Receives weekly load sheet from Production Planning Monday morning. Analyzes it to see what is overdue and what is expected during the week. (*b*) When overdue parts have not come to his department, calls the factory office expediter to locate them. (*c*) From the analysis may also need to transfer men within his own departments to satisfy labor needs, in which case notifies his foreman. (*d*) When he has no personnel available, calls other superintendents (who may have indicated their work is light in the weekly superintendent meeting), or (*e*) calls the employment manager.

6. (*a*) Receives weekly variance reports from the factory office manager on Tuesday. Checks off poor efficiency records and sends to foremen. (*b*) If effi-

Figure 3–1 (*Continued*)

ciency is poor for second continuous week, goes to foreman to find out what can be done to improve it.

7. Receives engineering reports, technical periodicals, etc., in distribution. Reads and files or forwards as indicated.

8. (*a*) Receives calls from his own foremen concerning special production problems. If he cannot answer over the phone, will go to foreman and discuss situation with him. (*b*) If problem cannot be solved, will call the chief engineer for help from the Engineering department, (*c*) the chief mechanic if it is a maintenance problem, or (*d*) another superintendent if the trouble seems to be in the latter's area.

9. (*a*) Receives calls from the Engineering department with regard to projects undertaken in his department, (*b*) from the Sales department with reference to the status of orders, (*c*) from the factory office with regard to records originating in his department. Usually answers from data at hand, but may have to go to own foreman before he can reply. (*d*) Sometimes he passes on the inquiry to the appropriate person, letting him handle it directly.

10. (*a*) Receives calls from chief inspector with regard to quality deviations in his department, and (*b*) from other superintendents on quality or production. Discusses situation with them to try to determine solution and, if necessary, calls in his foreman. (*c*) If he decides the trouble is in his own area, calls in the foreman to make sure that he will take the necessary steps to correct the situation.

11. (*a*) When one of his foremen has sent a requisition to the Employment department for a set-up man, group leader, or first-class mechanic, will interview a candidate after his foreman has seen the man, and (*b*) then discuss the candidate with the foreman and the employment manager.

12. (*a*) At the request of the union steward may discuss a problem in one of his departments, together with the foreman involved, or (*b*) if a grievance appears probable, with the manager of industrial relations.

13. Prepares layout sketches for changes in machine location and sends to Plant Engineering department with copy for the maintenance foreman. Receives a finished sketch accompanying the work order for initialing and transmittal to the factory office.

14. Conducts weekly meetings with his foremen to discuss department problems.

15. Attends weekly superintendents' meeting.

sweeping phrases. Every statement refers to an order or sequence that emphasizes the position of the manager in the work flow. Ignoring any technical know-how required, anyone could step into the job and know what he will receive, from whom, what he should do with it, and where it should go. In addition, he will know what day of the week a particular report comes in and, if tight scheduling of his time is necessary, even the approximate hour. If checking over a report requires him to initiate a contact to a foreman, someone in Production Planning, or the general superintendent, the job analysis tells him, in general, the conditions of choice. In other words, such job analyses follow the old field study adage telling who does what, with whom, when, where, how long, and how often, although the latter necessarily depends upon the frequency of specific situations requiring administrative action.

In many instances, the criteria for action are also indicated. The superintendent is looking for deviations in quality, scheduling, or variance in the reports he receives. He also tries to see what produced these figures in the daily operation of his departments. Perhaps machines are down or performing poorly, the material coming through is causing difficulty, or people are absent. These all upset the smooth routine and are reflected in the various performance reports he receives. The superintendent tries to make his foremen aware of each type of problem and has them call to his attention the ones they cannot handle. Consequently, he goes to others when he perceives a deviation or the possibility of one. Conversely, his foremen come to him with deviations they cannot correct, reflecting departures from anticipated operating behavior.

Classifying Types of Activities in the Job Description

The individual sequences of interaction or the work flows that make up the job of this superintendent fall into several groups. In some cases, he is simply processing reports like those on daily inspection, machine load, and production, that come to him for analysis. Much of this is only paper handling because, if there is no significant deviation, the reports are automatically filed, like the engineering reports or technical periodicals he reads, initials, and places in his out-basket. In other cases, his analyses require him to contact someone else, perhaps one of his foremen or another superintendent. He is also on the receiving end because his foremen, other superintendents, the chief inspector, etc., come to him with things.

Besides just reading and working alone or with others, the internal character of his interactional contacts vary. He interviews candidates for skilled or semisupervisory jobs, refers inquiries to the person who should handle them, meets with his foremen, and negotiates informally with union representatives. Grouped in this way, as in Figure 3–2, each of the activities that make up his total job can be crudely classified into a pattern of activity.

Although the analysis in Figure 3–2, does not list all the different patterns of interaction or administrative behavior that an executive follows in the various work flows in his job, it does include a good many that can be objectively classified. An executive makes inquiries, interviews, trains, ne-

Figure 3–2

SUPERINTENDENT'S JOB DESCRIBED BY PATTERNS OF ACTIVITY [1]

(Administrative Patterns)

Consulting, Advising, or Interviewing

2. (*d*) Where machine-load chart indicates that equipment is down for mechanical reasons, goes to chief mechanic to determine whether the fault is routine maintenance, operating, or machine construction.

11. (*a*) When one of his foremen has sent a requisition to the Employment department for a set-up man, group leader, or first-class mechanic, will interview a candidate after his foreman has seen the man, and (*b*) then discuss the candidate with the foreman and the employment manager.

Running a Meeting

14. Conducts weekly meetings with his foremen to discuss department problems.

Negotiating

12. (*a*) At the request of the union steward may discuss a problem in one of his departments, together with the foreman involved, or (*b*) if a grievance appears probable, with the manager of industrial relations.

Transmitting Inquiries

9. (*d*) Usually calls from the Engineering department are passed on to the appropriate person, letting him handle it directly.

Analyzing Data

1. (*a*) Receives daily inspection reports from the Inspection department. Looks them over, marks each "out of limit" figure, makes comments on margin, and returns to the foremen.

2. (*a*) Receives daily machine-load charts from each of his departments. Analyzes to see what machines were down and for how long.

3. (*a*) Receives daily production reports from each of his departments, indicating what orders were run the previous day. Checks these off on his schedule sheet to know the current status of his production.

4. (*a*) Receives copies of orders from Production Planning daily. Checks them over to be sure that materials, dies, etc., are on hand and if he wishes special precautions taken. Sends to the foreman, and if he wishes to see the actual order in production, makes a note on the order for the foreman to notify him when the order is ready to run.

5. (*a*) Receives weekly load sheet from Production Planning Monday morning. Analyzes it to see what is overdue and what is expected during the week.

[1] Note that the number–letter designations refer to elements in the job description presented in Fig. 3–1.

Figure 3–2 (*Continued*)

6. (*a*) Receives weekly variance reports from the factory office manager on Tuesday. Checks off poor efficiency records and sends to foremen.

7. Receives engineering reports, technical periodicals, etc., in distribution. Reads and files or forwards as indicated.

13. Prepares layout sketches for changes in machine location and sends to Plant Engineering department with copy for the maintenance foreman. Receives a finished sketch accompanying the work order for initialing and transmittal to the factory office.

Analyzing and Initiating Action

1. (*b*) Where quality is out of limits as indicated by daily inspection reports for two successive days, goes to foreman to try to find out what is causing the poor quality.

2. (*b*) Reviews daily machine-load charts and if he was not notified by the foreman as to the reason (what machines were down) on the preceding day, goes to him to find out the cause.

2. (*c*) If he and foreman agree that faulty material caused the down time, gets a sample and takes it to the superintendent of the responsible department to request corrective action.

3. (*b*) Where daily production reports show that orders are running behind schedule, may request permission from the general superintendent to hold up other orders and then direct his foreman to reallocate the machine loads, or (*c*) may act directly if the over-all production schedule will not be thrown out of weekly balance.

5. (*b*) Where overdue parts have not come to his department as revealed by weekly load sheet, calls the factory office expediter to locate them.

5. (*c*) From the analysis may also need to transfer men within his own department to satisfy labor needs, in which case notifies his foremen.

5. (*d*) When he has no personnel available, calls other superintendents (who may have indicated their work is light in the weekly superintendent meetings), or (*e*) calls the employment manager.

6. (*b*) If weekly variance reports show that efficiency is poor for second continuous week, goes to foreman to find out what can be done to improve it.

Trouble Shooting on Initiation by Others

4. (*b*) Foreman calls him when production planning order is ready, and he goes down to department to watch operation.

8. (*a*) Receives calls from his own foremen concerning special production problems. If he cannot answer over the phone, will go to foreman and discuss situation with him.

8. (*b*) If problem cannot be solved, will call the chief engineer for help from the Engineering department, (*c*) the chief mechanic if it is a maintenance problem, or (*d*) another superintendent if the trouble seems to be in the latter's area.

Figure 3–2 (*Continued*)

9. (*a*) Receives calls from the Engineering department with regard to projects undertaken in his department, (*b*) from the Sales department with reference to the status of an order, (*c*) from the factory office with regard to records originating in his department. Usually answers from data at hand, but may have to go to own foreman before he can reply.

10. (*a*) Receives calls from chief inspector with regard to quality deviations in his department, and (*b*) from other superintendents on quality or production. Discusses situation with them to try to determine solution and, if necessary, calls in his foreman.

10. (*c*) If he decides the trouble is in his own area, calls in the foreman to make sure that he will take the necessary steps to correct the situation.

Pattern of Behavior Unspecified

15. Attends weekly superintendents' meeting.

gotiates, sells, makes speeches, conducts meetings, and transmits information. Also, and this is sometimes overemphasized, he supervises.

But, supervision is not a single pattern of interaction (as illustrated in the listing of the superintendent's activities given in this chapter); it is really a combination of many distinct activities. Subordinates are given orders that result, at least in part, from the time the supervisor spent working on reports, schedules, etc. If the orders involve getting his foremen to take corrective action, for example, it is not just a matter of making a concise request. He has to learn the reasons for deviations, perhaps by interviews, decide whether any changes in scheduling or operations are necessary, and then persist in getting over his point of view to make sure that changes in his subordinate's behavior are forthcoming.

Under the general area of supervision, he also acts as a trouble shooter. If one of his foremen needs help, he may have to intervene with another foreman, another superintendent, or an engineer. He delegates responsibilities to his subordinates and may want verbal reports on what has been accomplished.

Traditionally there has been a great deal of emphasis on these different patterns of administrative behavior. There are literally hundreds of books on selling, interviewing, supervision, and other patterns. Unfortunately, most of these how-to-do-it prescriptions group a host of behavior patterns under a single heading. The reader who is seeking to improve himself often finds it difficult to distinguish these differences or even recognize the pattern when it is theoretically being employed. The situation in which the superior says he is delegating but his subordinates insist he never allows them to do anything on their own is all too familiar. The difficulty is simply the absence of any precise criteria on which to classify *delegation.*

Adding the Time Dimension

In developing these criteria, it is necessary to borrow another tool from engineering practice, to add the "time" element to the "motions" of the job. However, time for the executive is more complicated than for the lathe operator. Consequently, the kind of time study must be adapted to the realities of the work-flow sequences just identified.

A crude separation can be made between the total time spent in contact with others and in isolation. Yet, this is misleading because the patterns of interaction required by the diverse activities of the manager are important in determining the time dimensions of his job. They are analogous to the variety of arm and body motions made by the machinist to complete an operation. Consequently, it is important to identify how long it takes a given manager to do each of the motions in his job—training, delegating, disciplining, trouble shooting, etc.

As already observed, many of these administrative patterns have several subtypes. For example, in his interviews, the superintendent may follow one pattern when talking to a prospective employee, another when trying to find the cause of a machine breakdown from a machine operator, a third when trying to get recommendations for a major operating problem from the chief engineer, and a fourth when handling a discipline case. Each has different quantitative characteristics, and the time spent varies accordingly. Granted, some executives are so limited they use the same pattern in every situation, but ordinarily a competent executive is capable of using half a dozen, even though his skills in employee interviewing or training, for instance, may not be as professionally developed as the specialists in the Personnel department. However, if he is unable to employ a wide range of administrative patterns, he may end up as a specialist himself.

With instruments now available, it is possible to observe and classify each of the interaction patterns according to the time characteristics of give-and-take between the manager and the man he is contacting.[6] The same data also provide a good approximation of the total time required by the manager under study for each type of activity.

[6] Cf. Eliot D. Chapple, "The Interaction Chronograph: Its Evolution and Present Applications," *Personnel,* vol. 25, 1949, pp. 295–307.

Frequency of Use

To establish realistic managerial work loads, the frequency of any given pattern must be known. Because each managerial activity is evoked or stimulated by a particular situation, the problem is actually one of determining the frequency of occurrence of specific incidents. If there is no job turnover, the superintendent rarely has to interview applicants. If quality remains high, he does not have to correct his foremen, and so forth. The amount of time he devotes to each component of his job depends upon the frequency of deviations from standard operating conditions.

Thus, in planning jobs, the difference between the machine operator and the executive is really one of degree. The machine operator repeats his work within a day. He is expected to turn out so many parts daily (each having a time constant with permissible variations) and schedules are set accordingly. With the executive, a much longer time span is needed to encompass all the various components of his several administrative subpatterns. The day, the month, the quarter, and the year must be budgeted in terms of the time constants for each component in each of his several work flows. Of course, this part of the job is controlled by the accounting calendar around which organizational activities are centered.

The other components of the job, besides the activities and interactions resulting from the close of an accounting period, the receipt of a report, etc., appear unpredictable at first glance. However, because the conditions that set these components in motion can be identified, the frequency of their occurrence can also be determined. Although the exact moment when the telephone will ring cannot be predicted, the probability that a manager will have so many calls during any given period can be computed easily and the upper and lower limits estimated. If this were not possible, telephone companies could not plan their telephone exchanges, and city-wide or nation-wide systems would be inconceivable. The organizational problems can be resolved by similar means.

The problem facing the superintendent in the job analysis in Figure 3–1 is an obvious example, where his foremen come to him with the difficulties that arise. If a machine breaks down and delays production, the foreman contacts his superintendent or asks for a decision on switching production. If quality is lower and too many parts are being rejected, the superintendent may question the inspection superintendent or the superintendent preceding him in the work flow. By adapting the kind of statistical methods used in statistical quality control, both the probability of such crises and also the number of contacts and the amount of time required to correct them can be estimated. In other words, the unpredictable aspects of an executive's job become predictable after the flow of work is analyzed.

Frequency plus Duration

Figure 3–3 shows the superintendent's job broken down into its various job types, the average durations of contacts, and a few of the salient differ-

Figure 3–3

THE JOB OF THE SUPERINTENDENT

Contact and Interaction Differences by Administrative Patterns [1]

(One week = 2400 minutes)

Administrative Pattern	*Number of Occurrences or Contacts*	*Average Duration*	*Total Weekly Time*
Consult, Advise, or Interview			
2. (*d*)	1/week	35	35
11. (*a*)	1/week	50	50
11. (*b*)	1/week	65	65

Interaction Pattern Required: Sufficient energy to conduct relatively long contacts; ability to listen, to get people to talk so as to obtain information from them; also has to be able to give advice or suggestions—to "sell" or put over a point of view. The pattern is one of continually shifting from give to take, from getting people to talk and, from what they say, being able to talk in turn combined with adaptability to a wide variety of personality types.

Run Meetings			
14	1/week	60	60

Interaction Pattern Required: In smaller meeting manager needs to be able to listen and operate at slower pace than at larger meeting where larger number of contacts have to be managed and the interaction speeded up. Must be able to take initiative quickly and many times take advantage of lulls to shape direction, must have sufficient dominance to maintain control. Capacity to get a variety of people to talk and accomplish purpose within a limited period of time.

Negotiate			
12. (*a*)	1/2 weeks	25	12½
12. (*b*)	1/2 weeks	15	7½

Interaction Pattern Required: Requires ability to restrain oneself from too much talking and frequently allowing the other person to talk himself out.

[1] Note that the number-letter designations refer to elements in the job description presented in Fig. 3–1.

Figure 3–3 (*Continued*)

Relatively low initiative guards against too early offers; the capacity to wait out the other person as well as the ability to ask questions and not be maneuvered into quick reactions are important.

Administrative Pattern	*Number of Occurrences or Contacts*	*Average Duration*	*Total Weekly Time*
Transmit Inquiries			
9. (*d*)	7/day	2	70

Interaction Pattern Required: Ability to restrain one's discussion to a minimum and to concentrate on completion of brief contact; essentially initiating to someone else each time information comes to you: responding like a "switching center."

Administrative Pattern	*Number of Occurrences or Contacts*	*Average Duration*	*Total Weekly Time*
Analyze Data			
1. (*a*)	1/day	10	50
2. (*a*)	1/day	15	75
3. (*a*)	1/day	10	50
4. (*a*)	1/day	15	75
5. (*a*)	1/week	45	45
6. (*a*)	1/week	30	30
7	3/week	20	60
13	1/month	20	5

Interaction Pattern Required: The greater the length of time required for this, the more the executive must *restrain* himself from initiating contact or engaging in lengthy contacts or being too quick to "jump in" before completing his analytical work. Must tolerate isolation.

Administrative Pattern	*Number of Occurrences or Contacts*	*Average Duration*	*Total Weekly Time*
Analyze and Initiate Action			
1. (*b*)	2/day	30	300
2. (*b*)	3/week	10	30
2. (*c*)	2/day	20	200
3. (*b*)	2/week	30	60
3. (*c*)	2/day	40	400
5. (*b*)	2/day	6	60
5. (*c*)	1/day	10	50
5. (*d*)	1/day	20	100
5. (*e*)	1/day	10	50
6. (*b*)	2/day	15	150

Interaction Pattern Required: Takes action on basis of evaluation of reports. Again, the number of people to be contacted is critical. If the number is large, a great deal of initiating ability is required, with substantial quickness and flexibility, in order to complete all the contacts necessary to solving the problem. Adequate dominance is needed to cope with difficult contacts who accept initiations reluctantly.

Figure 3–3 (*Continued*)

Administrative Pattern	*Number of Occurrences or Contacts*	*Average Duration*	*Total Weekly Time*
Trouble Shooting			
4. (*b*)	1/week	5	5
8. (*a*)	2/day	10	100
8. (*b*)	2/week	5	10
8. (*c*)	2/week	15	30
8. (*d*)	2/week	20	40
9. (*a*)	1/week	20	20
9. (*b*)	1/week	10	10
9. (*c*)	1/week	10	10
10. (*a*)	1/week	5	5
10. (*b*)	3/week	5	15
10. (*c*)	1/week	5	5

Interaction Pattern Required: Waits for someone else to take initiative to him and then takes action; encourages others to come to him. Either gives answer in the original contact or takes initiative to bring in other people.

Unspecified Pattern			
15	1/week	60	60

ences that are responsible for the variations in each of the interaction patterns.

Figure 3–4 gives similar breakdowns for various executive positions to illustrate the wide variation in the distribution of time for an industrial relations manager, a sales engineer, a production planner, and a research director. Not only is the allocation of time different for each type of administrative action, but, of course, the work flows for each also differ. No matter how specialized any job appears to be, it is obvious that several administrative patterns are required to carry out the full scope of the organizational position. The more managerial the job is, in the sense of supervising the work of many individuals, the greater the number of patterns required to carry it out.

There is an important by-product of this time analysis. In assessing the relative cost advantages of new processes or systems, companies often neglect the managerial cost component. Of course, they calculate the number of supervisors to be assigned directly to the new activity; but they overlook the ways in which the new work-flow system may involve many levels of management above the one directly responsible for its operation as well as the supporting staff personnel utilized for emergency operations. Unfortu-

Figure 3–4

TIME DISTRIBUTIONS FOR FOUR EXECUTIVES

(One week = 2400 minutes)

***A.* Industrial Relations Manager *B.* Chief Sales Engineer *C.* Production Planning Manager *D.* Research Director**

Administrative Pattern	*Number of Contacts*				*Average Duration of Contact*				*Total Weekly Time Required*			
	A	*B*	*C*	*D*	*A*	*B*	*C*	*D*	*A*	*B*	*C*	*D*
Consult, Advise, Interview	2/day	–	1/week	5/day	23	–	30	32	230	–	30	800
Run a Meeting [1]	1/month	½/month	–	1/month	60	60	–	60	15	7.5	–	15
Negotiate	7/day	–	–	–	40	–	–	–	1400			
Sell	–	4/day	–	–	–	60	–	–	–	1200		
Make a Speech	–	2/week	–	–	–	60	–	–	–	120		
Training	–	–	–	1/day	–	–	–	34	–	–	–	180
Analyze Data, Read Reports [2]	–	–	–	–	–	–	–	–	125	60	780	800
Analyze and Initiate Action	4/day	6/day	12/day	10/day	10	16	25.3	7.3	200	480	1520	365
Trouble Shooting	10/day	–	1/week	–	6.2	–	30	–	310	–	30	
Unspecified Pattern [1] (Attending Meetings)	2/week	5/week	1/week	1/day	60	120	60	48	120	600	60	240

[1] The number of contacts (instances of give-and-take) and interaction patterns in which each superintendent participated at these meetings was not observed; only the total duration is known.

[2] The number of instances in which a superintendent analyzed data or read reports not leading to action is separated out to contrast it with the pattern immediately following; i.e., only the total time per week spent is given.

nately, higher management is frequently doing the job of a first-line supervisor. If these managers were compelled to record the time they spend in a subordinate's department and took this expenditure of managerial time into account, the real costs of many departments would soar astronomically. Unfortunately, accounting traditions do not encourage this, and, as a result, managerial time, the most expensive and scarce resource of an organization, is frequently dissipated.

Personality

The final factor in determining the time dimensions of each managerial job is the personalities of those with whom he deals as well as his own. Just as different activities require different lengths of time, personality adds another variation. If a subordinate is difficult to convince, the manager must spend extra time explaining and persuading. If another constantly quarrels with the union steward, the manager may have to provide him a decompression period to blow off steam to maintain some semblance of equilibrium. Or if a subordinate speaks slowly, the manager may need to take extra time to get the full problem.

Figure 3–5 summarizes the time distribution by administrative patterns by the superintendent in Figure 3–4, including the time he spends alone, and compares him with another superintendent. Although both individuals have essentially the same work flows and supervise the same number of foremen, there are sharp differences in the distribution of time. Superintendent A has fewer but much longer contacts. He spends more time by himself than Superintendent B, and yet uses more of his time interviewing his foremen and the engineers, as well as giving instructions to the foremen. Superintendent B is almost always on the receiving end; his foremen are constantly coming to him; he spends little time on records; etc. Superintendent B rarely meets with his foremen; A does so on a weekly basis. On the other hand. A has infrequent contacts with the union steward, and B is heavily involved.

The time requirements for any given administrative pattern are not fixed absolutely. From day to day, and from person to person, there are variations in the measurements obtained from a given executive. Consequently, the statements about a particular pattern are based on averages, and the expected variation in the values making up the average must be considered. This is determined by the personalities of the manager and of those with whom he deals, measured in terms of interaction. Because this can be measured with precision, the ranges of time deviations and the statistical limits

Figure 3–5

TIME DISTRIBUTIONS FOR TWO SUPERINTENDENTS WITH SIMILAR WORK FLOWS

(One week = 2400 minutes)

Administrative Pattern	*Superintendent A* *Number of Contacts*	*Average Duration*	*Total Time*	*Superintendent B* *Number of Contacts*	*Average Duration*	*Total Time*
Consult, Advise, Interview	3/week	50	150	2/week	50	100
Run Meetings [1]	1/week	60	60	1/6 weeks	60	10
Negotiate	1/week	20	20	2/day	28	280
Transmit Inquiries	7/day	2	70	20/day	2	200
Analyze Data [2]	–	–	390	–	–	60
Analyze and Initiate Action	14/day	20	1400	5/day	10	250
Trouble Shooting	5/day	10	250	16/day	18	1440
Unspecified Pattern [1] (Superintendents' Meeting)	1/week	60	60	1/week	60	60

[1] The number of contacts (instances of give-and-take) and interaction patterns in with each superintendent participated at these meetings was not observed; only the total duration is known.

[2] The number of instances in which a superintendent analyzed data or read reports not leading to action is separated out to contrast it with the pattern immediately following; i.e., only the total time per week spent is given.

It should also be pointed out that for simplification in presenting totals to make the contrast between the superintendents obvious, those contacts involving interaction with more than one person, as in trouble shooting, within a single continuing situation, have been omitted. Contacts here, in contrast to the data presented in Fig. 3–4, mean situations. This eliminates the need for fractions.

derived from the study of repeated samples of executive contacts can be calculated.

Because organizational planning must be based on real people, human personality differences, as they affect interaction among people, must be treated as equally predictable elements of the job. Just as the frequency of telephone calls or machine breakdowns can be predicted, so the reaction of particular personalities in particular situations can be predicted with statistical regularity. This subject will be discussed in Chapter VII. Although the actual moment on a given day the superintendent will have a problem with a certain subforeman cannot be pinpointed, the frequency of occurrence and the time spent can be estimated within specific limits. This is sufficient to use in planning jobs and determining the time required to accomplish them.

Use of the Time Dimension

Most managers are already concerned with how they spend their time: There is never enough time within the working day to accomplish everything. When they have time to think about it, they wonder if they are distributing their efforts in the best way. Are too many pieces of paper coming across the desk? How do I keep up with the mail and the reports that deluge me? Am I slighting certain people, even my most important subordinates, because others continually demand my attention? How often do I duplicate other people's work or get involved in problems I should leave to someone in the department? How often am I unable or reluctant to follow certain administrative patterns or prefer to use others that significantly lengthen or shorten my contacts and affect my relationships to people in the organization?

> I should have handled that quality problem in three minutes; instead, I wasted three-quarters of an hour giving the foreman a sales talk on quality.
>
> If I had spent a little time interviewing the methods engineer on what was going wrong with the new run, I wouldn't have had to spend three days in meetings with engineering or find myself getting called down to the front office.

This kind of speculation and second-guessing leads to the most obvious and least appreciated fact of organizational design: The working day is only seven or eight hours long and there are only so many days in the week and weeks in the year. In other words, regardless of what is planned for the executive to do, he has only so much time in which to do it.

If many executives did all that was assigned to them, they would work twelve to sixteen hours a day. Except when they take paper work home at night, they are limited because the major portion of their motions involve other people, whom they cannot take home. So, unless the others also work the same number of hours, the executives are unable to do what theoretically is expected of them, so they avoid certain jobs, spend a few minutes on others so they can report progress, and concentrate on what cannot be avoided.

One of the most extreme cases of time pressures damaging job performance is the Federal government, that convenient symbol of much that also occurs in business. Many senior officials during two-year terms of office, which tend to be the average, never have the time for a lengthy and thorough conversation with their key subordinates. They are constantly behind, in terms of maintaining the countless contacts with political figures and important spokesmen outside of their agencies or departments. Although these contacts may be an essential part of the official's job, the time they take keeps him from other equally important parts. Time, the most valuable asset of an executive, disappears if its use is not properly evaluated.

Work-Load Determination

By analyzing each executive's job in terms of the work flows he has to perform and computing the time characteristics of the activities and interactions that constitute them, the organization can be planned in realistic terms. What has been done, in fact, is to combine the human and the engineering aspects of the work, recognizing that they are mutually dependent.

Now it is possible to look at the actual time distributions of given managers and determine their reasonableness. Is a given executive overworked —or is his time just filled with "busy work"?

To answer such questions, the frequency with which situations requiring managerial action occur (usually deviations from normal operating conditions) must be determined from the records. The executive must use one or more of the administrative patterns already measured, varied by the known personality characteristics of the participants, to deal with these stresses or disturbances. Given these data, the time required to execute the administrative patterns for each situation can be computed. By doing this with every situation and comparing the results with the actual time spent, an over-all assessment of the reasonableness of the work load can be obtained as well as more detailed analyses of whether the executive is allocating his time to deal effectively with all significant operating disturbances.

By knowing the quantitative elements of the job and making repeated sampling observations, it is possible to ascertain how much an executive varies in his time distribution from the limits set by previous performance. If he does so significantly, we can then ascertain whether this is correlated with changes in performance on other jobs that require him to spend additional time restoring operations to standard or reflections of an individual shift in attention or competence. Thus, it can be determined whether or not the executive does his job within reasonable limits as it is presently defined. In a sense, each man sets his own standard for his organizational position.

Avoiding the Creation of New Jobs

Beyond this, the work-load analyses provide a means to improve the organizational system. The expansion of the administrative patterns carried on by one executive into separate jobs is a major malady affecting most companies. Rather than determine the frequency of a given stress and the administrative behavior required, many firms simply build a new position around each problem. If such stresses occur more often than usual management demands that something be done, even though there are no criteria to judge the problem accurately. So, the easiest solution is to give one man the full-time responsibility. If employees who are sent out to handle house calls are poorly trained, as indicated by a series of customer complaints, a training director is hired. If Department A repeatedly complains it is held up because essential parts are not being sent by Department B, an expediter, reporting to the general superintendent, is appointed to run between the departments and Production Planning. Wherever there is stress, real or assumed, some person is nearly always appointed to take over the responsibility or, even worse, a committee is set up. In a short time, administrative personnel proliferate and the organizational channels become clogged with unnecessary interactions.

The drive toward specialists and specialization is enhancing this growth. Because of insufficient skills or time or the presumed advantage of using a professional, management assumes specialization will result in a better job. And it probably will, except that no one has analyzed, in terms such as those described, how often a particular pattern is required and how much time it actually takes. The newly hired specialist can hardly be blamed for finding as many uses for his specialty as he can and for selling them to management as parts of an essential program!

The personnel department of a division in a major company serves as an example of this proliferation. In 1948, personnel activities for 1500 employees were carried out by a personnel manager and a girl who doubled as secretary and clerk. In 1958, there were six executives and eight clerks in the personnel department although the division actually had slightly fewer employees, about 1400, and there had been no increase in turnover or union activity. In addition to the same personnel manager, an employment manager, a training director, a wage and salary administrator, an industrial relations manager, and an employee welfare manager had been added to the staff plus eight clericals.

In 1948, the personnel manager and his clerk performed all these various jobs, although how adequately they did so can only be a matter of opinion without making the kind of analysis described here. Because the manager was not replaced, the importance of employing specialists for each job was apparently the deciding factor. Unlike the case used by Prof. Parkinson to illustrate his law, these six men are not writing the same report. Each is busy expanding his specialty that was made possible by the organization of the company even though one man was able to pay some degree of attention to each before.

It was stated above that management might justify such an expansion because of insufficient skills or time. Yet, essentially this means *time,* unless the skills are so unusual they cannot be acquired by the ordinary manager. Generally, there is not enough time to learn the skill or the job is so constituted that the manager cannot spend as much time on it as the situations demand.

This kind of work-load analysis will also highlight cases in which a particular executive, because of personality limitations, cannot carry the full load required by his position. For example, he may take substantially more time than required by most managers for trouble-shooting interviews. Conversely, another staff manager may avoid long selling contacts with coworkers and, as a result, fail to convince them that his ideas are worth considering. If such individual weak points are revealed by timed observations, it may be necessary to reassign certain segments of the job to others and, if the work load permits, allow the executive to add activities that are more compatible, in terms of time, with his own personality strengths.

The Manager's Job and Human Relations

There is room for wide misinterpretation in the statement that the job of the manager is to manage his human relationships. Most people believe that human relations is the organizational equivalent of the Golden Rule. As a result, emphasis on human relations adds fuel to the fire—which is more important, happy employees or high productivity?

A semantic argument is unnecessary. There is no reason why good human relations should not be synonymous with mutual trust and understanding, two-way communication, and the absence of interpersonal friction.

But, at the same time, it must be recognized that every aspect of organizational life is essentially human relations, or, more precisely, the interaction of its members that can be measured. Production involves the simultaneous coordination of people who must pass paper, materials, or points of view among themselves in some carefully controlled sequence. Giving orders, like handling grievances, involves channeling interpersonal contacts at a highly explicit rate and direction. Discipline, training, negotiation of union agreements, or purchases from vendors all involve observable patterns of human interaction. Such organizational innovations as delegation and decentralization can only be described in terms of human relations because they establish definite patterns of interaction both between boss and subordinate and also staff and line. In other words, the definition of these administrative patterns depends upon the use of interaction measurement. It allows the executive to make precise statements about any manager's behavior that can be used in planning his job and, consequently, in setting a standard of performance for him to meet.

After the narrowness that caused the separation between the human relations of supervisory relationships and the human relations of work flow and organization is overcome, then the question can be approached in specific terms of what the basic work flows that are essential to the business operation require from the manager in subsidiary work flows. This provides a tool for organizational planning far removed from the philosophical principles of the past, and organization engineering in the sense of Mary Follett can then become a reality.[7]

Conclusion

The manager's job is neither elusive nor unmeasurable. Nor is it simply a matter of the "right" attitudes toward people or the memorization of textbook principles. The manager's basic function is maintaining or stabilizing several interrelated work flows. Job descriptions can be written describing these work flows clearly and further specifying the conditions or signals that tell him something needs to be done to avoid breakdowns or inefficiencies. Most of these "somethings" involve detecting deviations and having interaction with one or more people in the organization, started either by the manager or by one of his subordinates, superiors, or fellow supervisors. These various interactions, called administrative patterns, are the "motions" of his job, and they are described in quantitative measurements, each outlining the type of interaction pattern required if the contact is to improve the situation or bring the system back to normal. The motions are actually more complicated because some administrative patterns, such as interviewing, have a number of subtypes that are further varied by personality differences.

Time standards can be established on the basis of the administrative patterns used by the manager in the several work flows and the calculation of the incidence of stress signaled by deviations which bring the manager into action. With these data the reasonableness of the work load for each manager can be assessed: Is his span of control too wide or too narrow; is he overworked or underutilized?

Managerial time and energy are among the most valuable resources of any organization. At present a great deal of effort is devoted to evaluating

[7] H. C. Metcalf and L. Urwick (eds.), *Dynamic Administration: The Collected Papers of Mary Parker Follett,* Harper & Brothers, New York, 1941.

the efficiency of hourly workers with the assumption that a few, simple success formulas or high motivation would solve the work-load problems of the executive. A closer look, or even a cursory one, inside most contemporary business organizations provides little reassuring evidence that this assumption is justified.

CHAPTER IV

THE DEVELOPMENT and USE of ORGANIZATION CONTROLS

The volume of paper that passes over an executive's desk in any American company would suggest that too much information is provided, not too little. Yet, a few casual questions about the value of all these forms, reports, memos, and correspondence would create the impression that there is probably no substitute for going into the shop or the field and finding out for oneself. Most managers are in fact sensitive about their lack of adequate information! "We wish we knew how things were really going down in the shop" is a typical remark.

But organizational complexity, both geographical and administrative, makes such personal observation impractical. In addition, only a kind of administrative extrasensory perception, not possessed by most people, would enable the executive to know what to look at, whom to ask, and what information to request.

Many companies preserve the fiction that top management is in close touch with what is going on at the first level. The executives sally forth from time to time to "look into a problem," but usually plenty of advance warning reaches the department through the company grapevine. Even though there are ceremonial virtues in such visits and the possibility that some exchange of information may occur on a variety of subjects, the yield is liable to be strikingly low even if an agenda is carefully planned. Besides the natural tendency of divisional or plant managers to spruce things up and sweep the problems under the rug in their front office, the framework for pinpointing difficulties is simply not present.

Accounting Techniques May Not Provide Control

The information available to the executive, or even top management for that matter, touches only a segment of the total operation, and most of this is primarily designed to fit the special needs of the accountants. Historically, these reports develop out of and have been strongly influenced by the public function of the auditor. The balance sheet and operating statements of the company are prepared for the stockholders and for the government, and they relate only incidentally to the operating needs of management.

Unfortunately, although management should be evaluated in terms of the financial statements of the company, the statements are not built up from the realities of operation of the smallest unit, which for organizational efficiency would be a unit work flow, and then combined into larger systems until the total organization is described.

Instead, the accountants have started with the total company and then tried with growing sophistication to set up similar reporting systems for smaller units. The Chart of Accounts, through which income and expense are assigned to organizational units, reflects and is patterned on the functional classification of organization activities. As a result, endless effort is expended on distribution of expense, prorates, and all the other fictions that make it possible to put the dollars somewhere to produce a statement that can finally be audited.

Skillful executives learn to maneuver within this framework because they know they are judged by what the figures show. "Balloon squeezing" then becomes a major art; one tries to make his financial statements look good by shoving expense off on less astute colleagues. Although the total picture of the company does not improve, the steady flow of reports are the index of performance for top management that determine the method of reward and punishment, no matter how unreal.

Thus, in some companies, as experienced accountants know, more executive energy is devoted to manipulating the figures than improving productive efficiency. But such behavior is a product of the incentive system management itself designs by using such auditing procedures as control measures of managerial effectiveness. The manager who plays along is responding as might be predicted with this type of situation.

James Worthy, vice president of Sears Roebuck, who is well known as a perceptive student of these problems, described this same problem:

> The effectiveness of the organization as a whole may be judged in terms of physical output, or volume of sales, or the P&L statement. But where the internal structure of the organization is broken down into a series of functional divisions, there are no "natural" standards of performance and management is forced to exercise considerable ingenuity in inventing controls which it can use for administrative purposes. Unfortunately, contrived controls such as these, so far from facilitating inter-divisional cooperation (which is one of their chief purposes) often

become themselves a source of conflict. The individual supervisor or executive is under strong compulsion to operate in such a manner as to make a good showing in terms of the particular set of controls to which he is subject, and often he does so only at the expense of effective collaboration across divisional lines. This conflict is likely to be particularly acute when two closely related functions report up two different administrative lines and operate under two different systems of standards and controls.[1]

But where the game becomes more serious for the organization is the difficulty of proceeding from a line on the operating statement to an individual's responsibility. Who is responsible when expense is up and income down? Even if it is assumed that the accountants completely describe the operation of the company (which is not usually the case), only a series of shaky fictions can lead from the operating statement of the smallest unit to the summation for the total company. Who should be held responsible, and can any single individual justifiably be accountable for what the figures show?

Top management people are actually even worse off than those on lower levels because they have to depend so much on what the figures show. Making decisions on the basis of what financial reports reflect, as they must be made, assumes the figures are organizationally defined. The action taken is often completely unrelated to the problem. Consequently, management tries to supplement the decisions that they are compelled to make when the "figures" show some significant change through the use of personal visitations, hunches, or special studies.

Moreover, as pointed out in Chapter II, company financial records are often produced for the convenience of accountants, not management. Accountants are responsible for the financial accuracy of their statements, so it is only natural that this should be an overriding concern. The profit-and-loss statement must be ready for the directors at their monthly meeting or for inspection by the banks or insurance companies which provide financing, and it must be balanced to the last penny no matter how much time it takes. Therefore, under the present rules of the game, the operating statements on which internal operation depends are always after the fact, matters of ancient history. They are of no use to the executive as a means of control. This is ironic because the chief accounting officer is the controller, illustrating the semantic difficulties of the word "control."

Controllers are generally concerned by their uncertain relationship to top management. Having the tools of budgeting and accounting in their hands,

[1] James C. Worthy, "Some Aspects of Organization Structure in Relation to Pressures on Company Decision-Making," *Proceedings of Fifth Annual Meeting of Industrial Relations Research Association* (ed. L. Reed Tripp), IRRA Publ. no. 10, 1953, p. 77.

they do not know why they do not have the full responsibility for control. For them, the term implies the detection of deviations and the authority to require the guilty party to correct the situation forthwith. Although they concede the manager has the first responsibility, at heart they usually consider themselves as watchdogs of the operations of the company, ready to bite.

The Real Meaning of Control

The reason for the ambivalent treatment accountants received from management is the real distinction between keeping records and the administrative behavior that makes the records actually happen. Management, often only intuitively, is aware that record keeping indicates what has happened, not what is going to happen, and a controller can play his part in management only as control is limited to anticipation and prediction. The problem, therefore, can be reduced to asking, "How can we predict from our records, whatever they are, that a deviation is *about to take place* in the near or distant future so we as managers can take preventive steps in advance?" Because the whole orientation of the controller, who is trained as an accountant, is toward the production of accurate but after-the-fact reports, it is little wonder he often fails to understand that what he calls "control" does not mean the same thing to management. The field of management accounting is working in this direction, but, as mentioned earlier, it is not yet adequately synthesized with the organizational realities.

What is required to develop a system of controls for the organization? To find out, it is necessary to go back to the work flows of the company that are the ultimate sources of record keeping and ask, "Do managers now get information on every point of disturbance so they can anticipate disturbances before they happen?" In most companies, executives do not, but it may be worth considering the part the unit work-flow supervisor plays in managing disturbance and with what the work-flow system manager and his staff of specialists are necessarily concerned.

In the old-fashioned days, the foreman operated entirely by "feel." Constantly disdaining records of any sort, his ear told him a machine was beginning to slip in its performance and his eyes detected when the material was slightly off in specifications. From close moment-to-moment contact, he could tell if an operator was upset, and, by constant and continuous effort, he was able to anticipate every kind of disturbance to the smooth flow of work in his shop and take corrective actions.

Now, the foreman has become an executive or, some would say, a clerical employee, who is more liable to be found in his office than on the line. Like his superiors, he is kept busy preparing and studying reports, many of which are only peripheral in his operation. To supervise his department, he needs exactly the same kind of data coming to him that his predecessor obtained from direct contact. The same information affects stability of operation (and costs). The span of his control, using management terminology, depends *not* on the number of people to be supervised but on the frequency and duration of disturbances within his work-flow unit and the length of time required for him to correct them. Thus, two considerations need to be made in planning his job: the ease with which disturbances can be detected, and the freedom he has to do something about them.

The nature of the work-flow system he has to work with, however, imposes real limitations on what he can do unaided. If his equipment has a high frequency of mechanical problems or his processing difficulties stem from another unit work flow in the system, intervention by the work-flow system manager, that is, the second-level supervisor, and his specialists is necessary. Perhaps a study of the machines that are causing trouble by the mechanical specialist (staff) will lead to action to lower significantly the frequency of machine problems as a source of disturbance, and concentrated attention by the manager on coordination between two unit work-flow groups will reduce delays that introduce an erratic element into his operating system.

However, both the first-line supervisor or foreman and the work-flow system manager and his specialists need continuous data on the various technical and human problems of the constituent systems. This involves a reporting system to identify the specific sources of deviation from smooth performance. If the span of supervision is to be increased to a total unit work flow, work flows cannot be split into small segments in order to make it possible for an experienced foreman to anticipate trouble before it happens. A further difficulty with that approach is that too few foremen have such operating perception; because it is largely intuitive, there is little possibility for the specialists either to recognize a problem or to diagnose it. Under the old system of organization, the foreman usually regarded the specialists as interlopers and there was no conceptual and objective framework of analysis for them to use to talk effectively to each other.

Staff projects should be a product of the control system, not of someone's ambitions. Most of the specialists—engineering, personnel, methods, etc.—are present to make improvements in the functioning of the organization. Unfortunately, unless the control system identifies the sources of difficulty, staff activities are likely to be independent of the work flow. Someone who has an idea "sells it" to a manager, and a major staff activity is underway. Unless there are adequate controls to assess the degree of improvement resulting from such programs, it is likely that they will fail to accomplish their assumed objective. The criterion should be the contribution of a particular staff activity in reducing the frequency or the severity of a particular type of disturbance, whether its source is disturbed employees, equipment, or systems.

Use of the Statistical Quality Control Concept

Modern statistics has provided a means by which controls in the sense used here, can be provided with great power and effectiveness. Best known in the area of quality control, the principles can be stated rather simply. Something is in control when the limits within which past variation will repeat itself in the future can be predicted. Although nothing will be exactly the same each time it is measured or counted, as long as the variation falls within statistically defined limits, predictions can be made for the future. If, after a condition of control is shown, the measurements suddenly or gradually move outside the established limits, it is assumed that some unknown or assignable factor has intervened.

To use one illustration of quality control, inspectors take routine measurements of samples of parts that are being manufactured. If the measurements begin to fall outside the limits set up by past performance, it signals trouble. Perhaps the machine is going out of adjustment, the material has changed its metallurgical composition, or the operator is not following instructions. Therefore, the signal set up by consecutive sampling tells the supervisor that action is needed, and he must investigate to find the cause for the significant deviation in the values.

Identifying Source of Trouble

In more advanced systems of control, the probable causes of deviation are also controlled. Routine measures of revolutions per minute, machine settings, etc., are made to prevent the machine from causing trouble; routine chemical analyses of the raw material are performed; and the operator's performance of instructions is checked. As a result, the supervisor's time is saved because the amount of trouble shooting is reduced to a minimum and the guesswork technique to locate the source of poor quality is eliminated.

These various types of statistical control systems are important because they anticipate the source of difficulty or disturbance long before it becomes evident by methods of observation. Thus, quality defects that are not apparent in the inspection of individual parts do show up through sampling by the statistical trends toward greater variability, although for some time thereafter there is no increase in the actual rejects by usual inspection techniques. The application of this theory to situations where stability or repetition can be determined makes possible the prediction of disturbance before it happens. This provides the supervisor with the opportunity to correct it before the operation of his work-flow system is seriously affected.

Using the yardsticks of interaction measurement, based on the time and frequency of occurrence, a statistical control system for organization, exactly comparable to the controls of quality or productivity, is available. The only difference is that the mathematical properties of the frequency of intervals of action and inaction follow a different law than the normal law introduced in elementary statistics. From the point of view of understanding control, this is irrelevant and of concern only to the mathematicians who work out the methods of sampling, the methods of calculating limits, and the amount of change that signals trouble.

As a consequence, two interdependent systems can be used: the measures of quality and quantity and their dependent variables, such as machine performance, etc., and the measurement of action and interaction. A shift in interaction can cause a significant deviation in quality or output; and a disturbance in the even flow of work changes interaction. Consecutive samples from both of these areas provide the supervisors with the data needed for control. If controls are set up to obtain samples from all potential assignable causes shown by experience to be sources of trouble, they automatically prescribe for the supervisor the pattern of remedial actions to take and where to take it. Thus human relations variables are subject to the same type of control as production variables.

Job Descriptions Determine Controls

All of this is just another way of looking at the concept of the job of the manager or, for that matter, of any organization position. The previous chapter described how the various administrative actions of a supervisor could be broken down into categories such as supervising, negotiating, or interviewing. Each supervisor's job represents a combination that is determined by the work-flow system under his jurisdiction. To maintain a stable system he must initiate or respond to certain types of contacts. (In the face of constant technological and personnel changes, such a system must avoid stress-creating disturbances to be successful.)

Heretofore, management has found it difficult to exercise effective controls over these supervisory positions, just as it has encountered difficulty in assessing the performance of most employees doing nonroutine work. Many organizations assume their managers are doing a good job until a situation becomes serious and involves sudden resignations of key people or a revolt ranging from a wildcat strike to a delegation sent to the office of the president. As observed before, management had only unreliable methods to measure individual performance. Frequently the lame excuse is offered that everyone is interdependent and the individual does not work alone, so it is necessary to wait for trouble to show up in the statistics.

But what are these "statistics"? They are measures of quality and quantity already mentioned. However, two problems are associated with them. Frequently by the time they reveal trouble, it has already been very costly to the organization. Secondly, even after discovering that a particular sales office is below its budgeted level of sales, no one knows who or what to blame. Possibly fault can be found with the measure itself; if income is lower in that section of the country, there is no money available to create sales. Even if that approach fails, it is still difficult, even impossible, to identify who made the mistake because so much modern business activity involves group efforts. The contribution of the individual, or lack of it, is hidden in the activities of the group.

But when checks are set up on the fulfillment of specifically defined parts of each job—the number of contacts with potential customers, contacts with market research when specific field problems arise, prompt managerial response to complaints or grievances, etc.—it is possible to assign responsibility for deviations from predetermined standards. More important, it is possible to predict where organizational problems will occur and, just as vital, what can be done to head off serious difficulties.

In this analysis, controls are not a separate part or tool of managerial activity; they are integrated with every aspect of the job, indicating again that the argument of work versus human relations has no merit. By designing control systems that relate unexpected changes in work output variables with unexpected changes in interaction patterns in key jobs, it is possible to deal with operating problems realistically. It is not enough to know that a particular piece of equipment is causing trouble, i.e., is out of control. Management needs to know what part of the day-to-day functioning of the human organization is responsible and who should prevent the recurrence.

The Place of the Dollar Component

This brief discussion may not have made it evident that all measurements or counts involve individual units or dimensions. The number of parts produced or handled is counted, and the time necessary to do the work and the organizational contacts associated with the operation of the total work flow are measured. Nowhere has the dollar sign been raised; the accountant, for purposes of control, has been left out of the picture.

On the other hand, it should be evident that a dollar value can be attached to each of the units being measured. The cost of the time spent in doing a job, either by the actions required or the interaction connected with it, can easily be calculated in the same way dollars are traditionally applied to rejects and the accepted product. If a deviation occurs outside the established limits, the dollar cost can be estimated. Variance is after all only a means of costing the deviations.

Curiously enough, at the level of control, the dollar is secondary. Its value fluctuates with changing costs of labor, materials, and market conditions. Units and time are much less variable yardsticks, so unless the product changes, there is a constant basis for comparison on the operating level.

In top management, however, the dollar is crucial in translating what happens at the work-flow level into profit and loss. Management usually encountered difficulties heretofore because it was unable to move from dollars to the elements they represent with any precision. Thus, when faced with problems of control, dollars and the unit-time complex could not be isolated from each other. Prediction of deviations from the limits that budgeting and cost accounting try to set becomes effective once the dollar is used as a multiplier at the work-flow level of the basic time units comprising the flow.

Control systems are thus available for both the organization and the product. Management controls can be provided systematically by extending the techniques used for the single unitary work flow to the whole operation. Therefore, the total control system is simply an accumulation of its constituent parts. Because one can proceed from the total down to each of its components, top management can make decisions regarding whole work-flow systems since the financial evidence is a multiplication of the operating results of the control system itself.

A separation of finance from the elements to which the dollar figure is applied by top management could lead to a revolution in the realm of "management accounting." Starting with the Chart of Accounts, an accounting reorganization would be necessary to make the dollar directly reflect its counterpart in the operation of the business. But, whether this occurs or not, it is essential that management give explicit consideration to controls as a means of anticipating future developments.

Conclusion

Forecasting and long-range planning are discussed a great deal today and are of primary concern to decision-makers or, more properly, the theorists who developed this area into a major topic in business studies. Such discussions necessarily involve consideration of the validity of the methods used to make predictions. Too few attempts have been made to extend the tools at hand systematically to all business variables that can be measured. The complex subject of the future—five, ten, or fifteen years ahead—should be considered only when short-term predictions can be made.

There is still much work to be done before people will be able to say with confidence how the corporation will behave tomorrow. At the very least, adequate systems of control should be introduced at this time; controls are a basic element in the structure of any organization, whether it is private or governmental. They provide a primary incentive and indicate where the individual members of the organization should apply their energies. Most important, they are the signal that should bring into action one or more of the supervisory techniques already described, and perhaps staff activities as well. Without adequate controls to direct managerial efforts, time and energy are wasted, and potential crises are ignored while smoothly functioning activities receive needless attention.

Finally, controls are the most important means to detect organizational defects that require the types of restructuring described in previous chapters. Malfunctioning work flows, badly placed executives, and ineffective supervision persist under present accounting and administrative controls. Organizational controls should uncover sore spots and, more crucially, detect potential weaknesses before the costs become great. They are the essential bridge between the organization structure and administrative behavior.

The authors are well aware that a large number of well-qualified accountants have been trying to overcome many of the defects described in this chapter. Such developments as variable or flexible budgets, responsibility accounting, and direct costing are examples of recent efforts to improve managerial controls. However, accountants frequently find management both unresponsive and uninformed about the use of such controls and, more important, the organization structure unyielding when they try to modify it. The manager is not sure what information he wants or for what purpose, only that he wants facts. He frequently assumes that there are package systems, ready-made for his operation. All of this is contrary to the notion of controls as integral parts of the management of the work flow.

CHAPTER V

TECHNOLOGICAL DETERMINANTS of WORK-GROUP BEHAVIOR

No experienced manager likes to hear situations described as static and unchanging. He knows that reality, at least for most organizations, is far removed from such an ideal state. Every supervisor is buffeted by change almost daily, in some cases hourly. Unexpected breakdowns, absences, or rush orders cause upsets. In addition to these presumably "uncontrollable" factors, employee or union rebelliousness may threaten in the background. The sudden grievance challenging a management decision and the implicit or even explicit threat of noncooperation, ranging from an excessive following of the "rules" or a slowing of work to excessive clumsiness and work stoppages, add to the problems of the manager.

The manager's job is basically one of stabilization. Undertaking a number of activities, he seeks to stabilize the work flow. He tries to maintain equilibrium in the pattern of work relationships in the face of a never-ending series of disruptions, resulting from changes in schedules, equipment failures, absenteeism, worker complaints, and labor disturbances.

His pattern of behavior must change to meet these new challenges. No matter what the source, they all consume valuable time. Yet, the supervisor must also maintain other essential work-flow contacts and be able to return to routine work patterns quickly, regardless of how personally threatening or upsetting the crisis is.

His work load, the number of employees he can supervise, and the measurements of his effectiveness in performing his job all involve computations of the total number of these stabilizing actions (administrative patterns) and their respective required time dimensions. Thus, the crucial determinant of the supervisor's work load is the frequency of occurrence of stress or crises that need attention. If the operation is functioning smoothly and everyone is doing his job with adequate results, the pressures on the manager are minimal.

The authors believe the type and frequency of these disturbances (and therefore the supervisor's work load) is determined in large measure by the organization decisions of management. The way department boundaries, technology, and layout distribute workers and jobs is crucial in shaping the work load of the supervisor.

A realistic appraisal of industrial-relations problems suggests the work group is the focal point of many day-to-day crises facing the supervisor. This is an old story to the student of collective bargaining who has observed challenges to management authority, threats of strikes or slowdowns, resistance to new work standards and incentive rates. They are usually centered in a discontented group, not an individual.

The field of industrial relations has assumed these work-group-centered upsets or protests were a random variable, at least from the point of view of the manager. Department X may require a great deal of supervision today to mollify the malcontents who threatened a work stoppage, but tomorrow the difficulties might shift to Department Y. The first outbreak may have been started by a troublemaker and the second could be a consequence of a poor supervisory decision. And so it goes; one day here and the next day there, with a welter of possible causes and effects.

Close observation of the incidence of such problems belies the simple assumption that they are random. The distribution of crises requiring supervisory attention is patterned, not a chance-cause system. One can predict with reasonable accuracy the relative frequency with which a particular work group will "act up." Not only do the same work areas within a plant maintain rather constant patterns of behavior, even though their personnel and management may change, but also these similarities extend to intercompany comparisons as well. Certain work groups have an industry-wide reputation for their behavior, which is almost the same in companies with good labor relations and those with bad or ineffective policies. Put in another way, management can predict in what areas technical changes or new incentive rates will be smooth and effortless and in what areas such transitions are likely to cause problems and of what types, so they can plan accordingly.

For many reasons, it is useful if the manager can predict which parts of his organization are most susceptible to these problems and which areas require special attention and large allotments of that scarce supervisory skill, the ability to cope with crises. With such predictability, supervisory assignments and time budgets can be made to obtain the maximum effectiveness from the available supply of supervisory and staff personnel.

The Functions of Work Groups

To understand these observable differences in group behavior, it is necessary to re-examine the function of the group in regard to its members and to the organization. The field of human relations has stressed the importance of the group, and management is often told it must learn to work with groups because employees, under many circumstances, do not respond to company action as individuals. It is almost commonplace to speak of the supervisor's responsibility for learning to deal effectively with his subordinates as an informal group with unique leadership, beliefs, and customs. Research in recent years has given rise to a whole new concept of leadership that involves the utilization of such group methods as conferences, group decision, and representative shop government. Thus, with few exceptions, groups are recognized as being important, but frequently for the wrong reasons!

Relation of Social Cohesiveness to Worker Satisfaction

In a series of pioneer studies, Elton Mayo and his colleagues found that employees sought and required social satisfactions in their work. If these were absent because of such factors as physical isolation or rapid turnover, individual discontent damaged organizational effectiveness. The emphasis on providing social satisfactions at work has not faltered in more recent years. It has been aided and abetted by such hypotheses as those of George Homans: The greater the opportunity for interworker contact, the greater the positive feelings of mutual goodwill and friendship.[1]

The result has been an overemphasis on social cohesion. It has been argued that the administrator must build tightly knit groups by providing maximum opportunity for social interaction within the limits of the work situation for his own good. Consequently, because assembly lines and automation reduce opportunities for widely and evenly dispersed worker communication, they reduce social cohesiveness as a result of the more modest level of mutual liking that develops with reduced interaction.[2] Such innovations, therefore, must lower worker morale.

Some interworker contact is undoubtedly essential to satisfy the need for

[1] George Homans, *The Human Group*, New York, Harcourt, Brace and Company, Inc., 1950, p. 133.

[2] William A. Faunce, "Automation in the Automobile Industry: Some Consequences for In-plant Social Structure," *American Sociological Review*, vol. 23, no. 4, 1958, pp. 401–407. This paper is an extreme example of this point of view.

group membership and identification, and management probably should recognize this social need. But, beyond this point, the provision of additional social satisfaction, per se, may benefit neither employees nor the firm. There are other factors that are much more crucial.

The Work Group as a Redress Channel

More important than socializing to both its members and management, the work group enables individuals at the bottom of the organizational hierarchy to initiate action for others. The manager who is under stress can usually reciprocate by directing action to his subordinates, but the organizational pyramid places the workers in such a position that they have no one to whom they can initiate, even though technological, managerial, and supervisory changes eventually are directed to them. With the exception of a few unusually dominant personalities who can take it out on the boss, they have no regular channel, other than their own groups, to direct these pressures and regain their equilibrium.

Consistent with the analysis of personality that will be presented in Chapter VII, the group provides its members with two types of critical satisfactions. First, the group internally provides an audience of responsive listeners to whom the individual can express and satisfy his need for interaction. Secondly, the work group, not the individual as is frequently assumed, is typically the means by which frustrating work conditions such as an oppressive supervisor or an overly tight incentive rate can be changed or modified. Some groups actually magnify the amount of grievance activity in excess of what might be predicted with the prevailing wages and working conditions.[3]

Relations of Informal Groups to the Union

Most individual members depend upon the support and solidarity of a group of like-minded fellows to initiate action to union and management. The local union cannot automatically serve the numerous and often conflicting needs of all the members it represents. Few political organizations, in fact, are responsible to an unorganized group of individuals. Insofar as like interests are represented in the informal group, their expression will be

[3] The other highly important function of work groups has purposely been neglected in this discussion. Their organization, the jobs included or excluded, and the physical proximities and barriers of contact have highly significant effects on the production process itself. For work operations requiring interworker cooperation and coordination, the intimate tying together and development of mutual responsibility that can be achieved within the confines of the face-to-face group can make a vital contribution to performance. Criteria for judging this and defining work-group boundaries to facilitate this objective, however, have been discussed in Chapter II.

amplified many times beyond the single voice in the department meeting or individual grievance in the union files.

Differences in Work-Group Behavior

To the individual worker, the group is important as the means by which he can participate in the organizational process, by which he can initiate as well as respond to action, and by which he can balance the varying pressures and strains directed upon him by his supervisor and management. Groups differ greatly, however, in their abilities to provide this kind of satisfaction and to act as stabilizing or unstabilizing forces in the organization. They also differ significantly in their patterns of interaction with both management and union representatives, in their methods of participation in the formal or informal grievance procedure and internal union politics, and in their responsiveness to change.

What are these differences in group behavior that can be predicted and used to improve managerial effectiveness? What do these groups look like to the supervisor or the administrator faced with the problem of maintaining schedules and work efficiency in a department or a plant?

Types of Work Groups

A recent field project encompassing thirty companies attempted to answer this question. When the data derived from the study of three hundred work groups were assembled, it became apparent that there were consistent and predictable differences in the manner in which a given group would relate to both management and the union. Furthermore, there were striking similarities among many of the groups in their characteristic style of behavior. Four rather distinct types of groups, classified according to the persistent behavior they demonstrated, were observed. The names given to them are primarily a convenience or a shorthand method of referring to a set of distinguishing characteristics, not an explanation of the differences. They are: erratic, strategic, conservative, and apathetic.[4]

The Erratic Groups

The most distinctive characteristic of some work groups was their tendency toward erratic behavior. This statement means there was no apparent

[4] Most of the remainder of this chapter is extracted from a recent publication by one of the authors with permission from the publisher.

Leonard R. Sayles, *Behavior of Industrial Work Groups; Prediction and Control.* Copyright, 1958, by John Wiley & Sons, Inc., New York.

relationship between the seriousness of their grievances (from the point of view of the employees themselves) and the intensity of their protests. Issues that both management and union observers considered minor, that is, problems that probably could have been settled satisfactorily by a brief discussion, developed into a major uprising or a mass demonstration such as a wildcat strike without warning. At the same time, deep-seated grievances may have existed within these groups over long periods of time with no apparent reaction in terms of group behavior. Union leaders have suffered consistently because of this type of "split personality." Petty grievances often became nearly insolvable problems because of rash strikes and demonstrations, and important cases languished in the grievance procedure because there was no support from the rank and file for the efforts of the union officers to convince management that "this is really important to the men."

By management evaluation, this explosiveness placed such groups at the top of the plant "dangerous" list. In fact, a great deal of the time and energy of both management and union officials devoted to the grievance procedure was concentrated on these tension areas. Even so, the managers and union leaders often admitted frankly they did not understand what was really going on in such departments. "You just don't know what to expect," was a typical descriptive assessment.

There was some scattered evidence that this kind of group is subject to sudden changes of atmosphere, that is, a department that had been a source of endless grief to all concerned, literally overnight, became one of the showplaces of the plant where unanimity and harmony prevailed. At some later time, it may just as suddenly revert back to its earlier condition.

In some instances, due perhaps to their ready inflammability, members of these groups occupied positions of leadership in the union during the early organizational phase when emphasis was on the ability to rally immediate, aggressive support for the union. In later years, when more mature skills of bargaining and strategic patience were required, top union positions were filled by representatives of other departments.

The Strategic Groups

In many plants, one or two groups were at the center of most of the really important grievances, important because they involved major economic considerations. Often these groups were also a part of the core of the union "regulars," who kept close track of how well their specific economic interests were being advanced by the officers. Time after time, they succeeded in electing one of their number to top union office, even when they comprised only a small fraction of the membership. These departments were not characterized by sudden flashes of activity; rather, they were shrewdly calculating pressure groups that never tired of objecting to unfavorable management decisions, of seeking loopholes in existing policies and contract clauses that would be to their benefit, and of comparing their benefits with those of other departments in the plant. They demanded constant attention for their problems and reinforced their demands by group action.

Unlike the erratic work groups, however, the amount and kind of pressure the strategic groups exerted was carefully measured, both against the objectives they sought and the immediate strategy of the total situation. Thus, management was startled with a sudden display of aggression only if surprise was chosen from the many weapons at their disposal. In the manner of some actors, they could "turn it on or off" ("it" referring to such concerted activities as slowing down work) as the occasion demanded. To that degree, their behavior was predictable. This consistency was regarded as a virtue by both management and the union.

Such groups are often at the heart of the union as well as of the grievance activities in their plants. The way management handles the difficult problems that arise in such departments is a prime factor in determining the existing climate of industrial relations. These departments are the real trouble spots where management and union decisions are likely to be vigorously and shrewdly challenged in the interests of improving the economic position of the employees concerned.

The outsider would probably be amazed at the brashness and unceasing economic pressure of the strategic groups. These characteristics do not fit easily into the everyday concept of the grievance procedure as an appeal channel reserved for protesting only inequitable management actions. These work groups use the whole range of collective bargaining tactics to obtain benefits for themselves that are quite apart from any inequitable management action. (In the process, they may set off a lengthy series of inequity complaints from other, weaker groups and establish new standards for the plant as a whole on such matters as appropriate work loads, leisure time, incentive earnings, and countless noneconomic working conditions.) As pacemakers in the struggle to better themselves, they attract and require an unbelievably high proportion of management and union energies.

The Conservative Groups

Of all the groups observed, the conservative groups were the most stable, in that they were least likely to use concerted action without warning.

The niche they carved for themselves was often so satisfactory, in terms of compensation and working conditions, that it was more common for management to have grievances against them than for the men to have grievances against the management. It was not unusual to find the company negotiating with the group for a higher level of output. This goal was sometimes difficult to achieve even when bonus systems and group strength guaranteed that all additional effort would be reflected in higher earnings.

This kind of group is much more moderate in its grievance activities. On the surface, at least, there was little evidence of turmoil, trouble, or concerted activity. At some time or times in the past, such a group had exercised its strength, but, once proved, their strength, like that of any great power, was accepted at face value by those whom it affected, until they could match it with greater force.

Representatives from these groups might be termed the senior statesmen of the plant negotiation machinery. Pyrotechnics are usually out of place, although when occasion warrants, a quick stoppage is always a possibility.

Because they are aware of their latent strength, such groups do not demand the immediate service often insisted upon by the erratic or strategic groups. They accept the time-consuming routine of the various channels and red tape of the grievance procedure without exploding from frustration. When made to wait, weaker groups are more likely to fear loss of the grievance unless they do something, and quickly. As others have observed, those with greater power can usually wait more patiently to secure satisfaction. Most of the men in conservative groups could probably find an adequate number of jobs requiring their specialization available in the local labor market if the company does not provide satisfactory employment opportunities. As the elite of the plant labor force, they are self-assured, successful, and relatively stable in their relations with management and in their own internal affairs.

On occasion, they exhibit ambivalence toward the union. They may experiment with leadership and then leave active union affairs indefinitely. They may even withdraw from the unified bargaining unit in favor of some craft union that will better represent them.

The Apathetic Groups

By almost any measure, the apathetic departments were the least likely to develop grievances or engage in concerted action as a means of pressuring management or the union. Although occasional incidents did occur, compared with other groups, these workers were not inclined to challenge decisions or attempt to gain something extra for themselves. Surprisingly, however, these departments were not ranked highest by management for consistent productivity and cooperativeness.

These groups were also less prone to engage in union politics or participate in the internal life of their unions. Petty jealousies and interpersonal problems were somewhat more common than in the other groups and cohesion less strong. Although management and union representatives could identify certain influential members of the group, real leadership was dispersed among a relatively large number of individuals.

Variations in Type of Informal Leader Selected

In an important sense, the personality traits of the informal leader or on occasion the union official through whom the group deals with management and union are the crucial links between potential action and any action taken. Although the leader does not determine the actions of the group, the group usually selects an individual whose characteristics suit its demands. The authors' data in this area are only suggestive at present, and the descriptions of leaders' behavior are highly incomplete. It appears, however, there is a significant relationship between the personality type that appeals to a group and the kind of group involved.

Apathetic and, to a lesser extent, erratic groups frequently seem to permit the leadership function to gravitate to highly aggressive individuals with a strong need to dominate the situation, both within the group and in its relations with management and the union, as leaders. These individuals tolerate no competition for the center of the stage; they must have the last word in every encounter. An interesting characteristic, and certainly a most unexpected one from the point of view of many management officials, is the readiness with which these leaders can, on occasion, transfer their censorious remarks from the company to the rank and file. While describing their roles in precipitating a wildcat strike or a serious verbal attack against the company, they may comment that the company is making a mistake by not promoting them to the personnel department.

Their striking and appealing personality characteristics, which set them apart from their coworkers, make them the obvious choice of groups that wish to be dominated or to follow a "spellbinder."

In contrast, the strategic and conservative groups generally select individuals who are temperamentally better suited to responding to actions initiated by the group. Because they are able to give a consensus toward problems, these groups utilize a leader who will do their bidding and not assert his own will. In fact, any attempts for leadership by members within the groups that are considered overbearing, inflexible, and irresponsible are rejected as being dangerous.

The leaders of these groups are less colorful. Although they may be intellectually committed to an antimanagement viewpoint and determined to press certain grievances with great vigor, they are not aggressive for the sake of being aggressive. They express their hostilities in controlled convictions, not emotional outbursts and, therefore, are much easier to negotiate with.

Factors Causing Variations

These behavior differences are not randomly distributed. Regardless of the plant in which they are located, the quality of supervision, or the expressed policies of union or management, certain kinds of work groups are strategic groups. The behavior of others, again with identifiable differences, is nearly always described as erratic. What are the qualities determining the type of group that will develop?

Significance of Technology

In looking at the organization chart and work flow or layout of an industrial plant, certain predictions can be made confidently regarding the behavior of the work groups found in specific spots. Concentrations of jobs with certain characteristics are probably centers of industrial relations problems. Jobs with other characteristics enable one to predict the absence of such frictions.

Upon analysis, it appears that all the relevant variables in group formation depend on the technological system used by the company to organize the work process. The degree of independence or dependence among workers in the flow of work, the number and similarity of jobs concentrated in any one location, and the indispensability of any part to the whole are largely determined by the kinds and quantity of equipment, required skills, and plant layout.

Industrial relations problems are generally attributed to individual worker and manager characteristics and the nature of the work situations. These problems supposedly continue because the jobs are unpleasant, repetitive, mechanically paced, heavy, dirty, or exacting in terms of the quantity and quality of output required. However, it appears that the group structure erected by the technological process is actually a more basic and continuing determinant of work-group attitudes and actions. How then does technology shape the behavior and differences in patterns of these groups?

The Importance of Common Interests

Generally, and this is not surprising, adjacently located employees who operate different kinds of machines or perform different tasks combine less often in pressure campaigns to attain mutual goals; they do not have enough in common. These are frequently the apathetic groups.

What seems essential for verbalizing complaints and uniting people to seek redress is reinforcement or a *resonance* factor. Reverberation is provided by people having identical experiences, such that each employee can hear his own grievances repeated and magnified. Particularly in erratic and strategic groups, a man who tells his mates of a job problem finds that they share it. With sympathetic repetition, the problem grows in importance. A group of like-minded employees may convince one another not only that something *should* be done but, more important, that it *can* be done.

This means that, other things being equal, the greater the number of workers affected by some aspect of the work environment, the greater the likelihood that they will act in common against the problem. These are groups of employees with the same supervisor, job classification, or type of job.

More serious problems of organizational instability occur when disturbed individuals in one department transmit their stress to employees in other departments. If the second group also becomes disturbed, their changed interaction patterns may act as an additional stimulus for the first group. The likelihood of this happening, as well as the rapidity with which a group becomes disturbed, depends upon the rate at which all or most members of the group are exposed to the changed interaction patterns.

What distinguishes the erratic from the strategic group if the resonance variable is characteristic of both? To help answer this question, it would be instructive to observe work groups where interdependence among employees is imposed by the technology. They contrast sharply with work groups in which the members work independently.

Homogeneous Crews

These work groups are usually composed of from three to twelve employees. Although they must work together, each man does an identical job. Crews loading or unloading materials, sanding automobile bodies, or stripping the selvage off paperboard cut for cartons are examples of homogeneous crews. Resonance is at a maximum because the work throws them together. But, in every case the authors observed, the behavior of this type of group was erratic not strategic. Why?

Part of the explanation may be in the intimacy of their relationship. Because of the high frequency of interaction, slight problems are quickly magnified as one employee stimulates his coworkers. Such work groups are incapable of long, carefully planned attacks on management or union decisions they dislike. They react immediately and often unwisely. Their inability to restrain themselves makes carefully calculated pressure activities unlikely.

Homogeneous crews have another handicap. Because of the close, almost family-like relationships they foster, it is difficult for them to ally themselves with more inclusive, larger department units, a unity which is necessary to process many important problems through union channels.

Interdependent work operations also have a delicate internal balance; new members can "quickly sour the whole bunch," in the words of several management officials. Although it is difficult to incorporate a new member because of the intimate coordination required by the process, at the same time, it is easy for the new member to extend his influence after he is accepted. For this reason, too, spontaneous changes such as shifts from low to high output, no grievances to many grievances, or docility to a wildcat walkout can be expected from these groups. Communications are almost immediate and reinforced by the completely shared experiences of the entire group. Thus, a really embittered employee or a highly satisfied worker with leadership potential can both have startling effects on the attitudes and behavior of the other workers.

Crews and Assembly Lines

Work crews and short assembly lines in which each employee has a different job need internal unity more than an aggregation of employees who work independently. The technologically interdependent workers must come to a mutually acceptable decision concerning the pace of work and total output. Although the high frequency of their interaction makes them a tightly knit work team and social organization, the conflicting needs of the several occupations included in the group (with different job classifications and skills) can prevent these same units from taking concerted action to attain work-group goals. In departments that contain a number of similar crews or assembly groups, unity among all of them for common goals is difficult to achieve because of the self-enclosed character of each of the component units. Similarly, these groups are not free to select and change their informal leadership; the functional work leader selected for them (the straw boss or crew chief) usually dominates the situation.

Consequently, the members of such work crews or short assembly lines do not engage in prolonged, carefully planned concerted activity on their own behalf. They are either apathetic or, in a few cases, erratic. In part, this may be because of their internal promotional ladder (moving up to the level of crew chief) and because they have less need for, or less tolerance of, participation in such outside groups as the union if the work process necessitates a high level of interaction. More tolerant of (or more accustomed to) highly dominant, inflexible leadership, they allow their own leaders to act as straw bosses and, in many situations, to fill in as first-line supervisors during the temporary absences of foremen, a dual responsibility that normally would not be permitted in groups of technologically independent workers.

Crews and assembly groups are more often involved in such demonstrations as wildcat strikes than other groups. Although such strikes are not a regular occurrence, frustrations build up in a group with no systematic means of expressing discontent, the problems become cumulative. The crew or short assembly line may appear to be relatively satisfied for a long period, and then a sudden explosion may occur, and the men engage in a serious walkout, exhibiting erratic behavior.

Long Assembly Lines

Longer assembly lines, on which workers are restricted in their interaction with workers on either side of them, may inhibit the development of an informal group, as Walker and Guest observed in their study of automobile assembly lines.[5]

A study by Zaleznik of an assembly line consisting of thirty-five workers found it encouraged the formation of tightly knit pairs of workers that, in turn, caused a number of operators to be socially isolated. The workers in the study were stationed at a moving belt doing simple wiring and soldering operations. According to Zaleznik:

> An operator could talk easily only with workers on her immediate right and left. From the point of view of any one worker, her only possible spontaneous group during working hours consisted of two workers and herself, or a group of three. A threesome, however, tends to make a very unstable group because of the likelihood of pairing. It is easy, therefore, for some operators at least to find themselves socially isolated. Once something goes wrong, there is considerable interaction, but under conditions of extreme tension and anxiety.[6]

[5] Charles R. Walker and Robert Guest, *The Man on the Assembly Line,* Harvard University Press, Cambridge, Mass., 1952, p. 79.

[6] A. Zaleznik, *Worker Satisfaction and Development,* Harvard University Graduate School of Business Administration, Cambridge, Mass., 1956, pp. 120–121.

This kind of behavior is typical of the apathetic groups observed by the authors.

Breaks and Imperfections in the Work Flow

Many erratic groups were located at points in an assembly or material flow situation where there was inadequate opportunity for workers in different parts of the operation to communicate. These two or more sections needed to coordinate their actions to avoid breakdowns and other mishaps, many of which not only could hurt production but might also result in lost incentive earnings or additional physical labor for the employees. However, because of the plant layout, physical or temporal separations kept the segments apart, making adequate communication impossible. This resulted in production difficulties that simultaneously erupted into employee-management fireworks.

The same erratic chain reaction of process problems followed by a number of grievances or complaints was observable. In such operations as electrolytic refining of metal or metal plating, these problems frequently contained several uncontrolled technical factors that affected the quantity of output in relation to employee effort. If earnings were less than expected, the employees became resentful and frequently focused their discontent on the work standards, which they declared were unfair. This resentment further diminished output, and management, in reacting, placed direct pressure on supervision and employees to bring up their output levels. Such an increase in downward-directed pressure can result in a further decrease in employee output and cause, in turn, more management pressure. Thus, a modest technical problem can create a sharp, downward-spiraling productivity curve, and the work-standard grievances are the additional by-product. In all such cases, there is a high probability that technological factors upset habitual routines and that the emotional responses of the workers to these upsets further hinder production.

Indispensability

There was evidence that work groups who were in a position to halt production used this economic power to get material gains for themselves. This characteristic was frequently found in strategic groups.

In a carefully documented study recently completed by Prof. James Kuhn, of Columbia University, he finds there are striking differences in the wildcat strike records of companies in the rubber tire manufacturing industry and of firms manufacturing electrical goods. Technologically, these two industries are at opposite poles. Many individual groups, by taking concerted action in a tire plant, can throw thousands out of work. This interruption of routine creates a strong backlash because groups who do not have the grievance causing the walkout are still subject to the stress of work interruptions. On the other hand, there is little fixed sequence of operations in electrical goods; interruptions caused by a slowing down of work or a strike of one group can be worked around. According to Kuhn, adequate banks of parts and the absence of continuous processing are responsible for the significantly smaller number of stoppages and work-flow disturbances in these types of plants. The greater leverage enjoyed by tire-plant workers increases the likelihood that management will acquiesce, reinforcing the use of concerted action weapons as a compensatory mechanism. Less immediate results in electrical manufacturing plants discourage the use of self-help measures as an immediate reaction to stress.

Note what Kuhn is saying. Individual work groups have enormous leverage in companies that follow traditional functional patterns of organization and where a stoppage in one department has immediate and drastic repercussions in adjacent departments. Minor frictions, causing modest interruptions in the work pace, snowball to major proportions. Employees quickly learn the lesson that a small number of them can put pressure on management many times greater than their size would suggest.

Research by the authors shows that efforts by management to expediently placate one group with generous grievance settlements often leads to more instability by creating inequities in the wage and benefit structure.[7] In addition, difficulties in employee relations that change the rate at which work moves through and between departments create stress for employees. Sudden changes in production schedules, combined with actions initiated by several levels of management seeking to maintain some semblance of normal productivity and the circulation of union and informal leaders within the work group, upset the normal pattern of intragroup and employee-manager relations. The result is often a spiraling of personnel difficulties. (An analysis of spiraling morale problems is presented in Chapter IX.) Personnel and line managers recount distastefully the disturbances during periods of high-grievance activity and labor trouble. The authors contend it is an inevitable result of this type of plant organization. Relatively autonomous departments, organized on a unit work-flow basis, show little of this epidemic pattern. Problems are self-contained, and the work group finds itself in a different position.

[7] Leonard R. Sayles, "The Impact of Incentives on Inter-Group Work Relations," *Personnel*, vol. 28, no. 6, 1952, pp. 483–490.

Selection and Development of Supervision

To date, emphasis has generally been placed on developing "qualities of good supervision" on the assumption they are universally applicable. Although certain general principles are applicable to almost any relationship involving superiors and subordinates, the behavior of the supervisor is only a part of the relationship. Appropriate behavior for the supervisor is conditioned to a substantial degree by the reactions of his subordinates. The supervisor does not supervise in a vacuum. Each action he takes produces some response by his subordinates, and the response varies according to the work group supervised.

Thus, a supervisor who deals successfully with the men in Department A may not necessarily be just as successful with the men in Department B. Different skills and temperaments may be required, depending partially on the pressure groups within the two departments.

As might be expected, the authors found the largest turnover of supervisors, the concentration of complaints about supervision, and concern over the problem of good supervision were in departments and work groups that demonstrated erratic and strategic behavior patterns and where concerted activity was greatest. Management believed these areas required the strongest leadership and the most able supervisors, that is, men who were not afraid to assert their authority and command recognition as leaders. These general attributes are not easy to define or assess in potential supervisors.

Supervision of Erratic Groups

The erratic group usually requires the most capable type of supervisor. He must be highly stable, self-confident, and able to comprehend the group forces with which he is working. By definition, these groups do not respond in any completely predictable manner, and he must realize that the onset of some of their aggressive reactions may be beyond his control. The likelihood that even the most intelligent decision-making and skilled leadership performance will still meet periodic demonstrations is difficult to tolerate and discourages men of lesser talents.

The reactions of his superiors are also a critical factor. They must recognize that the behavior of the group he supervises is not always rational and even the perfect supervisor cannot eliminate all concerted activity. Many of these activities are inherent to the group itself and its position within the total plant organization. By understanding these problems and by supporting the supervisor, they can strengthen him and bolster his position.

Supervision of Apathetic Groups

From the point of view of supervision, the apathetic groups, which show almost no concerted behavior, are almost equally difficult. There is little evidence of leadership within such groups, and the department is often fractionalized into a number of competing or antagonistic cliques and subgroups. Under these circumstances, the supervisor has difficulty in securing any consistent reaction from his subordinates. A decision may be strongly supported by one group but opposed almost as strongly by one or more others. Consequently, attempts to win agreement by means of consultative supervision before taking action may be doomed from the start. Almost by definition, there is no consensus within the group. Although morale is not overtly bad, the real danger lies in this deception. Because few protests or requests are made directly, the supervisor may have a sense of false security, yet worker dissatisfaction may be rampant beneath the surface and affecting the work effort.

Therefore, the supervisor must comprehend the structure of the work group clearly and be able to work with a complex set of forces and a variety of personality types among informal leaders. He must also be able to somehow balance the interests and demands of a number of cliques.

Supervision of Strategic Groups

At first glance, a group with strategic patterns of behavior may appear to be difficult to supervise because of its well-organized militancy. However, its predictability, its concentration of leadership in a small core group, and its outspoken nature provide a more receptive environment for effective leadership than work groups with apathetic or erratic behavior. The supervisor may be able to develop the necessary negotiating skills to maintain operations if he realizes the men in his particular department are critical, challenge policies that are accepted in other departments without question, and frequently set the patterns for the entire plant. He must also be temperamentally able to accept initiations of action from subordinates. If the group is unionized, the supervisor must be thoroughly familiar with collective bargaining techniques and the structure and function of the local union. This requires knowledge not only of the literal meaning of the union contract but also of its numerous applications in specific situations throughout the plant, often representing informal agreements. Management may have to help him develop the ability to accept challenges to his authority in such a way that subordinates are assured of a real hearing for their complaints without his abdicating leadership in his department.

Issues concerned with output standards are particularly difficult to handle in such groups. Where a "fair day's work" is a matter of judgment and where work load standards cannot be precisely controlled, the supervisor has to rely on his own skills to achieve group acceptance of reasonable productivity; he cannot rely on the firm decisions of the standards department as can supervisors in many machine-paced groups.

Supervisors of a strategically oriented group can use its informal leaders to facilitate the supervisory job. Because of the essential unity of the group, the informal leader accurately reflects the sentiments of the group and, in turn, has some influence on group opinions.

Supervision of Conservative Groups

A number of managers reported satisfaction with the supervisors of conservative groups. However, these supervisors may be receiving more credit than they deserve because conservative groups respond more readily to the accepted practices of "good supervision." These groups can assume responsibility, are cohesive, and speak affirmatively. Their complaints usually reflect objectionable conditions.

The leaders of conservative groups often make competent supervisors, and, even more important, the groups readily accept such a change in an employee's status. These employees are accustomed to responding and deferring to their most skilled and able coworkers and transfer this pattern to his new position as supervisor. In many cases, the choice for promotion made by management is an obvious one to the group. Thus, the transition is painless, as compared to the serious conflicts that often confront the newly promoted supervisor in departments where potential leadership skill is not evident to both management and employees.

Conclusion

Human relations advanced when management recognized that workers band together in informal groups. The next step is observing the enormous differences among these groups and their responses to management and the union. Actually, management creates some of its industrial relations problems because of its technological decisions. Differences in group behavior and the variation in the supervisor's industrial relations work load result from the interworker contacts established by the flow of work.

The strategic and conservative work groups can act as compensatory channels to help re-establish the equilibrium for disturbed employees. Apathetic and erratic groups do not provide this kind of constructive channel. They are usually trouble spots in industrial relations, troubles which are self-perpetuating and crisis-producing in the organization.

The criterion for a good group is not found in its expressed attitudes toward management. Many complaining, apparently disgruntled, and protesting groups (who score consistently low on plant attitude surveys) take in stride methods and personnel changes that would upset other groups and still maintain their productivity. The criterion is therefore related to the behavior of the group when its members are under stress. Differences in the way groups react to and resolve or add to the stress can be described in observable interaction patterns.

Supervisory success or failure may result as much from the type of group supervised as from the skills employed. The span of control of the supervisor should be related to the frequency and types of problems generated by the groups he supervises. Identifying these differences in group behavior patterns contributes to more effective supervisory assignments, evaluations, and collective bargaining.

The authors' comparative study of work groups suggests a subtle distinction between the groups that fail to provide adequate redress procedures because they are unable to take concerted action (the apathetics) and the groups that add their own unstabilizing influence to the plant environment by starting more concerted activities than necessary to provide an adequate outlet for employee discontent (the strategics and the erratics). Of the two groups that overcompensate, the erratics are a far more serious problem to management. They commit themselves to abrupt and sometimes illegal action, and if management or the union threaten reprisals, they do not have the internal organizational constraints to enable them to save face while retreating. The conservatives represent an ideal. They assure their members of adequate protection and still exercise the self-control to assure themselves they will not suffer from their own indiscretions while initiating action to management and the union.

CHAPTER VI

THE MAN, the JOB, and the ORGANIZATION

Management frequently has taken one of two extreme positions in organization. To some, the relationships that are presumably established by the formal organization chart are sacred; the line of authority and the division of labor thus prescribed are more durable than individual personalities. Executives should conform to the job descriptions of the organization chart, and people, not the pattern, must change or adjust. At the other extreme are those pragmatists who argue the man makes the job and the type of organization cannot be determined until the occupants of the interconnected rectangles are selected.[1]

The authors contend that a more realistic middle ground must be established. To the administrator concerned with the problems of developing an organization, management is a constant process of tinkering with people, with the jobs, and with the structure of authority to create the teamwork necessary for improved performance.

"Tinkering" is an accurate description of what the executive has to do, because, apart from his own capacity and experience, he has had few tools to combine people and jobs. He can get the techniques of planning the flow of work without regard for personality from industrial engineering, some empirical notions about formal organization structure such as line and staff, span of control, etc., from the philosophy of management, and a variety of testing procedures intended to provide some information about the individual from psychology. But, when the executive tries to put together these three kinds of information and their underlying principles, he is in trouble.

Each represents a completely different universe, and there are few if any common concepts or methods to bring them together. The engineer is con-

[1] It is disturbing to read in a recent survey of organization studies that personality "has been virtually excluded from traditional organization theory."

Daniel J. Levinson, "Role, Personality, and Social Structure in the Organizational Setting," *The Journal of Abnormal and Social Psychology*, vol. 58, no. 2, March, 1959, p. 170.

cerned with time, sequence, and rate; the management specialist with functions, responsibilities, and authority; and the psychologist with traits and attitudes. Organization, however, results from the technology, the systems and procedures, the structure of authority, and the personalities of the individuals doing the work. An underlying stratum of uniformity common to each of these elements is needed. Because they are interdependent, it is important to be able to predict what will happen if any one of them is altered. If the work flow in a particular department is changed, how will it affect the structure of authority and the adjustment of personalities? What will happen if a new supervisor is brought in or the responsibilities of the present boss are changed?

What Is an Organization?

Questions on the possible effects of changes need to be answered. They can only be answered by adopting the concept of organization as a system of relations between people, in which the interactional behavior of the individuals concerned is the common factor uniting technology, structure, and personality.

Each person reacts differently to the stresses in various organizational situations, and in turn, each individual interacts with the persons surrounding him and affects their reactions. The technology, systems, and procedures of operation and control inextricably bind people in a web of routine that is given structural form by the division of labor and responsibility so imperfectly represented by the organization chart. The people concerned cannot be treated merely as interchangeable units. Each box on the chart of organization, whether large or small, contains a different personality and temperament from those surrounding it. The lines that connect boxes or the empty spaces between, which seem to imply that two boxes are forever divorced from any contact, are travesties as representations of the human relationships with which the manager has to deal. The flow of work and varying tempo of operations force widely different personalities to work together within this network of personal relationships. The resulting stresses create many of the management problems that affect the operating statement and the balance sheet.

If an organizational system is made up of individuals with varying capacities for interaction with others, these capacities can be determined at the managerial level only by watching how individuals behave with other people. Furthermore, different organizational positions provide varying opportunities for each individual to adjust to other individuals.

The human relationships within the organizational structure do not occur in a vacuum. The patterns they follow, in fact, their very existence, are determined in large part by the techniques, processes, spatial layout, paper systems, etc., that carry out the purpose of the organization and make up the sequences or flows of contacts between people. These technical patterns determine where individuals come into contact, in what order, how often, and for how long; hence serve to facilitate or hinder the interaction between individuals. They control the interaction patterns comprised in the organizational structure, just as the test tubes and complicated glass linkages of the chemistry laboratory control the rates at which chemical processes can occur. To perform a different experiment using the same compounds, the chemist changes his arrangement of tubes, beakers, and piping. Any change in the technical elements that alters the flow of contacts, also changes the organizational relationships of the individuals involved, even though the personalities are the same. In turn, the personalities in the organizational system modify its structure, although all the technical constraints remain fixed, for each individual's needs differ if he is to achieve a state of equilibrium in his relations with others.

Organization in this sense constitutes the environment within which the executive must move and perform. If people are to be fully utilized within the organization, their capacities must be evaluated within this framework of organization.

Observing the Organization in Action

How should people and the organization be matched to each other using this point of view? What should be looked at, what techniques should be used, and what kind of results are obtained? Actually, as we shall see, this concept of organization gives the administrator a number of methods for evaluating the organizational structure and the people working within it. He can, in fact, observe and measure organizational behavior on the basis of an operational definition of organization.

The key to the approach is given in the question, "What should be looked at?" The answer is observing the way people behave with one another on the job and their interactions in the daily routine activities in the company. As stated in Chapter III, a number of distinctions can be made by observing how an executive spends his time. The difference in the amount of time he spends by himself and in contacts with other people can be observed as well as the different people with whom he has contacts. Although he initiates some contacts with people, it can be seen that others contact him. His relationships with his boss, the department head who precedes him in the work flow, and the different personalities in his own department can all be observed.

By studying what takes place within these contacts between people, further differentiations can be made. Some people behave much the same no matter with whom they are talking. Others have a wide repertory of behavior. They can talk freely and easily if the need arises, or they can listen. If necessary, they can be quick or slow to adapt to the other person. Some people take over a contact and try to control the course of action in varying degrees and appear to dominate those with whom they associate almost constantly, but others give up almost automatically if there is any competition. Moreover, people vary tremendously in their capacities to continue acting.

Different jobs require the individuals holding them to take part in significantly different numbers of contacts throughout the day, and each contact varies in the amount of interaction required to accomplish its purpose. For example, the "good" supervisor is supposed to explain the reasons for a decision to his subordinates rather than tell them what they should do in a curt fashion. However, the supervisor must have an adequate amount of energy to talk with many subordinates throughout the day and give relatively long explanations. The "do this" or "do that" type of supervisor is not necessarily operating under a different managerial philosophy. He is just not able to sustain longer daily contacts.

Variation in Job Requirements

As every person is different, so every job differs in its behavioral requirements. A salesman, for instance, obviously must have a high degree of energy and drive to initiate numerous contacts. Because he meets a wide variety of people, he must also be flexible enough to adapt to other individuals. A machine operator or a bookkeeper, who has few contacts during the day, does not need these characteristics. The need to listen, to dominate a situation, to show initiative, or to act quickly or slowly varies in importance from job to job.

Jobs differ in their inherent interactional dimensions and also according to the personalities that fill the surrounding organizational positions. The personality of the supervisor is an important factor in the selection of any of his subordinates. Similarly, if two or more executives must work together closely, the personality of each one is an important element in his job descriptions.

There is likely to be a small number of key jobs that are the center of communication networks within every managerial group. Persons holding these jobs must either respond to a constant stream of requests for action or initiate a wide variety of contacts themselves. Because top management is not always aware of the unusual interpersonal requirements of these positions, they can frequently turn them into bottlenecks in the chain of relationships.

In part, this lack of awareness results from the type of job descriptions used in the organization. Job descriptions rarely indicate the behavior required of the man who is to fill a particular job. They describe his responsibilities and authority and perhaps the necessary experience but seldom the actual interpersonal requirements of the job. Such terms as "will coordinate with," "has functional responsibility for," or other abstractions with no real operational meaning are used. Yet, as observed in Chapter III, job requirements can be established in terms of the number and type of contacts required of the individual to carry out successfully the relationships inherent to the job.

The contacts of each individual on the job can be measured and his behavior with different people described. A job description can be prepared from this information to tell when an executive is to act, with whom, and for how long. Thus, he can budget his organizational expenditure of effort.

How Personality Limits Decentralization

The care, or lack of care, with which people are fitted to their jobs determines their day-to-day relationships and performance, and throughout the entire organization, the smooth functioning necessary for success. Every organization is strongly influenced at the top level by the personalities of its management and the ways in which these men express themselves through policies, methods of operation, and the formal structure of the organization itself. Top executives naturally view the organization in the light of their own predilections, and consequently, many policies as well as the organizational means to implement them reflect their individual personalities.

Sometimes these policies, apparently based on "sound business reasons," run into unforeseen difficulties. Decentralization, often undertaken in the belief that it will increase the efficiency of the company, affords three pertinent examples of interplay of personality and organization.

In the first case, a large manufacturing company was setting up its major operating divisions as wholly owned but independent companies and, at the same time, adding new companies by direct acquisition. Because he was interested in further expansion, the president wanted each company to operate on its own with some corporate assistance, primarily of a financial nature. Although he consciously followed this organizational plan and set up its framework as completely as he could, he soon realized that he and his staff still had direct responsibility for running the supposedly independent companies until capable managers could be obtained for each of the separate companies. In other words, the organizational system could not operate unless the right personalities were placed as presidents of each of the subsidiaries. Although the organizational structure was changed, the president was still actually running a centralized operation.

As another example, a relatively small but rapidly expanding company was setting up a series of branch offices for its sales operations throughout the country. Both the president and general sales manager were concerned with the importance of selecting branch managers who would be personally compatible with management and who accepted their philosophy of decentralization and would make it work. In effect, each branch manager was to be the head of a small business with responsibility for his inventory, warehousing his products, and maintaining a service and sales organization. A system of incentives was designed by the company to further this attitude. Top management believed far greater results could be expected if this philosophy spread throughout the company than if each branch manager was directly and closely supervised by the general sales manager and his staff.

Interestingly enough, both the president and the general sales manager were alike in personality and temperament. Although both were highly flexible and adaptable and showed a great deal of initiative in their methods of operation, neither was particularly dominant. They both felt uncomfortable when they had to maintain control of situations. Their desire to set up independent proprietors directly reflected this preference to avoid situations that required constant and possibly critical supervision. However, the kind of men they found compatible as salesmen and branch managers were not dominant. In other words, they did not disturb management with too much opposition.

This deliberate choice of personality type actually conflicted with their small-business theory of decentralization because both branch managers and salesmen were responsible for collections and should have had dominant personalities. The company was operating in an industry in which credit risks were relatively high. They were far ahead of any competition, so the problem was not selling the product but getting paid for it. Lack of firmness in collecting payment frequently meant losing the chance of getting the money while the first enthusiasm for the product lasted. As a result of the organization pattern that management wished to follow, the firm ran the risk of serious financial difficulties because the men they hired had poor collection records. In other words, management had either to change the organizational structure in order to hire managers they liked or hire a different type of manager to make the existing organization work.

The third example of decentralization involved a manufacturing company in which one large, centralized manufacturing unit was broken up over a ten–year period and its various product lines put into a series of branch factories throughout the country. Here, too, the president wanted each branch factory manager to run his own operation as if it were an independent enterprise, although responsibility for sales, engineering, and finance was centrally held.

In this case, the president possessed extreme energy and initiative coupled with a high degree of dominance and inflexibility that made him concerned with every detail of the business. As a result, the managers of the branch factories were as subject to the control of the home office as if they were under the same roof. The kinds of men selected for the jobs were persons who could adapt to this tight control.

Training, Counseling, and Supervision

The foregoing examples illustrate one basic difficulty. Top management is often unaware of the possible conflicts between the kind of executive it wants and the requirements of the job it wants done. Another problem that is frequently at the root of the first is equally serious. Most executives are poor observers of the actual behavior of their colleagues or subordinates. Although they are occasionally aware of who is upset or who is relatively at ease, they cannot describe the conditions that caused either state or specify which actions are part of an emotionally stressful situation. Paradoxically, many competent managers are sensitive to the actions of their associates but cannot describe what they "see."

Without real knowledge about the on-the-job behavior of a fellow executive, it is difficult, if not impossible, to help him improve his effectiveness in organizational behavior. The present emphasis in management takes the form of "encouraging" a change of attitude. Yet, an individual's sentiments and beliefs are frequently beyond conscious control even if he can be made aware of them. Behavior, however, can be dealt with more objectively.

As members of management begin to realize how strongly organization and the success of the company are shaped by the interplay of personalities within the constraints of the jobs, they will become more concerned with the effects of their own behavior on others and, in turn, with the reasons for their different reactions to different people. They can learn their behavioral strengths and weaknesses and ways to control them from accurate knowledge of their own interaction patterns and those of the individuals with whom they deal. The following is a case in point.

An executive in a large company had been criticized by management for his inability to delegate authority. He was puzzled and upset by the criticism because he thought he consistently gave responsibilities to his subordinates. Actually, he had tremendous energy and initiative and was overly quick to step into situations if he did not think things were happening fast enough.

After he discussed his interaction pattern with a member of the personnel department, he began to understand that what he regarded as delegation was really an expression of a fundamental temperament trait; he preferred to do things himself rather than wait for others or take the time to persuade or assist them. When he issued an order or a request, he did not take time to explain the background of the problem, or find out how well his subordinate understood, or what conflicts might arise from other assignments, or the subordinate's capacity to carry out the order. Then, when a job was not done fast enough to suit him, this executive frequently took over and did it himself.

By working with the personnel officer, this man began to comprehend why management had criticized him and he developed a pattern of scheduling which allowed a mutually understood period of time to elapse after making an assignment before he took the initiative. He also tried to control his instinctive need to act and act fast. He learned to organize what he had to say before calling in a subordinate to give him an assignment. Thus, he could make his request in sufficient detail and make sure it was understood. By doing so, he overcame the immediate drive to act and be done with it and was able to listen and discuss things while making the assignment. From time to time, his best intentions and the regimen he set for himself were forgotten, but generally there was an impressive change in his manner of operation.

When Personalities Clash

An organization often has the means to turn unsuccessful patterns into acceptable ones. There are several paths that might be followed when conflicts and stress interfere with the smooth functioning of the organization.

One source of stress is incompatible coworkers. During their working lives, most individuals encounter people with whom they do not get along, and whose actions are disturbing and upsetting. After a sufficient number of unpleasant experiences, one person usually thinks anything the other does is all wrong, and it becomes increasingly difficult for him to think logically and objectively about the person.

What can be done to minimize such conflict? And is it possible to retain two valuable employees if they clash in this manner?

Change of Interactional Pattern

It frequently happens that the two have to work together. Consequently, it is important for each to understand both his own and his opponent's personality and temperament characteristics to learn what is disturbing about the other person and to develop a pattern to cope with it. This means both the interaction patterns involved and the interactional requirements of the job itself must be studied, to learn what other stresses are developing for each man concerned. Here are some examples.

A Conflict in Engineering. Two section heads in the industrial engineering department of a medium-sized company had been feuding almost since the day they were both promoted to their present positions two years before. Conflict, although not continuous, was never far below the surface, and the requirements of their jobs made the probabilities of trouble fairly high. One of the section heads was a methods engineer whose primary responsibilities were to develop new methods or processes in machine operation, to test them in the experimental shop maintained in the department, to figure cost benefits, and to turn the processes over to the installation section for testing in a pilot installation in the factory. The second man was in charge of the installation section. Whenever trouble occurred, the methods engineer believed the installation engineer changed the process or did not follow the method he specified. The installation engineer, on the other hand, was sure the basic idea was wrong or that the methods engineer did not take the practical requirements of the shop into consideration.

Because both men were good engineers and did their jobs well, the chief engineer did not want to transfer either of them out of the department. Yet he knew their disagreements were hurting production in the department. Further, both were bringing others into the feud. In an effort to solve the problem, the personalities of the two men were appraised, revealing interesting differences. The methods engineer had difficulty making contacts with others, and he was slow to take the initiative. Moreover, he was easily upset by criticism and withdrew and became petulant as a result. The installation engineer had a great deal of energy and initiative, and he liked to get things done quickly. He usually had little difficulty dominating others in the shop, but he was sufficiently flexible so the foremen with whom he worked got along well with him.

With the aid of the training director, the chief engineer tried to correct the situation. First, they discussed with the installation engineer the facets of his personality that disturbed his opponent. He began to realize he was too quick to take the initiative and dominated the methods engineer every time he raised an objection; in other words, his natural way of behaving, although effective in the shop, brought out instinctive unfavorable reactions in the other man. He saw that if he wanted to improve the situation he should try not to interrupt or take over the discussion when the methods engineer was presenting an idea but wait for him to finish. They pointed out to the methods engineer that one of his problems was trying to manage too many contacts during the day. They suggested that if he was under pressure or upset by other problems he should postpone seeing his "opponent" until the next day. They emphasized that everyone was subject to stress and that sometimes when he thought the installation engineer was being difficult, it might be that he, too, had had a rough day in the shop. In addition, the chief engineer worked out a schedule so each man could plan his contacts with the other rather than having the installation engineer go to the methods engineer every time he thought there was a problem. The training director made himself available when either of the two engineers felt things were becoming too difficult. He pointed out to them when and why they were becoming disturbed and stressed what they should do to handle the problem. Within six months the men had developed an adequate working relationship with a minimum of friction.

A Problem in Production Control. The manager of production control in a large company was having considerable difficulty dealing with the production superintendents. As a group, they were driving and dominant, accustomed to having their own way, and difficult to convince during an argument. As part of his job, the production control manager exercised control over the scheduling of production and, consequently, interfered frequently with what the superintendents regarded as the most efficient way to run their departments. Unlike the superintendents, the production control manager was not a particularly dominant person although he did have plenty of drive and initiative. When dominated by the superintendents, as he often was, he continued to try to make his point, although he realized this trait sometimes resulted in arguments he was likely to lose. Eventually he learned to wait for another opportunity rather than persisting against opposition that was too great for him. He made up for his inability to dominate at a single meeting by taking up the subject again later in the day or on the following day and with a new slant and new arguments. He followed this pattern until he won his point.

Frequently appraisals of personality and temperament imply there is a single pattern that characterizes a good executive. Not only does this concept ignore variations between different jobs in the same company (the sales manager has different interactional requirements from the controller, for example); it also ignores the differences in similar jobs in different companies because of the organizational climate special to each. The notion of a single pattern assumes that the properties making up the "ideal" executive are constant. However, by assessing his own behavioral strengths and weaknesses, the executive can learn there is more than one means to accomplish the same end, and accurate knowledge of his interactional pattern can become a tool to develop an effective individual style.

Job Redefinition

In building an organization, the personalities of top management and their mutual relationships, the ways in which they react to each other, and the ways in which these reactions are transmitted down the line must all be taken into account. It is also necessary to determine if effective organization changes can be brought about by redefining jobs to fit the available personalities of the company.[2] In many instances, a high turnover in a particular department is caused by the inability of the manager to carry out what top management thinks he should do. The problem often arises because the manager does not possess the personality characteristics to do the particular job as it is set up, even though he may otherwise be a capable individual.

As an illustration, a training director in one company could not develop effective working relationships with the managers of the many divisions

[2] An interaction analysis of job content often provides rather startling information regarding the differences between the jobs in practice and their theoretical definitions. For example, recent research on the position of the first-line supervisor suggests the effective supervisors spend more time with staff people and less with their own subordinates, contrary to earlier ideas. In fact, effective supervision probably had less contact with subordinates than poor supervisors, in opposition to much popular human relations thinking.

These interpretations were suggested by discussions with Charles A. Walker and Robert Guest, of the Yale University Technology Project, and Quentin Ponder, of the General Electric Company, who completed his Ph.D. research at the Graduate School of Business, Columbia University.

within the company although he had many other skills. He was competent as long as he concentrated on initial training in the training department, but he was unable to bring himself to make contacts with the divisional managers frequently enough to build up effective relations with them. This low initiative was reinforced by his inability to get his program accepted if any opposition was encountered, which was directly related to his low dominance. Although management believed training should be done on the divisional level, the training director almost always found an excuse to stay in the central training offices instead of going into other parts of the company. As a result, management finally replaced him. Of course, by redefining the job and splitting the activities and responsibilities, management could have kept this individual, but it would have meant that both areas of responsibility were full-time jobs and could not be handled by a single person.

Sometimes, the job can be slightly altered. In one company, the chief engineer was a somewhat withdrawn individual, who was slow and deliberate, with low initiative and dominance. Although he was a good engineer, he had difficulty supervising his division. This was made worse by the amount of time he was required to spend with the inspection department, which had been reporting to him for a number of years because of close tie-ins with inspection and specification work. The great disparity between his personality and the interactional requirements of the job indicated that either a new chief engineer had to be hired or the organization changed. Because the first alternative seemed inadvisable, inspection was changed and reported directly to the production vice-president. This reduced the interactions required of the chief engineer.

Analysis of individuals whose relationships are not harmonious may indicate that there is no inherent conflict between their personalities and that their inability to work together lies elsewhere. An example is the case study, presented in Chapter II, of the general sales manager and the credit manager of a manufacturing company who were constantly in disagreement. The sales manager complained that the credit department was interfering with the selling situation by refusing credit to old customers, writing letters at cross-purposes, and generally upsetting sales. The credit manager argued that management had given him the responsibility for sound credit policies that were being violated by the sales department which tried to get orders approved on poor risks. The battle became so intense the general manager of the firm almost decided to let at least one of the men go. However, assessment of each individual revealed no major personality problems or temperamental reasons for incompatibility. The problem was actually caused by a poorly organized work flow between the two departments. After this situation was remedied, the executives established a satisfactory relationship in the performance of their functions. The important factor here is that the two men were not incompatible, and the problems were removed by changing their organizational relationships.

Conflicting Requirements in Diversified Jobs

Another problem area in almost every company, particularly on the divisional or department manager level, concerns jobs that are almost impossible for a single supervisor to cover adequately. One of the most extreme examples of this is the department store buyer. First he must buy the merchandise, which means he must make frequent trips to the market and is often out of the store every month or six weeks for a week at a time. In addition, he is also the department manager and may have to visit several branch stores as well. Actually, he is responsible for the efficient supervision of the selling efforts of personnel, maintenance of stock, inventory, movement of goods, and all the other facets of the over-all management of the department. Thus, he has to see that merchandise is available when needed, that the proper papers are handled in the receiving operation, and that the merchandise for a promotion is on the sales floor when the advertisements appear in the newspapers. He must oversee the operation of the stockrooms and also be available to talk to salesmen. Finally, he is supposed to be on the floor during the busy hours to supervise his own salespeople.

When the number of hours in the day is compared with the number of contacts and activities he has to have, it becomes obvious that, except in small departments, the buyer cannot perform all these duties without neglecting several phases of his work. As a result, the buyers from department to department in any store tend to specialize. One may be particularly good in the market but poor in supervising; another may be expert at managing the paper work and controls and show a good figure performance but may be hard to deal with as an individual. Each specializes in terms of the particular limitations of his personality. This specialization is reflected in the organization of his department and the kinds of personalities that he employs. Thus, a buyer whose emphasis is on paper work and stockkeeping usually concentrates on these areas and prefers an assistant who can work with him on these duties. The buyer whose instinctive ability is to select and promote "hot items" may spend so much time in these activities that the detail of running the operation is left to assistants who receive little supervision from him.

Some stores have tried to overcome this problem by carefully outlining the duties of buyers, or by providing assistants who are supposed to "take up the slack." The problem, however, is more deeply rooted. The time requirements of the job make it almost impossible, for example, for the buyer to act as department manager giving adequate and continuous supervision to salespeople and still carry out his other duties. Many large stores have organizational systems with superintendents (who are really sales managers) in charge of the salespeople for a group of departments. Such a division of responsibility is limited to scheduling the salespeople's time and maintaining departmental coverage. Direct supervision of the selling force is still controlled by the department manager and his assistants. Because of the limited number of contacts he can manage during the day, a superintendent cannot give anything but cursory attention to the individual selling efforts of persons in the various departments assigned to him.

In one large department store the problem was handled on an individual departmental basis. Although it was realized that basically continuous selling supervision was needed within each department, the personality strengths and weaknesses of each manager and his assistants were determined first. Then the interactional patterns of their relationships to salespeople, stockroom help, and the various other individuals with whom they worked were analyzed. In one instance, the department manager, although technically competent, was a shy individual without much drive, initiative, or force. His paper work was excellent, and he preferred to spend most of his time in the office dealing with the strictly merchandising aspects of the job. His assistant, who had almost the same characteristics, spent a large portion of his time handling customer complaints, checking stock, and other activities that kept him off the selling floor. The salespeople received practically no supervision and, as a result, their performance was far below their potential.

The assistant was transferred to another department where the buyer required a good detail man because he was poor in keeping records but excellent in selling leadership. A new assistant who was brought in to supervise sales was selected because his personality showed the drive, dominance, etc., needed for this type of job. He was given full responsibility for the selling floor. The performance of the department improved almost immediately. The salespeople began to sell more aggressively, and the manager was able to devote his full attention to the part of the job he could accomplish effectively because his new assistant supplemented the qualities he did not possess.

The same process was repeated in other departments. The decisions on the type of organizational structure required were based on the people who were there, not an abstract theory of "sound" organization. Ideally, every department manager should be a potential divisional or general merchandise manager, of course, but the realities of the competitive market for manpower may make this impossible. Moreover, management cannot take lightly the moral responsibility for firing an executive it selected, trained, and promoted and whose length of service entitles him to consideration, particularly when he is weak only in some aspects of his operation.

Furthermore, few managements would take the risk taken by one unfortunate top executive who, on the basis of a "personality assessment" program conducted by a consulting firm, fired 70 per cent of the executives because they were considered incompetent! The process of organizational development is slow and continuous, and every move must be considered in view of the over-all picture.

Conclusion

The approach outlined here requires top management actively to assume responsibility for organizational controls. It cannot be put to one side and treated as something for concern only when a vacancy occurs and good intentions about organizational practice are discarded to make a decision on filling a job or solving an organizational crisis.

Analysis of the personality characteristics of all the individuals in the management group must be done on a continuing basis to determine how they affect one another if they must interact with any frequency, and, in planning the present and future organizational structure, to make sure the individuals selected will not bring out temperamental traits in each other that will create lack of cooperation, poor morale, or outright hostility.

At the same time, organizational responsibilities must be defined in interactional terms. Instead of such phrases as "he shall supervise" or "he shall coordinate," it is necessary to define the "who does what, with whom, when, where, and how often" that describes the flow of contacts occurring daily or on a weekly or monthly basis. By so doing, one can make sure that properly selected individuals can function as a team and that each knows his part and under what circumstances he is supposed to act and with whom.

Job descriptions then describe the actual flow of work in terms of the people who have to carry it out. In writing such job descriptions and working out the organizational structure in terms of the various processes necessary to operate the business, one can then learn to distinguish between the places where stresses occur between people as a result of bottlenecks in the work flow, poorly defined responsibilities, or clashing personalities. In practice, these crucial distinctions are often blurred in the confusion of recurring crises.

In other words, observation of behavior can provide management with the tools to effectively control its own destiny. The intuitive skills that the experienced executive brings to the solution of management problems need not be the sole guides; they can be supplemented and made objective and operational within the framework of this conception of organization. By using the unifying principle of interaction measurement, the influences of people and jobs can be analyzed and differentiated and rational decisions made as to necessary courses of action regarding technology, the structure of responsibility, and the particular people concerned. The success of a business depends upon the degree to which the total personality resources of the company have been assessed and utilized and effective working relationships developed in an organization, that is, upon the realities of human interaction.

CHAPTER VII

HOW MANAGERS CAN EVALUATE PERSONALITY

The previous chapter emphasized the importance of reconciling personality differences with organizational structure and job descriptions. Failures in managerial jobs and, in fact, in every other kind of job, are increasingly being attributed to "personality problems." Differences in aptitude, intelligence, skills, or training are seen as less important to success in salaried jobs than personality differences. The number of routine assembly-line jobs is decreasing because of automation, and the proportion of positions requiring contact with other people is growing ever larger with the expansion of service industries. As a result, many companies spend large amounts of money and time trying to assess the strengths and weaknesses of both job applicants and present employees.

Merely identifying the organizational or the personal problem as one of "personality," however, does not answer the question. The manager who is anxious to improve the functioning of his organization wants to know what the significant personality characteristics are and, even more important, how they can be recognized.

Limitations of Psychological Tests and Appraisals

It is a curious commentary on our highly pragmatic business society that most attempts to appraise the personalities of people who make organizations work are mystical and introspective. In everyday life, we recognize that what people actually do is what counts and tell our children that "Actions speak louder than words." Yet, research effort has concentrated on finding out what is going on inside the person through the use of ink blots, pictures, questionnaires, or the full-fledged treatment on the psychoanalyst's couch. What is learned from the resulting word patterns is highly difficult even for the experts to interpret. Too often their findings remind one of the sacred oracle at Delphi repeating the message of the gods in words so tangential to meaning that only the fact can prove the soothsayer right.

The dilemma everyone faces, of course, derives from concentrating on the internal goings-on of the individual. Everyone realizes how hard it is even to understand the significance of one's own reactions, but with these methods the executive is forced to jump from the unknown (or very tenuously known) to the actual behavior of other persons. Great novelists may successfully probe the inner workings of the human personality; such freedom of creation is not at hand for the manager.

Regardless of what technique is used, any theories about an individual can be substantiated only by what he does, that is, by his behavior in specific situations. No matter what words are used to describe his personality and temperament, they have meaning only if they help predict his actual behavior. Granted, of course, tests may provide other interesting and useful information, but from the managerial point of view, such information is often irrelevant to the organization. It may be fascinating to know an executive is "orally dependent," "ego inadequate," or, more traditionally, "moderately introverted," but the manager only needs to know how it will affect his actions in the company.

The desire to learn what makes another person act as he does also raises serious ethical questions. There is increasing resistance to an employer or prospective employer probing into the personal and private areas of an employee's mind. In spite of the assurances of the testers, information concerning mental health, much of which may be neither valid nor relevant, is often circulated within the organization. The result is more than an unnecessary gratification of curiosity; it is also a serious invasion of privacy, breaking down the division between the world of work and the world of private life. The authors seriously question the right of an employer to seek or know such information, even in the garbled form in which he usually comprehends it.

Actually, the terms and concepts used frequently fail to help the administrator identify the kind of performance to expect of the individual. Although they provide some notion of his over-all potentiality, anyone who has appraised employee performance knows how difficult it is to prove such predictions right or wrong. The persons for whom such tests are given usually hold jobs that do not permit easy assessment of output and productivity. As observed in Chapter III, totally new methods need to be developed to provide realistic appraisals for managerial jobs.

If the executive is to have any confidence in personality descriptions, he needs criteria that substantiate predictions on the job and enable him to say,

"When that happens, and every time that happens, a man will do this particular thing." He cannot do so with terms such as "oral dependency"!

Analysts are interested in reconstructing the state of mind, the attitudes, and feelings of the individual, and because they are trying to explain how these developed, they focus their attention on his early childhood. In business, however, answers are needed to the practical problem of predicting how an individual will behave in the immediate situation. Even the standard "personality" terms found on rating sheets, such as "cooperativeness," "initiative," "perseverance," and "motivation," present similar difficulties. "Cooperation" to one person may mean "obedience" to another, or one person's "perseverance" is considered "inflexibility" in another.

All of the terms applied to personality are generalities that are strongly affected by individual interpretations and the organizational situations of the moment. Several people may try to use them in the same way even though they cannot be defined objectively, but they should hardly be the basis for executive action.

The authors recently obtained performance appraisal information from several executives who worked closely with twenty-four employees in a large merchandising organization. Instead of giving evaluations of "loyalty," "ambition," and "motivation," the executives were asked to describe behavior, giving a picture of what their subordinates did under certain stress conditions (e.g., when someone "let them down" by not completing some work as promised), and what they were like when things were going well. No one thought the questions were difficult or threatening, and the informal interviews lasted as long as three hours. The results were surprising. Most of the managers had no idea of what their employees were like because they had never really observed them closely. When they were able to tell, more often than not, the behavior described was contradicted by descriptions received in previous interviews. The managers relied on subjective work interpretations, such as "He is a warm, friendly person but hard to get to know." These identify the individual, but they are useless in predicting the response of an employee to a particular situation or new job responsibilities.

Since the fashion at present is not to observe people on the job, there has been little real validation of most personality tests.[1] To be sure, many companies have a general "feeling" that they are or are not getting good

[1] Dr. Rains Wallace argues that there is an "almost total absence of criteria" by which any such tests could be validated.

S. Rains Wallace, "Contributions to Business and Industry," *Planning for Progress: What Advances in Psychological Knowledge Could Make the Greatest Practical Contribution to the Welfare of the Nation in the Next Ten Years,* American Institute for Research, Pittsburgh, Pa., March, 1956.

people as a result of their personality testing. But this is subject to the same errors and biases as the highly subjective rating scales employed by more "scientific" managements. Both are based on the same intuitions. Because of its unpretentiousness, the "feeling" may be the more useful and honest standard.

But since what the executive wants to know is how a person will act, why not note what watching him in a variety of situations actually tells us? This is the method most people use to evaluate others in everyday life. What is done in making such judgments can be isolated. (This method avoids any invasion of privacy because it relies on the *public* evidence that each individual displays for all to see.)

Personality characteristics that can be determined by careful observation will be described in the following sections of this chapter. Research indicates that these characteristics provide good predictions of job performance. This is hardly surprising because these personality factors can actually "be seen" in the way an individual carries out his job. Personality will be observed, measured, and defined by examining how the individual undertakes and maintains the relationships with others that are required by his organizational position.

Observation That Reveals Personality

To carry out this inquiry, it is necessary to accept literally the statement that management is concerned with people in situations. An executive, for example, cannot be taken out of his organization and considered alone. He is on the job, and most of his time is necessarily spent with others. Perhaps, as he sits in his office after the plant closes, his thinking or feeling may be significant, but it is possible to observe only what he is doing, not what is going on inside him.

Apart from the simple observations that can be made about his behavior when he is by himself, the bulk of the data will be concerned with his actions when he is with other people. This is when he reveals himself and when judgments about his personality and temperament can be made. The next step is to make observations that will provide accurate and objective criteria on which there can be agreement.

First, the criteria must be such that they can be applied to any situation with the same results. Two observers must not be able to arrive at different interpretations. The tools used for observation must be similar to those of the natural sciences; they must be statements of the order in which things happen with accurate measurements of quantity and frequency. Take the solitary executive, meditating at the end of the day. Whether it is significant or not, it is possible to observe how long he sits alone by measuring the time between the departure of his last visitor and the time he turns out the light and leaves. If during the day some particular event preceded this, and if this sequence occurs regularly, it might be possible to predict that given situation X, the executive will remain by himself after the closing hour. From repeated observation, it might be possible to observe that the length of time he spends in his office varies with certain aspects of the preceding situation that could also be measured.

Use of Time

Time, of course, is a fundamental yardstick. Applied to contacts with others in the company, it helps reduce behavior to more manageable dimensions. It can easily be used to considerable advantage within the organization to measure the length of contacts an individual has with others. At one time or another nearly every executive has said, "If I only had more time," or "I don't see where all the time has gone." Knowing how and with whom time is spent is as essential in planning jobs as in designing the organization.

There is another factor in length of personal contacts, namely, the length of time spent varies with different individuals. Sometimes this reflects the technological situation. Certain actions require more time than others. Buying a package of cigarettes is a brief exchange, but purchasing machinery requires substantially longer time to ensure that the machine will do the job claimed by the manufacturer. Although the organizational situation differs significantly in its inherent length, there is another variable that is even more basic in the use or misuse of time. This is the personality of the particular individual with whom contact is made. What does the measurement of time tell about this factor in actual situations?

Duration of Activity Periods

Obviously the length of time an individual talks can be measured. Or, because the words alone do not give the full impact of the time spent, it would be better to include the smiles, nods, and gestures that go along with his speech. Thus, his response and his action are measured from the first visible (or audible) sign to the last, when, for the moment, he is in repose. At that time, his silence, or more generally his period of not responding, can be measured until he starts to act again.[2]

[2] Cf. Eliot D. Chapple, *Measuring Human Relations, Genetic Psychology Monographs*, no. 22, 1940, pp. 3–147, for the initial statement of this type of measurement.

This constant alternation between action and inaction or speech and silence is the characteristic pattern through which human beings and all the higher animals go from birth to death.[3]

By measuring people against this scale of time, it is possible to see how they differ from each other. How often do minutes, and even hours, pass while a simple technical question is buried under the flow of speech of a more active individual who discusses every aspect of the problem at length and supports them with anecdotes that may even be unrelated to the problem. He is one factor in the disappearance of time if he has to be seen often.

The converse is also true. Some people are almost too monosyllabic. This does not mean that what they have to say is any more helpful for being briefly stated unless the other person likes to do all the talking; in fact, it is often difficult to get a question answered or sufficient details from them. The point is, as measurement shows, whether what is said is wise or foolish, that everyone's activity falls somewhere on the continuous scale from almost zero to (almost) infinity. The higher the level of activity, the more contacts one can manage and the more easily and freely one can talk.

Duration of Silent Periods

An independent variable is the length of silence. Some persons are extremely quiet. They differ among themselves in how long they generally act, but they have in common a noticeable interval between the end of one action and the beginning of the next. In contrast, many other persons cannot keep still. This does not necessarily mean they are constantly acting; rather, they give this impression because their intervals of silence are so brief. They stop for a second or two and then start in again. Sometimes their periods of action are relatively brief, but at other times they are long.

Because everyone learns the pattern of give-and-take from childhood, the listeners become the counterpoise of the talkative. We alternate, that is, when one person talks, the other listens and vice versa. To discover whether they listen, in the sense of comprehending, would involve probing inside individuals. Even the most attentive audience may not understand what a speaker is saying. The criteria can only show there was silence when another spoke. If this happened, there is greater probability that something was understood than if he was talking at the same time.

Although people may be classified as high, medium, low, or in between in the range of actions and the independent scale of listening or silence, the measurements will not show the same duration over and over again as if

[3] Not only is this immediately evident from everyday observation, but also a vast amount of research on "spontaneous activity" has been conducted.

people were controlled by a clock or metronome. Yet, people are actually controlled by clocks that prescribe not single values but a group of actions and another group of inactions.[4] Under certain conditions, these values repeat themselves quite regularly, although the amount of variation characteristically differs for each individual.[5] Some persons have a limited range of values to draw from, and others have a much greater spread.

Synchronization Depending Upon Other Persons

Not surprisingly, there is optimum regularity when the other person does not interfere. As two tennis players keep the ball moving back and forth in an extended rally, interaction is made up of a long sequence of exchanges in which each individual takes his turn while the other waits. Because measurements of time are being used, it can properly be said that their interaction patterns synchronize. One person is the perfect complement of the other. When there is rapport between two people, or when one person deliberately adapts his interaction pattern to create this situation for the other, as in certain types of interviews, the behavior achieves this condition of optimum regularity. Everyone has experienced and can easily see instances in which there is minimum constraint on the interaction. It is sometimes said, "He certainly has an appreciative audience," referring to the perfect matching of action and silence.

Such situations, unfortunately, occur only rarely. In fact, lack of synchronization is encountered more often than not. Lack of synchronization is exhibited in several ways, and their meanings in terms of situations within an organization are fundamental in providing the tools to manage (or at least to understand) the relationships of people within it.

Each job within the company involves a different personality in terms of the criteria already described. For example, the superintendent is high in activity and unable to keep still, but he is flexible, showing a considerable range both in his actions and silences. Much of his time is spent with the

[4] In *Spontaneous Activity of Mice,* T. J. B. Stier describes how chemical "clocks" control the durations of actions and inactions in two stocks of mice and how these appear to be genetic in origin, i.e., inherited.

[5] Eliot D. Chapple, "Personality Differences as Described by Invariant Properties of Individuals in Interaction," *Proceedings of the National Academy of Sciences,* vol. 26, no. 1, 1940, pp. 10–16, was the first demonstration of the regularity and unvarying character of periods of action and inaction.

G. Saslow, and J. D. Matarazzo, in "A Technique for Studying Changes in Interview Behavior," *Research in Psychotherapy,* American Psychological Association, 1959, summarize the literature on the reliability of interaction measures, including their own work and that of other investigators. In this chapter, we have tried to present the results of many years of such research in as easy a style as possible and, consequently, have not attempted to document the findings presented case by case.

chief engineer, who is silent for long periods, but is able to talk at great length with little variation when he does take the floor. When they are together, the illusion of harmony created as the silent engineer listens to the talkative and energetic superintendent, is brief. When the engineer begins to talk both are soon trying to talk at the same time. There is an extreme lack of synchronization in their interaction.

What happens depends on who can win, on which individual literally outtalks or outacts the other. This requires *persistence* or the ability to continue talking in spite of opposition, to dominate the other person, and for the moment to control the conversation. When one person dominates, the other person must either wait until the speaker stops to take his turn or interrupt.

Dominance

The ability to dominate, particularly when others are trying to take over, can be detected easily. At a conference or committee meeting, even though the exchanges may be rapid, it is easy to contrast the persons who continue in spite of interruption and who are able to hold the floor against competition with those who try to say something, are overpowered, and lapse into silence again.

The amount of dominance an individual possesses is relevant within the job in determining his prospects of finding adequate outlet and also the degree to which his organizational responsibilities can be fulfilled. If the people with whom he has contact are more dominant than he, he has little chance to give his opinions and ideas. More important, maintaining control is fundamental to many situations in managing. If the job requires conducting a number of meetings and the individual cannot handle interruptions that divert them from the purpose, the meetings disintegrate. In another dimension, time is also affected. Every executive needs to budget his time to perform his job, and if he is unable to control, he spends more time on individual contacts or meetings than is warranted.

On the other hand, overly high dominance can also be a problem. This is evident if, for example, the subordinate cannot report a crucial problem to his dominant boss, because he is cut off every time he starts to speak. There are also many other situations in which it is important to provide a "permissive" atmosphere. Research engineers discussing the best approach for a new design are not helped if one tries to impose his ideas on the others. A personnel manager listening to an employee's grievance makes the situation worse if he interrupts before the employee finishes.

The important element is not merely who can or cannot dominate another. Equally relevant is the change in behavior that results from being dominated or from dominating.

The dominance situation differs radically from the ideal state of optimum interaction. Two or more persons trying to act within the limits of their own individual patterns interfere with each other. Characteristically, people react against opposition or competition. Having to adjust, either by persisting and dominating or by giving up, significantly changes behavior. Persons who are easily dominated are automatically prevented from continuing action. When this occurs, part of a customary duration of action has been terminated. Observers cannot tell how long it might have been except from previous observations. Research suggests that people need to expend a certain amount of energy in contacts with other persons every day, so the individual who is continually dominated is under greater and greater pressure to find other outlets for this energy.

Immediate Reactions to the Stress of Dominance

Everyone has seen (and perhaps experienced) what happens when an ordinarily talkative individual is silenced by an overdominant associate, perhaps his boss or an equal. Regardless of the subject or the logic involved, the individual's inability to express himself is a serious source of stress. After such a contact, a physician may find a series of alterations in heart rate, blood pressure, and other physiological measurements. Time measurements also indicate radical changes in the behavior of the individual.

During the stress, of course, the change is noticeable. His actions become extremely short, and he is silent for longer and longer intervals as his attempts to break in are defeated. At the conclusion of the meeting a further change in his behavior can be observed before he returns to his normal patterns. Under the stress, he shows one set of temperamental reactions, and after the stress, another; each is characteristic.

Actually, the "winner" also undergoes stress that is revealed by the changes in his actions and inactions. He no longer (except in the rarest cases) behaves as he would normally. His actions are shorter and his silences shorter, and after the stress, he may also show further temperamental reactions.

The occurrence of opposition, which is a natural consequence of the differences in interaction in any situation, results in a fundamental shift in behavior. The extent of this shift, however, depends on the degree of dominance a person is able to maintain and the number of exchanges he needs to win to keep a balance in his interaction pattern. Individuals who are never dominated are rare. Everyone has a certain number of "wins" and "losses" that are expressed, in the observations of a given individual, as a percentage. He may dominate 10 per cent of the time, 50 per cent, or even 95 per cent. If the percentage is shifted or if he encounters someone with higher persistence, he may build up an energy deficit and immediately find another victim, such as his wife, a subordinate, or a taxi driver, to restore the balance.

Specific Reactions to the Stress of Being Dominated

It is possible to be much more explicit about the observable reactions of managers and employees to the stress of being dominated during a contact. There are several distinctive patterns of reaction, some of which can disqualify the individual from jobs where he has to work with people who can and do dominate him, and others which are less debilitating.

For example, some executives have the capacity to learn how to use a trait which makes it possible for them to deal relatively effectively with highly dominant colleagues or bosses. They cannot hold the floor in the face of any long interruption, but they come back into the conversation after allowing the other individual to speak. Therefore with repetition this *competitiveness* compensates for the lack of dominance. Repeated return efforts to gain the floor will tend to reduce the length of time the other person talks and, as a result, the subordinate will be able to stick to the subject he wants to talk about long enough to communicate important matters to his highly dominant boss.

Sometimes there is a slowdown in the behavior of an individual who is easily dominated. Instead of responding normally when the other person stops talking, there is an apparent difficulty to respond at all because of the domination and the reduction in opportunity to act. Such people become *passive* or *submissive*. They wait for the other person to take the initiative again and are unable to take their turn in regular interaction. Such a trait can be a serious handicap for an executive. Yet, there are many jobs where there is little competition or opposition, such as research engineers, draftsmen, etc., who work primarily by themselves, and being passive under stress is of no great importance.

In contrast to these types of reaction, other people show a pronounced increase in their actions under the stress of dominance. When the other person tries to maintain control, these persons talk faster and longer (and sometimes louder) than normally. Because they "protest too much," under relatively minor pressure, they are usually considered highly *defensive* and unable to accept criticism or to deal with situations when they are under attack. Measurement reveals successive increases in the duration of their actions as the other person tries to control the discussion. In many situations, competition is characteristic of the job, and the person who overreacts under minor pressure becomes an enigma and a source of disturbance to the person who unexpectedly encounters him.

After the Stress

Removing the stress does not guarantee that the individual will return to normal immediately. He has been disturbed by an attempt to dominate him and needs some time before he gets back to his equilibrium. The physiological disturbances of heart, blood pressure, etc., require time to return to normal. The muscular systems controlling interactional behavior parallel them because they are physiologically interdependent. Thus, the individual has to compensate for the changes in his behavior patterns caused by the stress. The effects of the stress are revealed by his actions after stress and their extent and duration.

The reaction under stress does not indicate accurately the strength of the reaction after it has ended. Many persons who manage their behavior well in a crisis are undone when it is over. Others who have extreme reactions under pressure apparently return to normal immediately afterwards. Therefore, an extreme reaction under pressure will not necessarily be followed by an extreme compensatory reaction after the pressure is removed. It is necessary to observe how people act both during and after a particular type of stress to judge their vulnerabilities.

The ways in which the individual reacts after the stress usually color the ideas others have of his whole personality. Measurements must be applied to discriminate what is seen, or to estimate the changes as objectively as possible. Without them an extreme reaction during or after a particular stress may be all that is remembered in summing up a person's personality and temperamental traits. People frequently forget that the reaction they see occurs only in one particular situation and so they fail to ascertain whether there are ways of changing the situation to reduce the frequency of the kinds of stress that incapacitate the individual.

For example some executives who can be highly dominant find the effort and the emotional cost so great they withdraw from contacts or talk briefly and abruptly after such encounters. One manager with this trait, whose periods of speech and silence under stress were brief, consistently found reasons not to have anyone whose dominance level reached his own work in his department. He resented any subordinate who accidentally challenged him and might go for weeks and sometimes months without speaking to someone who tried to dominate him during a conference. Because of the nature of the work in the department, the section heads needed to be dominant persons. Yet, the *petulant* reaction of the executive led to the selection over a period of time of a group of section heads who did only what they were told. Consequently, they were failures in operating their respective units.

Other individuals are unable to change their pace after a competitive situation. Under pressure, they speed up the give and take with shorter actions and usually shorter silences, and continue to do so after the pressure is removed. For example, later on they are unable to spend the time needed to discuss a problem with another person simply because they are still wound up. Instead of staying on the subject, they jump from one thing to another, and often start a series of contacts with people to keep themselves moving and interacting at the same rate as before. The result can be turmoil for persons in the organization who must absorb this high frequency of contacts, involving questions, demands, comments, and constant interference.

The degree of this trait is ascertained by comparing the measurements after the stress with those taken during the stress. Varying with the degree of the trait, the actions lengthen after a while and the silences become longer, returning to their normal patterns. In subjective terms, the people are called *excitable* or *impulsive* because they cannot relax at a normal rate and tend to bounce from person to person until the stress wears off. On the job, they cannot pay attention to or deal with problems except those requiring brief contact. Unfortunately, they try to handle more difficult and time consuming problems in the same way. They make snap decisions, and unless they can reconsider these decisions later in a more relaxed state of mind, they are likely to be arbitrary and unrealistic.

Sometimes a trait is not obvious. Except by measurement, the departure from a person's normal interaction after stress is not apparent. The individual possessing such a trait misleads the unobservant. Because there is no obvious reason to believe that he has just undergone a stress, others key their behavior to his normal pattern. But after the discussion starts, he does not behave as expected. Because people adapt their interaction rate to their experience with the individual, the lower activity he manifests may unwittingly cause others to dominate him and set the stress in motion again for this person. In dealing with such a person, it is necessary to watch for the sign of reduced output, shorter responses, and difficulties in listening that are warning signals. This kind of individual is frequently described as *oversensitive* because of his unexpected behavior.

A less common but difficult reaction to deal with in an individual, one of the general family of underreactions, occurs when he becomes silent for longer and longer intervals and his speech is almost monosyllabic after stress. The trait is obvious only in extreme forms, but the person sits and does not talk, contrasting with the others so far described who characteristically speed up both action and silence. These people are usually called *sulky* and resentful by their associates, who try to guess what is going on inside them. Behaviorally, they do not answer and stay away from situations in which they normally might play an active part. One executive, for example, had concentrated his energies and those of his department on a major promotional program for his product. The day after an argument with his boss on another subject, he refused to attend a dealers' meeting at which his program was to be unveiled.

In contrast to the preceding patterns of temperamental reaction after the stress of dominance, some people overreact and continue talking as if trying to make up for their reduced action earlier. Their actions are longer than usual for them, almost as though they cannot stop. Interestingly enough, at the slightest recurrence of the stress, there is a fresh flood of talk the moment the dominance is over, as if the individual were trying to talk his way out of future attempts at domination. The characteristic pattern with such people is to keep talking so the other person responds with the appropriate adjustment.

Frequently, such terms as *self-justification* or apple-polishing are applied to such behavior, but these express interpretations either of intent or of the content of what is being said. The overreaction itself is the objective test, because the underlying intent may be so well concealed that it cannot be detected. This pattern of reaction may be designed to please because it does provide a means of handling and perhaps preventing future occurrences of stress. People with this trait do not withdraw from contact. On the contrary, the problem often is to get them to stop talking (and out of the office) without dominating them and thus setting off another long speech.

Nonresponse Situations

In contrast to the lack of synchronization of two personalities whose action-inaction sequences interfere with each other are those who fail to synchronize as a result of not responding. For instance, one person speaks to another, but the second does not answer for an appreciable time; or when one stops speaking, the length of the other's response is far briefer than that for which the interaction pattern is set. This may happen either because the person habitually gives brief responses and his pattern of variability calls for a brief action, or, more commonly, because a temperamental underreaction on his part (perhaps to some previous stress) creates this appearance. If both are silent or have not interacted previously, one of the two has to take the initiative and start to act.

Initiative and Quickness

In either case, the absence of response creates a stress, and, as in the case of dominance, one or the other must act first, depending on the habitual degree to which both take the initiative and the daily net balance of initiating behavior remaining at that moment. Although one might think executives, almost by definition, should have a high degree of initiative, the facts do not bear this out. There are many people in responsible management positions whose initiative is well below the 40 per cent level because in their jobs others almost inevitably come to them. In other words, they take the initiative by acting first in a contact with another person in less than four out of ten situations.

Another variable that affects the capacity to initiate a contact is the rapidity of individual actions. Two persons with the same degree of initiative may both need to act at a particular moment to maintain their own equilibrium; if one customarily acts more quickly than the other, the slower will always be defeated. This, in turn, can produce serious temperamental reactions.

Taking initiative is so important a part of managerial folklore, it is worth emphasizing the definition used here: initiative is the observable occurrence of an action by one person after he and one or more other persons have been inactive (such as a person speaking in a group meeting after a long pause when no one apparently has anything to say or when walking through the plant he comes into such proximity to another person that one or the other cannot avoid speaking). With the use of simple observational tools, it is not necessary to guess why the person started the action but, more important, it is necessary to take into account *every* instance of initiative as part of the interaction. Some observable instances cannot be ignored simply because they do not appear sufficiently important to record.

Regardless of the rate of actions started by an individual in his daily interactions, situations vary in the degree to which initiative is required. An engineer or draftsman who works by himself for long periods of time has little need to make contact with others. Assignments are usually brought to him, so it is not important for him to be able to go to another person for help unless he has difficulties or does not understand instructions. High initiative is usually considered important for supervisors. Yet one cannot categorically say supervisors as a group require high initiative. Each case must be examined in view of the job situation to determine whether the technical processes demand the constant direction of a supervisor alert to rapid changes or whether the processes require a policy of laissez-faire most of the time. Some managers give instructions to subordinates so frequently the latter no longer take initiative themselves, preferring to wait to be told each step. Managers do not delegate when they tell people to do a job and then check every hour or so to make sure they are doing it right. The manager's inability to wait for the job to be completed and to see the results is a consequence of his level of initiative.

The range of readiness to act is equally variable among executives. Acting too fast may prevent people from getting their jobs done; acting too slowly may mean a catastrophe if, for example, a machine breakdown is imminent. In interviewing an applicant for a job, the inability to wait until the person works his way through an idea can prevent him from giving important information about his background; being in too much of a hurry in labor negotiations can prevent the discovery of the real issues and demands. Yet each of these situations can vary in its dimensions: hiring an executive requires a different degree of quickness from hiring a porter; waiting too long at the bargaining table may lose the chance of an agreement tentatively formulated.

The Stress of Nonresponse

After one person acts and stops, it is the other's turn. If he does not act while the first is silent, the time comes, sooner or later, when the first individual is again compelled to act depending on his initiative rate and quickness. He undergoes stress stemming from the break in the give and take; the other person should respond and does not, or, because he expected a long response and set his listening or silence interval for it, the second acted and finished and the two are out of phase with each other.

Encountering such a stress, the individual becomes disturbed and, as in the dominance situation, any repetition or prolongation of the stress elicits physiological changes. In the extreme, these situations cause the heart to pound and create numerous other bodily changes. The physiological responses cannot be classified simply by dividing the emotional reactions of maladjustment into "fear" and "anger"—the latter presumably associated with dominance and fear with nonresponse. There is no way to control the stress encountered in individuals' daily lives except in a laboratory. Almost no single situation represents one or another type of stress in a pure state. Failures to respond and interruptions are usually mixed even within a single contact.

Yet, proportionately, one stress occurs more frequently in certain relationships than in others because of the particular characteristics of the interaction patterns. Consequently, from the vantage point of observation, it can be seen that nonresponse introduces certain changes in any person's behavior. These changes relate to his basic need to balance his action-silence sequence and the percentage of times he takes the initiative.

Reactions to the Stress of Nonresponse

If a person does not respond and, after waiting, the first takes the initiative, he again expects a response when he finishes. If the person does not, the interaction pattern of the other shifts as a result of the stress. It does so in ways learned from childhood, through which he can presumably restore the give and take and thus eliminate the sense of stress he is undergoing. There are several patterns such a shift may take.

The most common reaction found, in business at least, is to speed up the tempo of the interaction. The actions and silences become shorter, thereby increasing the number of times a person takes the initiative and raising his average. The probability is that this will set up an imbalance in the other person and finally elicit an adequate response. Some people react much more drastically than others; their speech becomes terse, and they are inactive for only brief intervals.

People who are so extreme characteristically have difficulty handling situations. An executive, impulsively needing to get something, anything, to happen, issues brief orders but does not take the time to explain what he wants. Unless an order is routine, the subordinate may not be told enough to carry it out. As such people act more quickly, their silences also become shorter; if the other person tries to explain problems as he sees them, they do not listen. Frequently such executives do things themselves rather than explain them to their subordinates.

One of the interesting results of this type of temperamental reaction is that at certain levels of business, the "*do-it-yourselfers*" predominate in the executive ranks. This trait is highly useful on the lower rungs of the promotional ladder, particularly for first-line supervisors or assistants to department managers. Such people usually occupy jobs that require only the accomplishment of simple techniques and uncomplicated supervision of people to get the minimum done; by doing everything themselves, they can singlehandedly make up for inadequate performances of their departments. Because they work hard and appear useful, in its evaluation of potential executives management regards such people as highly promotable. Yet, after they have been promoted, the value of such qualities disappears. In higher management, the ability to get things done by others is often essential, and most of the problems cannot be handled at such a rapid tempo. Full discussion is a necessity for making a decision and cannot be avoided. Acting for the sake of acting when the desired response is not forthcoming, simply to relieve the stress, can get an executive and his corporation into serious trouble. This does not mean some degree of doing things oneself is not valuable, but measurement or careful estimate must be used to differentiate between the person who is willing to take the initiative quickly when needed, but who at other times is able to wait, and the person whose reaction to stress is almost automatic—the do-it-yourselfer.

In contrast to these people, there are others who react quite differently. Their tempo of acting slows down rather than increases. They become more and more silent as they wait for the other person to respond. Frequently, as they do so, what they have to say becomes briefer and briefer, so, in the extreme, they are silent and uncommunicative and take the initiative only after long intervals of waiting.

As a result, they, too, become unresponsive. If two people who react this way are brought together, they can precipitate each other into unending silence. For the ordinary person, not so characterized, however, who inadvertently sets off the nonresponse reaction in his partner, this withdrawn behavior comes as an acute stress. Persons who have a nonresponse characteristic make good negotiators because they can outwait the other person and their silence can put pressure on anyone for whom nonresponse triggers off the need to act. Typically, their brief actions are questions or guarded comments and, because they require an adequate response to relieve their tension, the direct question is the most useful device to get the give and take re-established within a brief space of time. Although such people might be called *questioning* in an attempt to picture their pattern of behavior, they are often subjectively referred to as *negative,* a term applying more to others' reactions to an individual's behavior than to their habitual use of "no."

In striking contrast to the individuals who are underreactors when confronted with the stress of nonresponse, many people are quite the opposite. Finding the other person unable or unwilling to respond, they become more and more talkative as if to fill up the void that otherwise would result. They *take the floor* whenever the occasion allows. If there is a momentary silence in a meeting, they jump into the breach, just as many salesmen do when, finding the customer is not responding to their opening pitch, they launch into an interminable presentation of the virtues of their product. Some people who react this way are self-starters who talk whenever they have an audience. Others are counterpunchers. After a period of not responding, the other person may finally take the initiative and make a comment. This is enough to set them in motion, and they talk far longer than they normally would. If the other person answers with reasonable alacrity and length when they stop, the stress is over, but if he is once again unresponsive, the same pattern of excessive speech may be repeated.

When channeled, this type of reaction to stress has its value; for example, when speaking in public, such as in meetings, in training sessions, before a group of executives, or when a salesman shows a line, responsiveness can hardly be expected at every item of a large group of ideas or products. In such situations it is important not to become silent because of the stress. In the extreme, of course, the individual may *talk rather than act*, but the world of business can usually find a niche even for this trait.

After the Stress of Nonresponse

After a stress is ended, as in the case of dominance, the individual does not automatically return to normal interaction. Although his pattern may synchronize with the other person (usually not the same person responsible for the stress) the release of pressure sets in motion compensatory reactions that must work themselves out before equilibrium is restored. As in the case of dominance, the temperamental reactions after the stress of nonresponse and their intensity cannot be foretold from the individual's behavior under the stress.

The observation and measurement of behavior must look for the individual's deviation from his normal or unstressed state. Some people show little reaction to the ordinary amounts of stress encountered on the job, and although minor changes can be seen, they are well within the ranges noticed in the unstressed pattern. If the severity and the duration of the stress were increased, of course, this would not be true, but for practical purposes the measurement is concerned with separating individuals whose behavioral changes show them to be easily vulnerable from those who are relatively unaffected by the ordinary stresses of business. Because so many people in the organizational world have pronounced temperamental reactions to major stresses, it is not necessary to worry how someone who returns to normal quickly and without obvious reaction might react under extreme and long-enduring disturbance.

The most typical pattern by which individuals compensate after a state of unresponsiveness is with a rush of speech that is often almost unending. Everyone has observed an associate who, after an unrewarding session with the boss, has to "*blow off steam*" and tell everyone all the details of what he said, what the boss said, and why the boss did not understand the importance of the point he was trying to make. Many a wife whose husband has uninterested and unresponsive colleagues in the office plays the part of the good listener and helps him smooth out his ruffled feelings and get ready for the next day.

In extremes, these long-drawn out performances are often accompanied by visible signs of emotional disturbances such as tears, a flushing of the face, a raised voice, or language that shows uncontrolled emotion. Yet, these are not always present because many people are so trained in self-control that such obvious indications of upset are inhibited. To the acute observer, however, the degree of disturbance is a matter of measurement. How much longer are these bursts of speech than his normal ones? Does he present a reasonable and logical argument (but still at too great length) or does he curse the boss in the refuge of the boiler room? People who cannot stop talking after this stress are said to "lose their tempers," but, as with many terms, this phrase is also applied to persons who, in "losing their tempers," are curt and petulant, such as the executive discussed in connection with dominance. "Temper" is about as precise a word as "emotional." All temperamental reactions are emotional, and many reactions, both overlong and overshort, are referred to as signs of temper.

The other major type of under-reaction after a nonresponse situation also is often perceived as a sign of temper. After experiencing the stress, the individual's actions become short and his silences brief in comparison with his normal pattern, although in the case of the do-it-yourselfers, they are not as reduced in length as under the actual stress. These people generally avoid further interaction. Unlike the individuals just discussed, who look for an audience to whom they can pour out their troubles, these persons want to reduce their interaction to a minimum. Anyone who tries to discuss a problem with them finds them curt and *impatient* with any attempt to spend much time on the subject. "You make the decision. Don't bother me, I'm too busy!" are the impressions they give, and certainly their behavior usually substantiates whatever subjective judgments others make. After stress, they are unable to adapt to the interaction patterns of others, and those who know them realize that the quick tempo, the brief actions, and the periods of silence are unlike their normal pattern.

Stress at First Meeting

There is one other common type of interactional stress that needs discussion, the one many persons find most difficult to handle. This is meeting new people or new situations. Nearly everyone knows a person who cannot bring himself to talk as freely and easily with a stranger or someone he rarely meets as he would with friends and old acquaintances. He is considered *shy* or possibly *reserved.* The symptoms are indicated by his brief actions and relatively long silences which are not like his behavior with persons he knows well. Other people, who are equally troubled by meeting new people, automatically react by talking too much. Because they are not at ease themselves, they are unable to stop to let the other person say anything. The push of speech through these long drawn-out actions releases the energy by which they finally are able to relax and reach their normal rate. Such phrases as *talk a good game* or *pretentious* are sometimes used to describe these persons and imply that others do not think they see a true picture of their natural or unstressed patterns.

The behavior of shy or reserved individuals may be misinterpreted by others. Because they are unimpressive at the beginning of the meeting, they make it difficult for others to adjust. Moreover, they convey an impression of awkwardness and low activity that may be far from the truth. On the other hand, their opposites, the overtalkative people, may suggest a remarkable degree of energy and activity that is not present after the rush of speech slows down or they are subjected to other stresses. Such overtalkative people often make a good initial impression in contrast to the shy person who usually does not. The trouble is that their introductory burst of energy is too often their only strength. In jobs requiring continuing high energy and capacity to deal with stress, these people often fail.

The Definition of Stress

Throughout this chapter, the three major types of stress the individual encounters in his interactions with other people have been discussed. First, he may encounter opposition or competition or generate it, when he or another person interrupts and takes over control, and the loser must stop acting and wait until the other finishes. In the second type of stress, the individual does not receive the response his particular personality requires from other people. Finally, if the contact involves a new person, a stranger, or someone to whom the individual is not yet accustomed, another type of stress automatically is produced. The reasons why poor work-flow design creates serious human relations problems, as described in Chapter II, should now be clear.

Stress, therefore, is the occurrence of marked behavioral deviations from a person's characteristic actions and inactions, i.e., when his interaction synchronizes with another individual. Such synchronization takes place with someone who complements his own basic interaction rate, either naturally or by a learned skill in adjusting to him. Absence of stress, therefore, occurs when the person is not being dominated or when he gets an adequate response from other persons. The degree of stress and its intensity both during and after the disturbance is proportionate to his natural or basic pattern of interaction; it is measured as a ratio in arithmetical terms. The greater the difference in value of the ratio from equality or one (when no change can be detected), the greater the stress and the reactions to it.

If people are closely observed in interaction, it can be seen that they differ radically in their capacity to synchronize or to adjust their interaction patterns to one another. But, there are intervals of give and take in any contact where synchronization does not occur, intermingled with intervals where the interaction is in phase. Stress is not an either-or situation; rather, it is cumulative in its effects. The stress increases as the lack of synchronization becomes more frequent and lasts for longer intervals.

A person's capacity to adapt and to vary his pattern of actions and silences to fit the other person, therefore, is crucial in determining the limits of stress and its cumulative influence. Some people have a wide repertory, but others are confined to a narrow range. People who can adapt to varying interaction patterns are usually called "flexible," and, those who are extremely limited, "rigid." If a person can adapt by choosing patterns that complement the other's, the frequency and duration of stressful intervals is reduced. If, on the other hand, he follows a set interaction pattern, he continually creates a lack of adjustment.

Stress, therefore, occurs automatically if people fail to adjust, but people vary in the degree to which a given amount of nonsynchronization affects their behavior. It is cumulative throughout the day, so a brief interval of stress in one contact may set off a reaction that is built up by stresses in previous contacts. Everyone is aware of how a situation that can ordinarily be taken in stride is upsetting after a "bad" day. Therefore, in appraising others it is necessary to determine their limits and how much they react after the stress begins to exceed their limits.

To summarize, stress is the product of the interplay between a particular individual, with his combination of personality traits, and a human situation that makes certain demands upon him and provides (or fails to provide) him with certain responses. It is possible to determine when an individual is under stress by observing and measuring the difference between his behavior then and his normal pattern in an unstressful situation.

The pioneering work of the Western Electric Hawthorne experiments showed the importance of stable routines to the individual. The evidence was largely derived from interpretations of what people said about working situations they found satisfactory and those found to be stressful. Of necessity, the methods used were anecdotal. Similar findings can be obtained by more precise methods, with the advantage that the stress-producing situations can be defined with accuracy, and the magnitude of the stress and how long the situation and the individuals involved take to return to the normal pattern can be determined from these measurements. The ability or inability of specific individuals to handle a given managerial job provides one of the best applications of this concept of stress.

Use of Stress Analysis for Organization Decisions

A warning needs to be sounded here. Part of the growing restiveness with the traditional human relations pronouncements on management skills has resulted in statements like these: "Many individuals function best when they are challenged; when they are under tension and not placed in a nice relaxing environment where everyone is 'nice' to everyone else. Stress brings out the best in people."

What do such statements actually mean? It is necessary to distinguish between their implicit concept of stress and the one used in this book. No one would deny that many individuals with high dominance, quickness, and initiative require and thrive in situations that provide them with opportunities to exercise these characteristics. Such a denial would be inconsistent with the authors' own research on personality. Many times these are highly competitive, fast-moving organizational environments where the individuals can express those personality needs for vigorous interactional situations to the fullest.

But these patterns of behavior do not elicit the disabling emotional reactions described in this chapter when the executive has the appropriate personality characteristics. Managers who are sulky, defensive, withdrawn, or excitable (to mention only a few temperamental characteristics) when they are confronted with or after they have engaged in a disturbing contact are those with vulnerable personalities. Stress that produces these incapacitating reactions is highly unproductive. Managers and employees do not function at anywhere near their intellectual capacity if they are upset and disturbed.

Recognizing that there are different types of stress, it is important to identify which individuals become ineffective under what kinds of organizational stress. Jobs can be analyzed to determine the kinds of stress they are likely to produce. Then, individuals who do not have emotional reactions under such stresses can be selected to maintain organizational efficiency.

Most evaluations of potential and present executives make the mistake of observing them in a normal (unstressful) situation. Jones may impress people with the way he conducts meetings, interviews subordinates with problems, gives orders, takes and holds the floor at crucial conferences, and works with a large number of people with dispatch and vigor. But, by chance, he may have been observed under conditions that were not stressful for him. What happens at a meeting if a more dominant person opposes his suggestions, if a subordinate fails to respond as expected on an important assignment, or if his boss ignores a well-considered request for additional budget allowances? In most managerial jobs, these are common problems. They are part of the day-in, day-out frustrations of organizational life. And, as most people have learned, the executive who cannot cope with these stressful interactions and loses his temper, starts many more contacts with subordinates, is unavailable or curt after such situations, handicaps the normal functioning of the organization until he regains control of himself.

Conclusion

Our emphasis on observation of the behavior of the people in our organizations, or relying on measurements of how they act normally under stress and after stress, will provide the manager with means of getting reliable indicators of performance. Watching and estimating the frequency and duration of interaction changes eliminates the need of psychologizing about the individual or prying into his inner-mind's secrets. They are not the mysterious workings of the mind which can only be inferred by indirection. Rather we have described the individual in terms of his observable behavior; what he does in the variety of relationships with other people that comprise organizational life. The great advantage of understanding the individual and being able to predict his behavior in the terms we have used is that it matches the way we have described organizational positions. Both utilize the same dimensions or variables so that there is no need to speculate on how an Oedipus complex might affect the ability of a purchasing agent to deal effectively with suppliers or on similarly vague and difficult attempts at judging the effect of personality characteristics on job performance.

Although precise measurement of the personality and temperament characteristics described require controlled interviews, timing instruments, and trained personnel, every executive should be able to improve his own observational skills to evaluate managerial capacity.[6] Through training emphasizing the observation of individual behavior in time, selection and placement decisions can be improved substantially. Unfortunately, most managers assess personality largely in terms of their own reaction to what an individual says, the attitudes and points of view he expresses, and their relationship to the executive's own sentiments.

Management Check List for Appraising Personality

The characteristics described in this chapter are summarized here somewhat more formally. The analysis makes a distinction between personality and temperament traits. This division is based upon a fundamental observation that certain traits are characteristic of everybody, and others are found in only a few persons and are apparent as reactions only during or after specific behavioral situations. Traits that are a constant part of the individual's behavior in all his relationships are called personality traits. Every individual has each one in varying degrees and can be ranged on a continuous scale for comparison with other persons.

The larger number of traits described are called the temperament traits. They appear as over- or undercompensatory reactions to given situations. Many persons show no evidence of possessing them, and the frequency and the magnitude of their occurrence vary in different organizations and, perhaps, in different societies. The important fact is that the same behavioral situation can have differential results in two persons. The temperament traits have been classified by the situations that produce them, so the observer should easily be able to identify the precipitating behavior and describe the specific reaction to it to determine which temperament trait is being manifested. Although individuals do not habitually manifest opposed reactions to the same situation, they may possess temperament traits that appear inconsistent.

Because each combination that occurs in any given individual varies in magnitude, that is, the intensity, of each trait, the possible combinations and permutations can be large. Further variations may be produced by

[6] A standardized interview has been developed in which these various traits are measured by having the interviewer change his behavior to provide minimal amounts of stress in a manner analogous to the scratch tests used to assess allergies. The reactions of the interviewee are timed by an instrument called the Interaction Chronograph. Cf. Joseph D. Matarazzo, George Saslow, and Ruth G. Matarazzo, "The Interaction Chronograph as an Instrument for Objective Measurement of Interaction Patterns During Interviews," *The Journal of Psychology,* vol. 41, 1956, pp. 347–367.

differences in magnitude of the personality factors that serve as the basic substratum on which the temperamental factors are constructed.

Personality Traits [7]

I. Level of Activity

A. At one extreme is the individual who responds to almost every question or comment with a long speech, who has boundless energy to express him or herself, and who obviously enjoys talking to other people.

B. At the other extreme is the individual who is almost monosyllabic, who gives brief replies, and with whom it is usually a struggle to obtain adequate responses.

II. Listening Ability

A. Again, at one extreme is the individual who can refrain from talking for relatively long periods of time and who would rather listen than talk himself. He may be low or high in activity, but when his action ends, there is a noticeable interval between it and his next action. Thus, he is able to listen to the speeches of those with whom he comes in contact.

B. The opposite, of course, is the individual who cannot keep still. His periods of silence are brief, sometimes almost imperceptible. Although his actions may or may not be long, they appear so because another speech is started almost as soon as one is finished, so the person appears to be talking constantly, even though it may be in short, quick bursts.

III. Dominance

A. High dominance is characterized by the ability to take control of most interactional situations. A highly dominant person, regardless of interruptions and competition from others, succeeds in "holding the floor" and making his points. He may also interrupt others when they are talking and prevent individuals of low dominance from expressing themselves.

B. An individual with low dominance is usually overpowered by others with whom he is in contact if there is any competition. He cannot handle interruptions or express himself in the face of opposition. When interrupted, he stops and lets the other person take over and never interrupts another individual.

IV. Initiative

A. An individual with high initiative is almost constantly starting some kind of action, physical or verbal, after a lull or a period of inactivity. Whenever he is in contact with another person, the chances are great that he began the conversation by going over to the person, telephoning him, or asking him to come to his office.

B. Low initiative is observable in the individual who waits for others to contact him. This person rarely, if ever, volunteers a comment or response if there is a lull in the conversation. He can spend long periods of time by himself without finding any reason to contact others, and he may even put off as long as possible the contacts he is expected to make until someone else finally forces him to start again.

[7] The descriptions of personality traits cover only the extremes of the spectrum. There is a substantial range of variation between these highs and lows.

V. Quickness

A. Individuals also differ in the speed with which they take the initiative. One type of person may start acting if he thinks something needs to be done or if things are not going as he thinks they should. His reaction is that he should do something about the situation immediately.

B. Another person may wait a long while before taking action, either because someone else may handle the situation or because he may not be sure of the best action to take. Although he may be aware of the need to act, he is not quick to do something himself.

VI. Flexibility

A. This term refers to the amount of variation an individual shows in the length of his responses. A person may vary considerably, according to the situation in which he finds himself. Sometimes he may be very talkative and have no trouble in speaking at considerable length if he thinks it necessary or desirable, and at other times be a quiet listener and give only brief responses when he thinks them appropriate.

B. Other people show little variation in their responses. They are either always talkative or they are always taciturn. They have little variation in the length of their responses, regardless of what the situation demands.

VII. Persistence

A. High persistence is found when an individual's actions are almost as long in facing opposition as in the period of relaxed adjustment (which determines his base level of activity). Attempts to dominate him have little impact on his usual behavior.

B. The length of action of persons who are low in persistence becomes much more brief when such persons encounter competition; in the extreme their activity becomes minimal and is radically different from their behavior under optimum conditions.

VIII. Hesitancy

A. When another person stops acting, people vary in the speed with which they respond or synchronize their interaction pattern with the other. Those who adjust almost instantaneously, pausing at the most a fraction of a second, are very low on the scale, almost having an absence of this trait.

B. Persons who are markedly hesitant consistently fail to respond immediately when their turn in the give and take occurs; in the extreme they wait for long intervals (of many seconds) before they reply.

IX. Overeagerness

A. Just as there are many persons who rarely hesitate before responding, so there are many who rarely interrupt or, if they do so, the lack of adjustment during which both people are acting is very brief.

B. On the other hand, the extremely over-eager, often called aggressive, consistently interrupt the other person and keep on acting for long intervals while the other person is trying to hold the floor. They may or may not be able to dominate, but characteristically the stimulus to act is when the other person is already acting.

Temperamental Reactions

I. Stress of First Meeting

A. Reserve or *shyness* occurs when a person's actions at first meeting are markedly shorter than usual. He does not relax and reach his average base rate until after the contact has lasted for some time. The shorter his actions by comparison to his normal ratio and the longer it takes for them to increase, the more acute the reaction.

B. Pretentiousness is a word sometimes applied to a person who markedly overacts at first encounters. His actions are markedly prolonged, (perhaps to "make a good impression.") The longer the actions, and the more time it takes to reach what are base values for him, the more severe the trait.

II. Stress of Nonresponse or of an Inadequate Response

A. When a person finds he is not getting a response, he may begin to act briefly, stop, initiate a short action, and repeat the sequence, that is, he reacts by taking the initiative or by doing something to elicit a response. This kind of person often has difficulty giving long explanations to others and often *prefers to do things himself* rather than get others to do them.

B. In contrast, another kind of person may go to extra lengths to get a response. He talks at great length, and when he stops and receives no response, he may pause only briefly before starting again. In extreme reactions, this person may talk rather than act; he frequently talks too much. Habitually, he *takes the floor.*

C. A third kind of person reacts to the nonresponse situation by *questioning.* He is more silent, perhaps wondering or questioning why the other person does not respond or what to do to get a response. This individual takes considerable time before starting action. In the extreme case, his actions are shorter, and he becomes more and more silent.

D. Coincident with one or another of these patterns of reaction to nonresponse, an individual may also show a marked increase in the degree to which he hesitates before responding, far longer than his normal pattern. This inability to respond when the other person initiates to him is often considered a sign of being *easily discouraged.*

III. Reaction following a Period of Unresponsiveness by Another

A. Instead of returning to his normal base rate when others adjust to him, an *impatient* person continues to act quickly and speak briefly and tersely after the stress is over. Whenever possible, he tries to withdraw from the situation and avoid further contact with the unresponsive person. The more acute the trait, the shorter his actions and silences.

B. A common pattern appears in the person who has to *"blow off steam."* Immediately after the stress, he has an unusual burst of speech. He finds it difficult to stop talking about his problems, and in the extreme is clearly overwrought.

C. Sometimes the individual who is questioning or negative continues in this pattern. Removal of the stress does not alleviate the reaction. The person continues to be withdrawn and brief even though the other person is now reacting to him. This kind of person is considered *distrustful* or *suspicious* because he still does not trust the previously unresponsive person.

IV. Stress of Meeting Opposition or Competition

A. Many people when they encounter opposition are easily dominated. When the other person comes in, they stop and give up. But rather than waiting until the other person finishes, they interrupt in turn and thus appear *competitive,* frequently dominating the other person by cutting him off before he finishes. In the extreme, such people appear combative, matching the other person tit for tat; the longer they are interrupted the longer they interrupt in turn.

B. The *defensive* individual overreacts when he encounters opposition or even the threat of it. As it continues, he talks substantially longer than his usual level. In the extreme, his actions become so long he appears unyielding or obstinate.

C. The effect of competition on certain people is to inhibit their capacity to respond when their turn comes. The winner who has interrupted and dominated them finally stops, and in the pattern of alternation, they should now act. The opposition they have encountered, however, makes them *submissive* or *passive.* They become extremely hesitant, far more than they ever are in their normal or base condition of behavior when they are in a situation in which the other person is adjusting relatively well to them.

V. Reaction after the Stress of Competition

A. A person who is considered *excitable* has difficulty returning to his base level. His actions are only slightly longer than when under stress; he acts too quickly, jumping from one contact to another. In the extreme, such a person is called *impulsive.* Although he may show a greater recovery, he does not reach his base values. Thus, the carry-over of the disturbance is not obvious, but the individual cannot talk easily and might be called *oversensitive.*

B. After any opposition, another kind of person may have a long rush of speech that appears to be an attempt to get the other person to respond and agree with him. This reaction is often called *self-justification* because the person talks at great length around or away from the subject.

C. Still another, after the competition ends, shows marked underreactions. Not only are the actions less than the person's base, but also they are briefer and quicker than under the *stress* itself. This kind of person appears curt and is commonly considered highly *petulant.*

D. In contrast to petulance, another person may increase his periods of silence markedly. His pace becomes slow, and the length of actions decreases. He withdraws into himself, saying nothing and responding slowly. Typically, such a person is called *sulky* and frequently resents the person who caused the stress. He *bears a grudge* which only time will heal.

By learning to observe, it is relatively simple to apply these criteria in evaluating the behavior of members of an organization.

CHAPTER VIII

THE IMPACT of the ORGANIZATION on EMPLOYEE HEALTH

Recently, some companies have been attempting to handle the personality variable in another way. Instead of stopping with selection and placement decisions, progressive organizations now try to cope directly with executive neuroses and the problem employee. Where once such "personality problems" were ignored or assumed to be inevitable, such companies as International Business Machines, Eastman Kodak, and du Pont now have major programs stressing mental health and psychiatric techniques.[1]

Unfortunately, some of the efforts to adapt psychiatry to the organization parallel those first used with personnel methods when personnel experts and their techniques were considered something apart from the regular, day-to-day business of the organization. Personnel matters were supposed to be superimposed on an already well-functioning operation. Similarly, psychiatry often is utilized as though it could provide ready-made solutions to the difficult problems posed by disturbed employees.

However, effective treatment for these employees requires methods that consider both the situation and the personality. Treatment and diagnosis can involve changes in situations (or organizations) as well as in personnel. So, the executive who is concerned with mental illness in the organization or, more important, with the physical illnesses such as ulcers, coronary disease, and high blood pressure that are set in motion or worsened by stress tries to isolate the real sources of stress and the connections between individual susceptibilities and the organizational framework.

To understand the possible uses and limitations of psychiatry in industry the concepts of personality, job requirements, and organizational structure presented in the previous chapters must be related to psychiatric concepts.

[1] Cf. *Wall Street Journal,* Disturbed Workers: Their Mental Problems Spur Industry to Push Psychiatric Programs, June 30, 1958, p. 1.

The Place of Psychiatry in Business

An examination of the practice of psychiatry in business highlights the present difficulties of psychiatry itself. Modern psychiatry is almost entirely concerned with the illness of the individual patient. In spite of the growing interest in social or preventive psychiatry, the actual practice, as opposed to the theory, of psychiatry has been largely restricted to the individual physician's office and the clinic. Even psychiatrists who are regularly employed in industrial or business institutions are primarily concerned with either directly treating members of the organization or advising management on executive problems. "Mental Health" activities are largely diffuse and essentially devoted to educating management to consider psychiatric disorders as medical problems.

Everyone who is familiar with present-day organizations in which people spend their working lives can imagine how psychiatry might avert human tragedies, but the current organizational structures and psychiatric methods of handling emotional problems make it difficult to fit psychiatry into the organizational picture. The reasons for this are partly practical—the cost of treatment, the dearth of psychiatrists and the great demand for their services, and skepticism of other branches of medicine, fundamentally stemming from theoretical problems of present-day psychiatry.

First, within the field, there is a struggle to integrate psychiatry with general physiology and general medicine, that requires a coincident acceptance of psychiatrists by other physicians. This will enable cardiologists, gastrointestinal specialists, and the other specialists who deal with diseases affected by emotion to have a common meeting ground with the psychiatrists who presumably are specialists on "emotion." Second, the theoretical framework of psychiatry must be revised and extended to include consideration of the precise effects of the organization on the production of disease.[2]

Limitations of Psychiatry in Organizational Situations

In its present stage of development, psychiatry cannot cope with the effects of organizational life on mental health. The major emphasis placed on the predisposing effects of early childhood on the personality frequently

[2] Doctors L. E. Hinkle Jr., and Harold Wolff of New York Hospital, Cornell Medical Center, report that physiological changes associated with attempts to adapt to environmental situations influenced the time of occurrence of all types of diseases, affected the health patterns of two-thirds of the adults, and were involved in the development of at least one-third of all illnesses experienced by a series of more than 3000 persons.

"Ecologic Investigations of the Relationship between Illness, Life Experiences, and Social Environment," *Annals of Internal Medicine,* vol. 49, 1958, p. 1373.

ignores the way in which specific organizational situations, in the family or on the job, predispose or precipitate an illness. Consequently, except where psychiatric practice is concerned with the immediate alleviation of severe symptoms, the usual solution of the personal problem is to "remake" the personality by trying to eliminate or substantially modify the effects of early childhood. From the business point of view, the conceptual framework of psychiatry does not provide a method that can be used organizationally to identify individuals who are, or more important who can become, vulnerable to specific types of stress, nor does it provide any means of defining what constitutes a stress and of determining its effects on a given individual.

Individuals are usually referred to the psychiatrist by immediate supervisors or through staff departments, particularly personnel and medical. Hence, referrals depend upon alertness of supervisors in the organization, and, in spite of films and educational effort, it is often low. Even if in principle one believed in giving a psychiatric examination, along with a physical examination, few organizations provide thorough physical examinations of all employees, even on initial employment. Moreover, it would be necessary to repeat such examinations at least annually, and although management might believe this is the only answer to its problem, the practical difficulties and the expense of such a procedure make it almost prohibitive. With these conditions, there is little chance of utilizing psychiatry on an effective, across-the-board basis in any type of organization, even if the necessary number of psychiatrists could be added to the payroll, with the possible exception of educational institutions.

The present orientation of psychiatry limits its usefulness to the organization, particularly in the crucial matter of case-finding. Because he has no way of dealing with the disease-producing aspects of organizational situations and of evaluating on a routine basis the propensities of any given individual to succumb to stress, the psychiatrist can do little more than increase the awareness of the members of the organization to signs and symptoms of emotional disorders. Then, he can only hope for enough time to screen out cases from the many leads that such a program might reveal. Moreover, because present psychotherapeutic methods are unrelated to the conditioning effects of the organization, they cannot be used as part of the treatment and are too time-consuming for practical purposes.

The authors believe the key to the problem lies in the conception of case-finding as defined in public health. Without a theory and a method to determine the points where there is a high probability of the disease appearing, the psychiatrist is operating much as the specialist in contagious diseases would be if he had no knowledge of the way malaria or bubonic plague are transmitted and of the factors that condition their rate of spread. It may be true that modern chemistry will at long last develop a true cure for malaria, but the knowledge of the part played by the mosquito, and by particular species of mosquitoes under specific environmental conditions, provides a much more effective and practical means of wiping out the disease than individual treatment of individual illness. The value of this point of view is in the broad area of case-finding that depends upon a thorough understanding of the causes of the various psychiatric disorders and the environmental factors that affect their control by psychotherapy.

Analyzing the Organization for Stress

As pointed out repeatedly in this volume, analysis of an organization begins by describing the flow of paper, materials, or people, and the contacts between people associated with these processes. And, as described in Chapter II, by studying their quantitative characteristics at any given point in the flow it can be determined whether the relationships between individuals occur within well-defined (statistical) limits or whether there are sources of stress derived from the technical factors involved. These conflicts may be caused by relationships of undefined regularity set up by the organization or by the personality and temperament peculiarities of particular individuals. By locating and isolating reasons for stress points in the organization, it can be determined whether the stress can be eliminated by changes in process or technique, by more precise definition of the organizational relationships of the individuals, or whether the personality of an individual is such that he is unable to operate within the interactional requirements imposed by the particular job. The technical variables can be isolated by studying the time characteristics of the daily contacts and determining whether they occur regularly or erratically and to what degree. The relevance of the personality variables, as described in the preceding two chapters, can be determined either by measuring the interactional pattern of the contacts between given individuals on the job or by a standardized interview. The individual's personality and temperament as expressed in interaction can thus be described.

Through the use of integrally related methods of analysis the congruence of each individual's personality and organizational position can be determined. Studies in the field of business and industry indicate that the individual's performance and his degree of adjustment or maladjustment are directly related to how well his personality and temperament fit the particular position in the organizational network. Experiments have demonstrated repeatedly that a transfer from a position for which a personality is not fitted to the proper one creates major changes in mood and performance; conversely, experiments have also shown the harmful effects when an individual is transferred to a position involving stress, even though the transfer may involve a promotion and substantial advantages in terms of recognition and salary. Too often, organizations reap the unfavorable results of hasty placement decisions; an effective person who is placed in a job for which he is unfitted may develop ulcers, high blood pressure, or heart disorders.

Professor George Strauss of the University of Buffalo completed a case study of the effects of major organizational changes on a group of skilled mechanics (set-up men). A series of changes were introduced in this manufacturing company that radically transformed their jobs. The changes involved the number and type of personalities to whom they reported and with whom they worked, the range of contacts with subordinates, and the frequency with which certain production crises occurred. Strauss reports that during the ensuing twelve-month period, seven of the total of twelve set-up men became ill. Although absolute proof is lacking, a large share of these problems would normally be associated with psychiatric disturbances.

Set-up man A: Died of heart attack that was attributed to overwork.
Set-up man B: Developed nervous twitches that became substantially more serious; is hospitalized with a painful back injury.
Set-up man C: Had constant complaints of stomach pains; was taken to hospital reportedly for an emergency appendicitis operation, but after three days of observation, no organic faults were detected.
Set-up man D: Had nervous breakdown; on advice of doctor left plant to work as bartender.
Set-up man E: Developed stomach condition.
Set-up man F: Was out sick for various reasons for twenty-three days in rush season quarter.
Set-up man G: Developed hernia, was out thirty-four days.[3]

Changes in organization or in the flow of work, on the other hand, can also transform the situation so persons once again become capable of effective and contented performance. In a number of instances, highly dis-

[3] George Strauss, "The Set-up Man: A Case Study of Organizational Change," *Human Organization,* vol. 13, no. 2, 1954, p. 23.

Additional cases of a similar nature can be found in the recent study of intra-management relationships in several large West Coast firms: Melville Dalton, *Men Who Manage,* John Wiley & Sons, Inc., New York, 1959.

turbed individuals, superficially at least, who might have been referred to a psychiatrist, completely lost all signs of pathological behavior and autonomic symptoms after the source of stress was removed by changes in the organizational structure. Such findings are not particularly novel. Their importance lies in demonstrating that the nature of the stress is highly specific and the same or a similar job can be made either highly disturbing or highly satisfactory with what might appear to be minor changes in the interactional pattern. Consequently, environmental stress cannot be dealt with in general terms. It must be specifically related to the interactional capacities of the individual and the patterns of interaction that are available to him in an actual situation.[4]

What Are the Psychiatric Problems of Business

In studying people in business organizations, the kind of pathological behavior that creates serious difficulties is seldom of the type encountered in psychiatric clinics and hospitals. The incidence of psychotic states, or what perhaps might be called prepsychotic states, is extremely low. Furthermore, although substantially higher than psychosis, clearly defined patterns of psychoneurosis and disorders that are familiar in the clinic are far less common and significant than types of pathological behavior classified by psychiatrists as psychopathological or "pathological emotionality" that is, manifestations of temperament. In other words, although the term "neurotic" is used to cover nearly every instance of emotional reactions and in some circles it is fashionable to refer to oneself as neurotic, the psychiatrist uses the term to mean a clear-cut behavioral entity.

What is found, as seen in the preceding chapter, are persons whose primary characteristic might be called "reactibility," in contrast to the restricted and rigid behavior patterns of the neurotic. When such people encounter stress, they underreact or overreact in ways that are loosely called "infantile" in psychiatry (meaning simply that they are most obvious in children). After being dominated, they may become sulky and try to avoid further contacts or they talk themselves out of the fancied threat by resorting to what in the extreme case might be called pathological lying. They are shy and reserved, or are apparently so concerned with making a

[4] In a three-volume study, Prof. Eli Ginzberg, of Columbia University, concludes that many soldiers who were rejected from the armed service for psychiatric reasons could have functioned satisfactorily in jobs that did not involve certain strains and pressures that were beyond their limits of endurance.
Eli Ginzberg, *The Ineffective Soldier,* Columbia University Press, New York, 1959.

good impression they cannot stop talking. They become impatient or lose their tempers when they do not get a response.

Each of these patterns can be measured by observation, and the degree to which each person is affected by them can be determined. Although these patterns may be found in forms of psychosis and neurosis and may color the impressions such people make, they are not the characteristic behavioral symptoms that prevent people from consistently adapting to others.

Temperament Characteristics in Different Organizations

Apart from such reactive people, there are, of course, also the individuals who are simply misplaced and whose personalities are extreme only in comparison to the kinds of people and situations found within a particular organization but who, in other contexts, would be quite at home and well adjusted. There is, however, a process of natural selection in business both in personality characteristics and in the presence of special kinds of temperamental factors. These seem to be related to the types of jobs and their interactional requirements as found in the various kinds of institutions.

Thus, the kinds of personalities found in a department store are different from those in a government bureau or in an engineering or manufacturing firm. This is not surprising if one thinks only of salespeople. But, although characteristics also vary significantly within the organization, the need for a fast pace and high initiative extends to all types of jobs in a store and thus differentiates them from jobs in other types of organizations. For example, in a random sample of 260 department store employees, slightly more than 30 per cent showed a significant occurrence of "persistence;" whereas in 500 individuals selected at random in a government agency, only 5 per cent of the sample showed significant degrees of this trait. In the same way, only 7½ per cent of persons in the government agency sample showed an indication of a type of emotional reaction that, when extreme, leads to uncontrolled, long-lasting outbursts, but 23 per cent of department store employees showed this characteristic. By the nature of their work, people in department stores might be expected to be more "temperamental." The facts indicate clearly that, with specific traits, this is indeed the case.

Significant Health Problems in Organizations

Such findings also indicate that the traditional types of cases handled by the psychiatrist in the clinic are relatively unimportant in organizations. This does not mean there is not a significant number of neurotics and mild psychotics or that it is not extremely important to identify them and deal with them. It does mean, however, that the personality problems that are of major importance in the operation of an organization and the health of the individual are those patterns of reaction in interpersonal relations (psychopathological in psychiatric terms) with which little has been done in psychiatry. Attention is often paid to these behavioral disturbances in child psychiatry, but in the adult they are loosely classified as neurotic, regarded as normal weaknesses or, in some special cases, used as reasons for exclusion from employment.

Moreover, little is known about the precise relationship of each of these temperamental reactions to the vast group of diseases developed by or made worse by stress. Generally, it is known that "emotional reactions," are responsible, but not which ones. Some of the most interesting work in this area was done in cardiology by Drs. Rosenman and Friedman. They have shown that the major factors contributing to the development of coronary disease are affected by specific stresses in the jobs of individuals. Accountants, working to complete an audit or close the books, showed significant increases in measurements of these various factors, only to drop off to more normal levels after the deadlines. Not only was this characteristic of the effects of the work situation, but also individuals with specific behavioral patterns had both higher levels of such potentially causative factors as serum cholesterol, blood-clotting rate, etc., and a higher incidence of actual coronary artery disease.[5]

From the point of view advocated here, much can be done to deal with these problems in terms of careful placement. Determining the degree of stress an individual can withstand, and evaluating the job opportunities in similar terms can play a useful part in adjusting people to their working environment more effectively. Nevertheless, it must be recognized that organizational realignment and the placement of individuals in terms of their organizational capacities cannot accomplish everything. Individuals will still be affected strongly by the impact of their relationships in other areas, notably the family. Increasingly, the psychiatrist and other specialists will have to consider systematically the interdependence of all the organizations in which an individual interacts, both in studying the development (etiology) of the illness and in the management of the therapy.

[5] R. H. Rosenman, and M. Friedman, "The Possible Relationship of Occupational Stress to Clinical Coronary Heart Disease," *California Medicine,* vol., 89, pp. 169–174, September, 1958.

M. Friedman, R. H. Rosenman, and V. Carroll, "Changes in the Serum Cholesterol and Blood Clotting Time in Men Subjected to Cyclic Variation of Occupational Stress," *Circulation,* vol. XVII, no. 5, May, 1958.

M. Friedman and R. H. Rosenman, "Association of Specific Overt Behavior Pattern with Blood and Cardiovascular Findings," *Journal of the American Medical Association,* vol. 169, pp. 1286–1296, March 21, 1959.

Framework for Future Cooperation

Using this concept of an "interactional" psychiatry, the individual practitioner will no longer have to limit his therapeutic resources to the administration of psychotherapy, although even here a vast development can be foreseen in the design of behavior patterns to fit the needs of varying types of personalities.[6] Rather, the physician will become the active manager of the patient's interaction in differing organizational environments, recognizing the requirements each can impose on the personality, and making deliberate use of their conditioning resources. In part, this trend can be seen already in the increasing concern with the interpersonal environment of the hospital ward, and the exploration of the possibilities for using social work in a more comprehensive plan of patient environment management. But, the efforts are not systematic, and the methods of analysis employed do not permit routine inclusion of the organizational environment. Today, the individual psychiatrist, confined to traditional methods, must in one hour set his skills against the impact of organizational relationships over the remaining twenty-three hours. Surely much progress has been made in psychiatry, but the victory can be achieved more easily by using the forces raised against the patient, as in Judo, rather than by struggling against them.

The organizational use of psychiatrists, from the authors' point of view, must be integrated with other medical specialties as part of what is coming to be called "comprehensive medicine." Although certain physical diseases are far more likely to be known to the medical department than the more specifically "psychiatric" disorders, case-finding and the evaluation of organizational stresses on individuals can become matters of routine administrative practice using the methods and techniques described in this book. If general management, or the personnel department as an integral part of it, is able to eliminate stresses by changing the work flow or the organizational structure, there is no point in involving the psychiatrist or internist in an individual's situation, unless, because the process of change is slow, the disturbance in the individual must be handled on a temporary basis.

If analysis of the organizational situation reveals an individual's personality has definite vulnerabilities in his present job, then the methods described here will enable management to determine whether there are other positions

[6] See Eliot D. Chapple, "Deliberate Use of Occupational Therapy to Rebuild Human Relations," *Bulletin of the Massachusetts Occupational Therapy Association,* vol. 13, no. 8, 1940, pp. 1–6.

in the organization in which he can make a better adjustment, whether some kind of individualized program (not necessarily "treatment") is necessary to help him adjust better to his organizational position, or whether training or treatment should be combined with transfer so the effects of the job and the supportive help of a psychiatrist or personnel specialist will make a successful shift.

In other words, the authors believe psychiatry cannot be practiced, in corporations at least, independently of the process of measuring both the individual's personality and temperament traits and the interactional stresses of the particular job. The organizational situation, therefore, is decisive. It provides the environment that sets off emotional disturbance in vulnerable individuals; so it must also provide the administrative means by which such disturbances can be corrected or alleviated. Psychiatry and the psychiatrist, however useful, cannot singlehandedly take over the responsibility or provide the techniques for organizational analysis and decision.

CHAPTER IX

MORALE: THE MEASURE of ORGANIZATIONAL HEALTH

As observed in the preceding chapters, management must be concerned with human satisfactions within the organization. Some of the ways in which the work flow, the controls, and the definition of executive jobs establish constraints and provide outlets for the individual personalities who implement them have been examined. Executive jobs, as all others, must be designed to challenge the capacities of the individual personalities who will fill them. Both company efficiency and the physical and mental health of key personnel are the potential rewards or the prices to be paid for these man-job-organization decisions.

But, the manager's responsibility and concern does not end here. Organizations are not static and all decisions do not have their predicted effects. Change originating both in and outside of the company buffets everyone, and the executive seeks to discover whether the over-all organization is standing up under ceaseless pounding. For his answer, the manager needs to have some measure of the current state of organizational health or well-being: How can the operations of the total system as a system be assessed?

This is not a new question. Beginning in the military and increasingly in business, many efforts have been made to evaluate "morale," the term employed to characterize the human product of organizational activity. In the armed services, morale has been regarded as the index of potential combat performance; in business, the degree of morale is presumed to directly affect company productivity and therefore profitability.

TRADITIONAL CONCEPTS OF MORALE

As a consequence, the management movement has long been interested in means to determine morale. Unfortunately, there has been less concern with establishing the dimensions of this concept and the techniques of measurement consistent with the definition. The relationship between productivity and human relations was conceived very simply as the presence or absence of this morale factor.

Thus, morale was used to explain good or bad organizational results, much the same way that physicists once used the concept of the "ether." Not knowing how electromagnetic energy was transmitted, it was satisfying, if not very useful, to assume that some mysterious element—ether—provided the medium. Not understanding why employees fail to do their best, it was reassuring to speak of "low morale."

When it came to measuring this elusive but potent factor, management turned to some of the traditional assumptions of the labor economist, e.g., the employee derives certain quantities of satisfaction from each of the elements in the work situation: his wages, working conditions, supervision, coworkers, type of work, etc. Added together, it was assumed, these satisfactions made up his morale. Much as the worker seeking a job is supposed to handle the arithmetical operations of evaluating alternative sources of employment in the labor market, the employee keeps score inside his organization. When the computer gives a low sum, his performance is supposed to drop, and, conversely, high readings are supposed to release pent-up productive energies.

Attitude questionnaires developed by both companies and consultants as measuring scales have been produced in numbers to take these readings. Vast sums are expended annually in their processing, although systematic, impartial analyses of the results fail to show any correlation between these attitudinal scores and employee job performance.[1]

This is not surprising. One fallacy in this concept of morale is the belief that summing up feelings about supervision, wages, intrinsic job satisfaction, etc., can produce a meaningful total.[2] As generations of statisticians have never tired of pointing out, one cannot add horses and apples together; a horse-apple index simply has no meaning.[3] Actually, there is no reason to believe these bits and pieces of employee responses to abstract questions can be used to predict behavior on the job. Common sense, bolstered by personal experience, tells us a person can feel his wages ought to be higher even

[1] Arthur H. Brayfield and Walter H. Crockett, "Employee Attitudes and Employee Performance," *Psychological Bulletin*, vol. 52, no. 5, 1955, pp. 396–422.

[2] Even economists, for the most part, have abandoned their notions of totaling the utilities derived from the consumption of individual goods and services to obtain the total level of utility and satisfaction attained by one consumer.

[3] Bassett Jones, *Horses and Apples; A Study of Index Numbers*, The John Day Company, Inc., New York, 1934.

though he continues to do outstanding work, and there are situations in which an individual recognizes he is being overpaid for not working hard enough. Employee expressions of contentment and loyalty toward management can be poor predictors of worker behavior. The constant complainers, if they can find suitable channels for the expression of their dissatisfactions and the means of redress, actually may be the more stable, more productive employees. There are also semantic questions. What does an employee really mean if he checks off on a form that working conditions are not as good as he would like or that his supervisor does things that he believes are wrong?

Morale is usually stated to be present in a group on the basis of subjective rather than objective criteria. The emphasis is on the way the members of a group feel not on the way they behave; little attempt has been made to give any explicit criteria that could be used for purposes of control.

An exception to this approach to morale was the study of the Relay Assembly Test Room at the Hawthorne plant of the Western Electric Company. Coincidentally with an increase in output, morale was said to have improved with five objective criteria used as evidence. These were: "(1) a decreased absenteeism; (2) an increased amount of social activity among the test-room operators outside of working hours; (3) an increased amount of socialized conversation during the day; (4) a willingness to help one another for the common good of the group; (5) 'pacing' each other in output." [4]

These observations are also limited in their value to the manager who wants to know how to bring about such conditions within his organization. There is a tendency to regard morale as a latent characteristic of the group or the individual, as something that only appears in times of stress. The administrator's problem is not primarily to recognize a state of high morale when he has it; his problem is to run the organization so this state is constantly present.

Although companies have been shocked to learn that what they have been calling "morale" and measuring as "morale" appears to have no predictive value, there has been no evidence of any decrease in the efforts to measure it. A manager probably recognizes intuitively that there are significant differences among employees in their responses to the organization over a period of time. The tangible quality that distinguishes the zestful, effective employee group from the ineffective, disturbed organization is worth evaluat-

[4] F. J. Roethlisberger and W. J. Dickson, *Management and the Worker*, Harvard University Press, Cambridge, Mass., 1939, pp. 19–179.

ing. Also, management wants, and badly needs, some way to assess the effectiveness of its personnel activities and to exercise controls in this area comparable to those developed for materials and finances.

Equilibrium and Morale

To develop these control measures and to identify techniques that contribute to a continuing state of high organization morale, management needs to re-evaluate the whole concept of morale. Previous chapters established the basis for a more tangible definition of morale that permits measurement. Its foundation is the distinction between the disturbed and the satisfied individual.

In discussing personality and temperamental reactions to stress in Chapter VII, it was emphasized that each person is characterized by a fundamental pattern of interaction. This basic pattern of activity and its associated personality factors represent a state of equilibrium for the individual that may be disturbed to varying degrees when he encounters a stressful situation.

Observation shows that in the extreme the various temperamental reaction patterns are accompanied by visible evidence of emotional disturbance, and the physiological evidence shows there are correlative changes in heart rate, blood pressure, rate of gastric secretion, etc. Consequently, one can assume that changes in the interaction patterns are part of the body's reaction to stress. If a person has to "blow off steam," he experiences the changes in rates of bodily processes known as emotion that can be measured by physiological techniques. The more upset he is, the greater the changes in his interactional behavior and the physiological changes that produce a variety of other symptoms of the disturbance within his body.

Physiologists call this condition the state of equilibrium or homeostasis. When a system is in equilibrium, the internal processes are maintained at a constant rate until such time as a small force is impressed upon the system. When this happens, there is a reaction to the force. After the force is removed, another reaction takes place to restore the system to its initial state.

For example, when an infection disturbs the body, a series of changes take place to counterbalance the effects of the virus. The body temperature rises, white corpuscles increase, and other changes occur as a reaction to the infection. After the infection is eliminated, the temperature returns to its normal level, the white count to its former value, and the body processes are said to have returned to a state of equilibrium.

Organization life provides analogous infections or disturbances to the individual that have been called stress. A supervisor whose personality is such that he cannot tolerate an unresponsive subordinate will react immediately if one of his employees fails to satisfy him. The reaction may take the form of unusually long speeches or even tirades directed to the subordinate, constant interruptions whenever the other speaks, or perhaps sulking uncommunicativeness. Even after the stress is removed, reaction continues for the length of time and intensity needed to restore the upset boss's equilibrium. This is compensatory behavior. The hapless employee and others in the department can easily detect how long it takes the temperamental supervisor to work this "hurt" out of his system simply by noting when he resumes his normal pattern of interaction.

Sometimes, of course, there is no apparent reaction to stress. Minor irritations may produce no readily observable change in behavior. However, if these disturbances continue through the day, their effects accumulate. These situations cause the surprise and sense of shock: "I don't know what came over him; we just exchanged a couple of words when he blew up right in front of me." A major disturbance can be triggered by what appears to be a minor cause if one does not know the past sequence of stresses.

Whether the stress is of major proportions for the individual or is built up over a period of time, the reaction is almost automatic. The autonomic nervous system, or the neuro-humoral system as it was called earlier, that controls bodily functions becomes upset.[5] The heart beats more rapidly, blood pressure rises, contractions begin in the stomach and the intestines as the body becomes ready to deal with stress.[6] This volume cannot discuss this evidence at length; the important point is simply that the individual has little control over what takes place.

Everyone has his limits of tolerance within which he effectively maintains his equilibrium. Outside of these limits that vary for different types of stresses, he experiences temperamental reactions as the body first changes its patterns of interaction to the altered environmental situation and then compensates for the disturbance in the process of getting back to equilibrium.

Efforts to Restore Equilibrium

What actually happens in the process by which equilibrium is restored is, of course, a function of the individual's distinctive personality and his reactions to stress, the full range of which we described in Chapter VII. He may reduce the length of his contacts with other people, or try to

[5] P. Bard, "The Neuro-Humoral Basis of Emotional Reaction," in C. Murchison *Handbook of General Experimental Psychology*, Clark University Press, Worcester, 1934.

[6] W. B. Cannon, *Bodily Changes in Pain, Hunger, Fear and Rage*, Appleton-Century-Crofts, Inc., New York, 1936.

eliminate them completely, or, following the reverse pattern, he may find listeners and talk to them for extended periods of time. The subject matter is of little importance. He may be berating one of his own subordinates or telling a colleague about the impossibility of working under a tyrant like his own boss.

Whatever the course of his reaction, it can be predicted that it will affect those with whom he comes into contact. Just as the original stimulating situation involved a stress for the individual, so his behavior provides stress for those with whom he deals during his readjustment period. Everyone has experienced the strain of interacting with someone who is upset and is compensating. Although his words may try to hide the situation, his actions indicate something is wrong. He speaks more briefly, talks more, or picks up his part of the conversation more slowly or faster than usual. As a result, the other person is uncomfortable because the contact is not within the normal scope for the relationship.

Within a given organizational context, individuals learn over a period of time what to do to minimize the impact of a stressful situation. These learned patterns of adjustment can either help smooth over the difficulty or they can have injurious effects on the organization. Again, because of personality differences, all employees are not equally able to learn these techniques.

For example, if a piece of equipment breaks down and employees are contacting him at a much more frequent rate, the experienced supervisor learns that if he calls his carefully cultivated friend, Joe in maintenance, and makes a special plea, the repair will be swift and the stress on him thereby shortened in duration. After a frustrating experience, the availability of a colleague to whom one can express pent-up feelings facilitates a quick adjustment to the stress. This is also evident in group behavior. Work groups have learned they can frequently eliminate or substantially modify the impact of certain management-imposed stresses, such as a change in the work load that will cause substantial interaction changes, by adroit use of such tactics as slowing down work and carefully timed demonstrations. As a result, the period of stress can be substantially reduced, for them, at least, and the tension reduction is observable in the increased productivity that often follows a strike. (Work-group pressure tactics were described in Chapter V.)

Adjustments to Long-run Changes

Most of the examples above have been of short-term kinds of disturbances, the unanticipated but typical breakdowns in the normal pattern of relations that cause stress. However, in most dynamic organizations the individual is also subject to more long-term change: the introduction of new personalities, a new job, or new organization systems and procedures. Each of these shifts means the individual must adjust to a new pattern of interaction.

For example, if a manager is transferred, his immediate reaction is frequently an effort to preserve the satisfying ways of the past, thus providing himself with a minimum of stress. If he was in equilibrium, he had fitted his job to his personality. However, the new job may require a different distribution of time and contacts. Perhaps, if he continues to spend the same amount of time consulting with and advising subordinates, his responsibilities for meeting with other department heads are neglected. The first signs of trouble are pressures that originate with other people who are subject to stress because the transferred manager fails to fulfill the requirements of the new job.

The manager may shift his pattern of contacts as these new pressures build up (e.g., frequency of contacts coming to him), causing tension and dissatisfaction. At first the new sequences of relationships will not be comfortable, but gradually the job will be accommodated to the needs of his personality and a new equilibrium attained. (The modification of the organization structure because of the mutual adjustment of jobs and personalities was described in Chapter VI.) During the adjustment process evidence of compensatory reactions might be observed as the manager seeks to regain his base level of interaction.

As indicated, these realignments of relationships create stress for other members of the organization who come into contact with the individual experiencing these long-term changes. Thus, if an executive becomes active in a political campaign, he necessarily increases his interaction within the framework of the party activities. At the same time, he decreases, by necessity, his interactions with his family and frequently, if encouraged, with members of his own company. The other people, in this case the family and the firm, compensate by increasing their contacts with each other to make up for the shift in interaction. Because such changes rarely occur smoothly, minor disturbances take place within these relationships during the process of adjustment. After the campaign, the executive's interaction with party members and voters drops markedly and the old pattern of distribution is gradually restored, with family members and fellow executives again increasing their interaction with him to match the initial state.

In general, the patterns of interaction that comprise an individual's total system of relationships become stable through habit. Each employee seeks to adapt his organizational position to fit the needs of his own personality. In other words, he seeks to provide himself with homeostasis or to minimize the number of times he must confront stressful situations. He resists attempts to change these habitual patterns either by other individuals or changes in work flow, job distribution, etc. As pointed out earlier, the individual operating within a state of equilibrium tries to avoid disturbance as best he can. When it occurs, his automatic reaction is to shift in a way to minimize the stress (for himself) and to return to his accustomed ways when the stress is over. This then is the reason for employee resistance to change, not the newness of the situation itself.

How can management make use of this equilibrium concept?

An Operational Concept of Morale

Morale can be defined from this analysis. Every organization consists of individuals in interaction, each of whom has to achieve and maintain a state of equilibrium. The basic problem of management is to organize these individuals in terms of the technical routines in such a way that equilibrium is maintained for all of them. Stated differently, the problem is primarily one of maintaining a proper balance in the autonomic nervous system for each individual. Or, conversely, the objective of management is to prevent situations that produce in the individual the more violent temperamental reactions and overreactions of the autonomic nervous system, with attendant loss of the ability to adjust, to coordinate, and to maintain the complex habits necessary to carry out most office jobs. If the individual is able to maintain this condition of equilibrium for any long period of time, he is physiologically in a state of high morale.

In fact, observers emphasize this aspect of morale in the individual. They comment on the zest of the people involved and the increase of well-controlled and purposeful activity. All these phenomena seem dependent, however, upon the state of the autonomic nervous system. If changes in the environment occur regularly, it is possible to adjust to them through effective organization and to return rapidly to a state of equilibrium. If organizations develop this kind of equilibrium, even the sudden and unexpected changes that upset the autonomic nervous system have short-lived effects. From the point of view of organization, therefore, the problem of morale is one of obtaining a state of equilibrium in the relations of the constituent individuals.

In its effects on human physiology, organization does not present a static picture because the interactions of persons are anything but static. Contacts between persons fluctuate from hour to hour and day to day, depending upon changes in the work process, in volume, delays, breakdowns, etc. On different days, different persons are brought into contact, and each differs in his capacity to adjust to others and his ability to lead or follow. In addition to changes in the actual routines imposed by technological considerations, i.e., new equipment and new methods, there are similar changes in personnel such as hiring, transfer, promotion, layoff, illness, and death. Each change in personnel, as each change in routine, brings about differences in the structure of the organization; new relationships must be formed and old ones abandoned.

When changes occur, and they are constantly occurring in the normal operation of any business, mechanisms and routines have to be developed by which the organization can absorb the compensatory interactional patterns of disturbed individuals with resiliency. These mechanisms and routines will be described in the next section. Their purpose is to permit the individual to work out his adjustments to change within the limits of his interactional capacity, without further disturbance to the organization. In such cases, the compensatory reactions of the individuals (involving changes in their interaction pattern) are short and followed by rapid restoration of equilibrium.

Therefore, high morale for an organization, industrial or otherwise, is a state of equilibrium in the system of relations such that disturbances to the equilibrium bring about changes in the interaction rates that are within the normal limits of adjustment and quickly followed by a restoration of the system to its equilibrium. Such an equilibrium can be tested in its members by the low frequency of temperamental or emotional reactions with their correlative changes in the interaction rates and by the high number of periods when a steady state exists. For the organization as a whole, such a condition of high morale can be tested by the degree to which the rates of interaction of the constituent individuals remain constant over a period of time in spite of change. Morale for an organization can, therefore, be measured on a continuous scale based both on the degree of stability of the system in the face of change and also on the length of time involved before equilibrium is restored.[7] The greater the stability and the more rapid the restoration of equilibrium, the greater the morale of the organization.

[7] Cf. the discussion in Chapter IV, pp. 72–74.

Differences in Organization Capacity to Absorb Stress

Some organizations are constituted, either through design or accident, so compensatory reactions that result from sudden changes in relations do not spread havoc throughout the organization. If a breakdown occurs in a manufacturing process or if a member of the supervisory group is absent because of illness, the compensatory reactions follow regular channels through which equilibrium is rapidly restored. In the terms used above, such organizations have high morale.

In other companies, however, minor disturbances may throw a large part of the organization into disequilibrium for several days, and a major change may seriously modify the organizational structure. Because of the nature of the equilibrium in a system of relations a disturbance that upsets the equilibrium of part of an organization may have spiralling effects if it is not taken care of.

As already noted, when one or more individuals are disturbed, they undergo a marked change in their rates of interaction. If the members of Department A are disturbed, this disturbance affects not only the internal relations of the department but also its external contacts. If the disturbance in Department A upsets the interaction pattern of its members with persons in Deparments B and C, they in turn may pass the disturbance on to other departments through their work relationships. The spiral results from the timing of these disturbances. It may take some time before the status quo in Department B is disturbed because a series of contacts is necessary before the whole group is upset. (Groups that are more prone to exhibit this were described in Chapter V.) In the meantime, Department A may gradually start back towards its equilibrium. However, if Department B in its turn becomes a disturbing force, Department A will be moved away from the equilibrium to which it was returning. If a number of departments are closely related to one another, a disturbance starting in one may spread to all of the others, with each one disturbing the others until the entire organization is in disequilibrium. Such cumulative effects can be avoided only if the organization is designed so the effects of disturbances are "damped out" as they spread from the original source.

Therefore, if an organization is to achieve a high state of morale, provision must be made in the routine relations of individuals in and between departments to safeguard against such cumulating disturbances. This can be accomplished first if each unit work-flow system is maintained in a state of equilibrium by eliminating as many sources of stress as possible, and second if structural mechanisms are installed by which compensatory reactions can work themselves out through specific channels of interaction so the state of equilibrium of the organization is restored.

Maintaining Equilibrium in Dynamic Organizations

Limiting Sources of Disturbance

If an organization, or each of its constituent departments, is to be maintained in a state of equilibrium, the primary problem of management is to adjust the relations of individuals to each other so disturbances are at a minimum. Three sources of stress must be dealt with. The first is the technical processes of the department. Inefficient allocation of work, material delays, an overly complex record system, poor design of the production flow are all common types of technical difficulties that upset employee equilibrium by disrupting the routine pattern of relationships. For example, Chapter V explains how points of "blind coordination" in a work-flow process (where employees must achieve close coordination and are prevented from maintaining effective communication because of the work layout) are breeding grounds for labor-management disturbances.

The second factor is the manner in which the specific personalities in the department adjust to one another in the work process. Can the supervisors maintain the requisite interaction patterns at a constant rate, and are personalities compatible with job assignments? [8] Some individuals may be maintaining their equilibrium at the expense of the rest of the department.

The third factor is the stability of the relationships of the department to other departments through the relations of the members. The processes of production and control can cause changes in these interdepartment relationships. A common situation is found in the relation of staff to line departments where high-initiative staff officers disturb the line organization by devising new methods of control, the installation of which provides them with constant opportunity to increase the frequency of their contacts and at the same time disturbs the balance between the members of the departments. C. M. Arensberg and D. MacGregor made a valuable analysis of reasons for disturbances in the engineering staff of an electrical manufacturing company. In their case, instability in the relations of staff and line officials, both in their direct relations and also in their relations to higher management, brought about marked instability in the equilibrium of the

[8] Cf. Chapters III and VI.

individuals concerned. As a consequence, the morale and efficiency of the engineers was markedly lowered.[9]

The Effect of Outside Organizations on Morale

The external relations should not be omitted in assessing the sources of disturbance in an organization. Each employee and manager is a member of several other organizations in addition to the company: his family, his clubs and societies, his church, his political institutions, as well as the stores and banks of which he is a customer and client. If disturbances take place within the firm, compensatory changes may occur in these outside groups which, in their turn, may again react upon the organization. Thus, a prolonged strike may bring about reactions in the political community that result in restrictive ordinances or legislation. It may even produce a series of modifications in all of the organizations mentioned.

If the management brings the organization into a state of equilibrium, the principal problem it faces is the way in which outside institutions create disturbances within the company. Direct sources of disturbance for the organization also come from the variety of external relationships that the company must maintain to operate. These include relationships with banks, insurance companies, government officials, vendors, and customers, among others. All of them directly affect the company.

Specific employees are usually assigned responsibility for dealing with these outside institutions. Those who negotiate with banks, unions, or vendors, or who undertake to sell or promote the products or reputation of the company all have the same need to maintain an equilibrium in their relationships. Economic and political forces cause changes in these institutions that have direct ramifications on the interaction of the external contact men of the organization. If changes cause them to become disturbed, their compensatory reactions affect those inside the firm who have no such external relationships.

It is worth pointing out that "abstract" economic and political forces can have a direct interactional impact on the indiaviduals making up the firm by operating on one of the most important and obvious outside institutions that affects members of the organization, the family. A number of studies, particularly those at the Western Electric Company, have shown the effects of family disequilibrium upon the ability of the worker to get along in his job and to produce. T. N. Whitehead, for instance, made an extensive

[9] C. M. Arensberg and D. MacGregor, "Determination of Morale in an Industrial Company," *Applied Anthropology*, vol. 1, no. 2, 1942.

analysis of the output of a group of workers in the Relay Assembly Test Room in which he showed that the output of individuals whose home environments were in an unstable state markedly decreased.[10] Family disequilibrium may have a more profound effect upon the organization if it involves not individual cases at random but large groups of families as a result of nation-wide forces. These include changes in the cost of living, changes in the ease of obtaining credit, and many other factors.

Controls for Stability

After a department or an organization attains a state of equilibrium, its permanence can be tested by the use of methods of statistical control described in Chapter IV. Periodic samples of the rates of interaction between individuals can reveal whether the changes fall outside the normal expected limits of variation. If there is a change, such a control system will tell where in the organization it occurred; further analysis can then suggest how to restore equilibrium. The advantage of such a system is that changes can be detected long before disturbances become serious or spiral. It provides a mechanism to keep morale on a high level. When changes in production methods or supervision are made, or when changes in personnel are imminent, these controls not only provide a way of determining how to introduce the change but also they enable management to see whether the change is working out as desired. Frequently routine changes in personnel or processes do not have routine effects on morale.

Compensatory Mechanisms

When disturbances occur in the relations of individuals, their compensatory reactions may spread the disturbance to all other individuals with whom they are in contact. If these disturbances are not to upset the organization, there must be an outlet for disturbed interaction rates. This outlet must be habitual and automatically called into operation when a disturbance occurs.

The most important of these compensatory mechanisms is the democratic process. Thus, if the ordinary citizen finds his equilibrium upset, he compensates for the disturbance, and thus relieves it, by increasing his actions upon his representative. The latter, disturbed in turn, acts upon the administrator until the circular series ends by a final change in the relation of administrator to administered, restoring the equilibrium. In societies

[10] T. N. Whitehead, *The Industrial Worker,* Harvard University Press, Cambridge, Mass., 1938.

where this democratic process does not exist, the compensatory reactions of the ordinary citizen must find an outlet elsewhere, his family, members of alien groups, and the like.

Ordinarily, the relations of workers to their immediate superiors are characterized by considerable instability because the first-line supervisor is at the bottom of the supervisory hierarchy and therefore constantly subject to the impact of disturbances passed down through a sequence of relations. Not only do changes occur in relations down the line, but also the first-line supervisor is the focal point for contacts from the various staff departments, who often restore their own equilibrium by using the foreman as a channel to work out their compensatory reactions. As a result of these various forces, the foreman has to find an outlet, and under ordinary circumstances, his outlet follows his habitual relations to his employees.[11]

From the point of view of morale, therefore, the workers are at the most vulnerable point in the organization. Under ordinary circumstances, much of the compensatory reaction finds its outlet in relations to others, increased interaction on the job if this is allowed, restricting the output rate, and the like.[12] The first-line supervisor can also be an outlet if his personality makes this possible. For example, an effective department head gave the authors the following description of his technique for dealing with disturbed subordinates:

> Two or three times a day one of my people comes in ready to throw a fit. One of the departments which services ours has let him down—they failed to get things here on time or sent the wrong stuff. What he wants to do is to go upstairs and really let them have it; he is mad enough to burst. Well, I just sit and take it. He blows off steam for maybe ten or fifteen minutes telling me all of the things that have gone wrong and how these so and so's keep him from getting his work done the way it ought to be done. Sure it takes time, and I get pretty tired of it, but I figure our relationship isn't going to be hurt by this temper tantrum. But if he goes upstairs, and they get an earful, this is going to damage the relationship of our two departments for some period of time. The result will be more, not less, failures on their part to coordinate with us, and I'll be the real loser.

Many supervisors cannot adjust to these increased interaction demands, and they end these contacts before the disturbed individual's equilibrium is restored.

When supervisors, because of their personalities or training, are incapable

[11] The Western Electric Company study was the first of many that demonstrated the instability in the position of the first-line supervisors. Foremen either adjust by passing on changes coming down the line to the workers under them or, in effect, become one of the workers and protect the group from actions of superior members of the supervisory hierarchy. Cf. Roethlisberger and Dickson, *op. cit.*

[12] Cf. Chapter V.

of providing this type of compensatory channel, disturbances spiral because upset subordinates do things that, in turn, create more stress for themselves.

Unions as Compensatory Channels

Although this is frequently overlooked, the union is one of the principal examples of a compensatory mechanism. Disturbances to the workers can be compensated for through the union machinery in which the members increase their interaction with union officers who, in turn, interact with members of management. With such a compensatory mechanism, sources of disturbances can be called to the attention of management and the necessary changes made in the organization to eliminate or alleviate the stress. If the union officers and the representative of management can develop a satisfactory adjustment, there is considerable possibility for effective union-management cooperation in increasing morale and making the company more efficient.

However, there are several difficulties here. Many managements make the mistake of assuming there should be no further disturbances after a union contract has been signed, and if they do occur, the union, not the management, is responsible. If sources of disturbance are not remedied, management is faced with increasingly militant unions because the compensatory reactions of the workers follow the union channels. The result of such a situation may well be low morale in the company and high morale in the union.

A second difficulty regarding unions ordinarily results from the first situation, namely, management refuses to respond to the actions of the union leaders. In this case, the unions by necessity become militant organizations, which means that there is great increase in the strength of the supervisory hierarchy of the union itself.

Under the influence of continual crises, union officials become much like the first-line supervisors in the company; they compensate for their own disturbance by increasing their initiations of action to the men. In such cases, the unions may gradually lose their usefulness as compensatory mechanisms. Actions started by the members of the union to their leaders to remedy some situations are followed by actions directed to the men, such as demands for greater cohesiveness, loyalty, and militancy. In such a situation, the union no longer restores the equilibrium of the workers. Although the union is not weakened, management finds that labor problems are not solved but multiplied.

There is an alternative to this situation that often occurs in association with it. In this case, union officials and members of management achieve a good adjustment and an equilibrium as the result of a much higher frequency of interaction with each other than that which the union leaders have with their members. A classic example was described by Nyman and Smith in their study of the strike at the Pequot Mills.[13] In this kind of situation, the union leaders lose their leadership because they do not keep the compensatory channels in operation.

The role of unions in furthering or inhibiting compensatory actions will be discussed in detail in the next chapter.

Committees

Various companies have tried to develop committees to bridge the relationships subject to these disturbances, but unless the committees can truly direct action to higher management (as would a union), as the "multiple management" plan of McCormick & Company is said to do, they do not provide compensatory activities in the sense used here. The committee is most effective as an outlet if it is composed of individuals in the same or similar positions in the supervisory hierarchy and whose activities overlap. In such cases, the committee may relieve tension, but it will not eliminate the basic source of stress. Except in a minor sense, it is not a structural compensatory mechanism. Indeed, it is likely to accentuate the weaknesses in the organization. If men of different levels are included, the committee permits more interaction but interaction in which the lines of authority still predominate.

One should remember, as shown in Chapter II, that such expediencies as committees are attempts to bridge a source of stress in the organization. Typically they are found in places in the work flow where separate organizational units are responsible for parts of what is essentially one unit work flow. Management assumes that by establishing a committee to provide liaison or to work out the problems between the various organizational units involved, the fundamental stresses resulting from the way the work flow was segmented can be corrected. The very existence of a committee in an organization or the proposal of one to deal with a problem is usually good evidence that a basic organizational weakness needs investigation! The correction needed is generally a matter of improving the basic organizational structure itself, not imposing a new time-consuming system. In this view, the time executives devote to commitee meetings is a serious waste of the scarcest of all company resources, management time.

[13] R. C. Nyman (in collaboration with E. D. Smith), *Union-Management Cooperation in the "Stretchout."* Yale University Press, New Haven, 1934.
A more detailed description of this process is given in Chapter X.

Morale: A Continuing Management Responsibility

While popular novels and commentators concentrate on the problem of conformity in large organizations, companies themselves are facing the consequences of accelerating change. The merger movement, new efforts to diversify products and services, automation, and changing concepts of administration are steadily bombarding the organization. In some companies, the resulting instability is disguised by preeminence in the market based on successful capital concentrations, patent protections, and control over distribution channels. Internally, many are unable to digest these changes and take maximum advantage of the financial, production, and marketing positions they enjoy.

The problem of morale depends upon the successful adjustment of human beings to one another within the framework of the technical processes in which they have to work. If individuals are to contribute their maximum effort, the organization must be so constructed that the kinds of situations that disturb people emotionally are rare. In a sense, human relations must be regarded as an engineering problem.

This kind of organization engineering cannot be carried on effectively by isolated personnel specialists within a company, particularly if their efforts are necessarily restricted to handling individual cases. The morale of an individual is so dependent upon the system of relations of which he is a part that little improvement is possible unless there are modifications in the organizational structure. High morale in an individual company can be attained only if the mutual dependence of the various parts of the organization is analyzed and if each change in the organization is evaluated for its effects on the system as an operating entity.

A stable equilibrium for an individual, as for a group or an organization, is one in which adjustments to change occur within the limits of tolerance of his interactional system. Just as with pulse rate or body temperature, individuals have characteristic interaction patterns. When an individual is pushed away from this equilibrium by stress, he shows compensatory reactions. If an individual or an organization is to withstand the shocks of a dynamic environment, the compensatory changes brought about by forced change must not throw either into a prolonged state of disequilibrium. In these terms, a company has high morale if first, the system of organizational relations provides habitual channels for compensatory reactions and thus for the maintenance or quick restoration of equilibrium for all concerned; and second, the organization structure itself is designed to minimize the possibility of stress by placing individuals into jobs with matching interactional requirements and by eliminating points in the flow of work that might become sources of conflict. These organizations are able to adapt quickly and efficiently to change.

High morale, then, is not a neat function of the sum of wage, job, supervision, and working condition satisfactions. Efforts to convert a problem organization into an effective working unit by correcting and improving each of these areas may prove fruitless. A different conception of the meaning of morale is necessary before corrective techniques can be developed. These require dealing with the organization as a system of relationships and introducing the interaction measurements by which it can be controlled.

The preceding has endeavored to present a concept of employee morale with two advantages: First, it is based on objective and, therefore, measurable elements, e.g., behavior. Operating management can make use of direct observation to control employee morale. Second, morale is not something apart from the production and work activities of the organization. On the contrary, its source lies in the same pattern of successfully designed and functioning organization routines as productivity.

Traditional approaches to the measurement of morale have not satisfied these criteria. Their emphasis has been on subjective feelings; they have no logical or research-proven connections with the production objectives of the organization. Therefore, management cannot use them for control purposes.

CHAPTER X

UNION-MANAGEMENT RELATIONS and PRODUCTIVITY[1]

Unions have developed because most hourly employees, as described in Chapter IX, are on the receiving end of many pressures and, in turn, find it difficult to adjust by passing these pressures on to others. Although strong pressure groups (particularly the strategic and conservative groups described in Chapter V) can provide a compensatory channel for the individual employee under stress, the more formal system of collective bargaining has developed to accomplish this function. Efforts by management to provide special channels for compensatory behavior, e.g., employee representation plans, "open door" policies, and employee counseling programs, have failed to provide this kind of outlet largely because employees were usually unable to obtain adequate responses in terms of behavior changes from persons they contacted in these channels. Even the pressure groups already described become more effective after the establishment of formal grievance procedure.

Above the hourly level, supervisors and staff officials can compensate for stress they experience by changes in their behavior to subordinates. With the exception of those in strong groups, however, hourly employees have no such outlet because they are on the "bottom." But, the union gives them the means to initiate action to other levels in the organization, to the boss, to his superior, and to the industrial relations department, all contacts that they could make by themselves only with great difficulty.

Thus, collective bargaining can help the organization by providing a compensatory channel and, thereby, a potentially more stable environment. Unions become a real part of the organizational structure as employee-

[1] A significant portion of this chapter is based on an article by George Strauss and Leonard R. Sayles, "The Scanlon Plan: Some Organizational Problems," *Human Organization*, vol. 16, no. 3, pp. 15–22.

The authors are indebted to Dr. Strauss for permission to make use of this material. He has not, however, reviewed the additions and deletions in the present material.

union members contact their leaders, who, in turn, interact with various members of management. The effect resembles that of the addition of any new organizational component such as a new staff department or a new level in the line.

The attention devoted to the field of collective bargaining as a special area of study is largely a reflection of the critical role unions can play in dealing with the instabilities and undissipated tensions in the organization. Ideally, and certainly in theory, the function of the union is to act as a stabilizing mechanism to provide an outlet for its members that will enable them to adjust to the ever-varying pressures created by new techniques, new standards, or new personnel, and to regain equilibrium.

Students of labor relations, of course, have found on closer examination many cases in which the results were not as beneficial as envisioned. Malfunctioning collective bargaining adds its own instabilities to the organizational system, after creating serious disequilibrium for the organization and its members.

The most typical problem of this kind was best described by William Whyte in his discussion of the impact of the interactions introduced by collective bargaining on both management and union leaders in the traditional hostile kind of relationship:

> In some cases we find that it is an established management policy not to originate activity directly for the union. In other words, management conceives of the union as a watchdog of the contract. Management transmits its orders and directions to the work force right down the line of authority from plant manager through foreman to worker. The union, then, has a function to perform only when it challenges decisions that management has made.
>
> This managerial approach has two consequences: It provides the union stewards and officers with so little scope of activity [expression of their own interactional energies] that they must be constantly seeking to find ways to challenge management's authority through the grievance procedure. In the second place, this approach limits union-management interaction to those situations in which the union is challenging management's decisions. If those are the only interactions between union and management, they inevitably tend to build up a defensive reaction on the part of management people. They come to see the problem as one of maintaining management prerogatives against the onslaught of the union. In such situations no cooperation between union and management is possible.[2]

Recognizing this, there has been a growing interest in organizational techniques to convert hostile relationships, the breeding grounds for additional tension, into more harmonious relationships.

Concomitantly, students of industrial relations have been seeking ways

[2] William F. Whyte, *Money and Motivation*, pp. 235–236. Copyright, 1955, by Harper & Brothers, New York.

to gain benefits from the presence of the union above and beyond its function as a compensatory channel for employee-initiated demands. They reasoned that these same channels might appropriately be used to uncover ideas and suggestions from the workers, who are closest to the work flow and therefore most able to see flaws in managerial methods and processes. Although their points of view and ideas are usually lost or discouraged by the normal hierarchical or downward channels of action and response, union-protected and union-serviced channels might provide this needed medium. In turn, productivity would benefit as workers contributed their insights and ideas and utilized their energies to improve the performance of the firm. These, then, have been the sources of the growing interest in union-management cooperation.

Union-management cooperation, as the term is typically used, refers to systems by which the union takes some responsibility for encouraging improvements in productivity in exchange for what it hopes will be more job security, higher wages (perhaps through the mechanism of a Scanlon Plan bonus [3]), and the opportunity for a broader role in plant affairs. The latter involves allowing the union, and sometimes the membership as well, to make suggestions and criticisms of management methods on a more regular and systematic basis than is usually possible in the hierarchically organized plant.

A close examination of the organizational effects of the efforts in this direction, both successful and unsuccessful, should give a better understanding of the significance of collective bargaining as a compensatory channel (in the organizational sense of the term) and of its possible effects on the stability of both management and the union.

Conditions Necessary for Successful Cooperation

Although it is easy to understand why continuous conflict and strife in collective bargaining is unsettling for the organization, it is less apparent that movements in the direction of harmony and cooperation can also produce instability. In the effort to remove the sources of conflict and stress, it is important to retain balance in all of the elements involved. Four distinctive aspects of a cooperative union-management relationship should be examined and their parts in the achievement of equilibrium from the point of view of the organization as a whole should be noted.

[3] The late Joseph Scanlon developed the proposals and was instrumental in their installation in a variety of industrial settings. He was Lecturer in Industrial Relations at the Massachusetts Institute of Technology. A collection of essays describing these efforts was published recently.

Frederick Lesieur (ed.), *The Scanlon Plan*, John Wiley & Sons, Inc., New York, 1958.

The Union Must Retain Its Ability to Initiate to Management: The union will probably agree to assist management in improving productivity only when the firm faces serious economic conditions, when some impending or existing crisis threatens the equilibrium of the officers, who may find themselves without a local union to administer, and the members, who may find themselves without jobs. Its cooperation may include (*a*) explaining and passing on information about changes introduced by management; (*b*) negotiating changes in contractual provisions that hinder production; and (*c*) encouraging workers to increase their efforts.

Care must be taken, however, that this does not eliminate the traditional activities of the union leader. If his capacity for activity and initiation of action is fully utilized in convincing the membership of the need to tighten work standards, eliminate wasteful practices, and generally work harder, it is probable that legitimate grievances will be neglected. Members under stress, who seek relief by interacting with their union representative, will find an unresponsive ear. Because the organizational changes imposed by the union-management reaction to the economic crisis typically involve severe stresses for employees, this is precisely the period when employees have greatest need for a compensatory channel.

If it is not available, in time the new system will destroy itself as an enraged membership throws out its old officers and perhaps "cooperation" with them.[4]

The Union Leaders Must Utilize Different Kinds of Contacts to Process Suggestions than for Grievances: Just as the union leader may come under more pressure than he can bear if he must respond to both management officials seeking improved productivity and a membership seeking relief from stressful situations, the manager, too, can find the cooperative relationship upsetting. Individual managers now have not only their own bosses dominating them, but also the union leader who may be pressuring for production method changes in the same way he handles grievances.

According to the authors' observations, joint union-management production committee meetings have involved great stress for managers. Many meetings are devoted to a constant stream of union-initiated complaints, such as: "There are too many engineers here; they eat up the bonus!" or "The scheduling department is all loused up; we can't get production out!" or

[4] The Pequot Mills Case is a classic example of this and to a lesser extent the well-known union-management cooperation in the clothing industry in the 1920's.

Sumner H. Slichter, *Union Policies and Industrial Management*, Brookings Institute, Washington, 1941.

Eliot D. Chapple, "An Analysis of the Pequot Mills Strike," *Applied Anthropology*, vol. 3, no. 3, April–June, 1944.

"Why doesn't management get some more fire extinguishers?" In such an atmosphere, management officials must have unusual flexibility to avoid becoming defensive and giving the same kind of reply. Indeed, these meetings may resemble those of the grievance committee in a hostile relationship, that is, individual suggestions may be discussed not in terms of their merits but as symbols of the power relationship between union and management. Under such circumstances, management may reject good suggestions merely as a reaction to the stress felt in the pressureful situation.

One union president admitted frankly that such sessions "give us a chance to get things off our chest [compensatory behavior for stress they are experiencing] and make the company officers look small." To maintain cooperation, these contacts must be substantially less stressful for managers, who may already be near the point of disequilibrium as a result of their normal job contacts.

All Levels of Union and Management Must Be Involved: This point will be discussed in more detail later in this chapter. Here it will suffice to say that cooperation must involve more than top union and top management officials. Every effort must be made to communicate with union members and lower management to obtain maximum benefit from a cooperative system. For commitments to be binding on the membership, the officers must forestall grievances and also convince the rank and file of their point of view. At the same time, suggestions from the membership must be encouraged.

Management must be careful that the supervisor's relationships are not endangered in a scheme of cooperation. If the new pattern of interaction is restricted to only the top levels of both organizations, it is unlikely that there will be constructive give-and-take over significant issues. More probably, management will be using the union official only as a sounding board to test out membership sentiment.

If management uses the union primarily as such, cooperation then extends only to highly general and abstract discussions of production problems or specific issues of secondary importance, such as cafeterias, washrooms, washup time, etc. Deep-seated problems will be avoided, and the level of accomplishment will be low. (British experience with Joint Consultative Committees sustains this point of view.)[5]

Top Management Must Retain Its Ability to Say "No": Just as the union has its function as an upward channel, management must also maintain cooperation in a balanced state without giving up leadership and conceding

[5] W. H. Scott, *Industrial Leadership and Joint Consultation,* The University of Liverpool Press, Liverpool, 1952.

to any and all union requests to keep union peace. Prof. Whyte provides a good description of an unbalanced situation and its effects:

> By following this policy, management adheres to the theory that it can win peace and a harmonious adjustment with the union through satisfying the demands of the union leadership as often as possible. They look fondly toward the day when their generosity will be rewarded—the day the union leaders will cease pushing their demands. Unfortunately for management that day never dawns, and if we regard the problem in terms of the pattern of interaction, we recognize that such an outcome is impossible. The union leaders, accustomed to originating action for management at a relatively high frequency, will not adjust easily to a situation calling for a cessation of their origination. Also, we should note . . . the strong control exercised upon the rank and file by the union leadership. As their demands are granted by management, the union leaders are able to offer constant rewards to the rank and file, thus strengthening their efforts to originate action down the line in the union.[6]

Needless to say, this pattern is nearly always unsuccessful for both parties in the long run.

Possible Effects of Union-Management Cooperation

After this introduction, it is possible to consider more specifically the impact of union-management cooperation on various segments of both groups.

Impact on the Union

What happens to the union under cooperation? Does it now approach all problems, including those with a direct relationship to increasing production, with a new feeling of reasonableness as management hopes? Does it dwindle away completely, as some members fear? Or are normal collective bargaining functions completely unaffected as claimed by union officials who advocate cooperation?

If union-management relations have been relatively harmonious prior to the introduction of cooperation, the amount of adjustment required by the union may not be great. Under such circumstances, grievances have normally been discussed in terms of problem-solving rather than power positions, and at times management has originated action for the union.

However, the authors' studies suggest that, as relations between union and management improve, there is a tendency for officers to withdraw from

[6] William F. Whyte, "Patterns of Interaction in Union-Management Relations," *Human Organization*, vol. 8, no. 4, pp. 14–15. Copyright, 1949, by *Human Organization*.

the members and for membership participation in the union to decline.[7] The officers may become so involved in management policy that they are not inclined to settle grievances that in many cases attack their own positions.[8]

A top company officer in one of the most publicized instances of union-management cooperation reports that each year he becomes more concerned that the union is losing its effectiveness. He is worried about the failure of the union to process legitimate grievances and the excessive willingness of its leaders to share responsibility for unpleasant work-load increases and incentive rate cuts. (According to the concepts presented in preceding chapters, the union is no longer functioning as a compensatory channel.) He believes the union can no longer provide a two-way channel of communication to the worker. As the union changes its role in the plant, it also sacrifices its ability to commit the membership completely and to alert management of trouble spots in the organization. This is a loss for management.

Under such circumstances, grievances may take an almost anti-union character. Wildcat strikes and other forms of self-help activity may be the members' form of protest. In another context, the wildcat strike was described as an act of last resort when more peaceful channels proved inoperative or unresponsive to the demands of a particular work group with grievances. Frustrations gradually mount and tensions increase with the number of unsettled problems and the inability of the group to demonstrate concertedly their needs to union or management officials. Then, some spark, perhaps minor in comparison to the backlog of grievances, sets off the issue. The ensuing walkout shocks both management and the union.[9] These strikes are the hardest kind to settle because the issues that caused them are usually not the basic problems.

Although union officials can express their criticisms of management shortcomings that hamper productivity, it is more difficult to deal with employee behavior that may be holding back incentive earnings and company productivity that could result in more job security and better wages. These are the goals of any union commitment to cooperation with management. In one case, the officers stated that because the main cause for low production was management inefficiency, such as poor scheduling, harder work by indi-

[7] Leonard R. Sayles and George Strauss, *The Local Union*, Harper & Brothers, New York, 1953, chap. 3.

[8] Slichter commented on Pequot Mills, "Union-Management cooperation turned out to be a process by which the leaders gained such a thorough appreciation of the problems of the company that proposals which seemed quite unreasonable to the rank and file seemed reasonable to the leaders."

Sumner H. Slichter, *Union Policies and Industrial Management*, Brookings Institute, Washington, 1941.

[9] Leonard R. Sayles, "Wildcat Strikes," *Harvard Business Review*, vol. 32, no. 6, November–December, 1954.

viduals would not accomplish much. Still, they felt a considerable amount of responsibility and were concerned because a large number of people had not made an effort. As one officer said, "These fellows just can't get it through their heads they should work harder." For instance, several officers made pleas to the members at union meetings, encouraging them to get to work on time because tardiness lowered everyone's earnings.

The officers realize that by urging higher production they run against long-established group standards and jeopardize their political position. Also, their traditional role is one of fighting rather than cooperating with management and is very different interactionally!

If the officers are to be successful in changing standards, they must involve the rank-and-file members in the discussions of problems. They must exercise substantial skills in human relations and be informal leaders themselves if possible. Yet the authors' studies with local unions suggest union officers frequently are not informal leaders.[10] Further, the kind of individual who would be interested in the technical problems discussed by a committee considering production suggestions would probably have less skill in consulting with his men than the informal leader. If this consultation is not carried on, the members may feel they are under new and greater pressure rather than that they are participating in the system.

In reviewing his experience in one company, Whyte describes the interactional conditions that are necessary if the officers are to carry out this dual function:

> In the Inland Steel Container Company case we observed a high level of down-the-line activity within the union, but we also saw the rank and file originating actively for the leadership. For example, the problem of the punch press department manifested itself through numerous daily originations of workers to their union leaders. Eventually Columbus Gary (the union president) responded to these pressures by taking the initiative with management in proposing a new plan for the assignment of jobs. He then called a meeting to present the plan to the workers. But before final decisions were reached, the rank-and-file workers had an opportunity to decide on the ranking of the jobs in the department. It is this active involvement of rank-and-file members, this skillful balancing of up-and-down-the-line activity in the union, that gives us part of our explanation for the remarkable level of cooperation we have observed in this case.[11]

Another question concerns the traditional union functions of collective bargaining under cooperation. Joseph Scanlon, who was a well-known expert

[10] The local president in one situation explained the complicated indirect method of electing members to the production committee that would work with management on the grounds, "We don't want this to become a popularity contest." In other words, he was looking for administrators, not informal leaders.

Sayles and Strauss, *op. cit.*

[11] Whyte, *op. cit.*, p. 238.

in this field, insisted that collective bargaining activities should be entirely separate from the plans with which he was associated. To ensure this, he required that union stewards and officers, except for the local president, be excluded from positions on the production or screening committees established under the system he installed.

In so doing, the union makes a gallant effort to divide itself in half, part maintaining the traditional structure of the local union and the rest devoted to cooperative endeavors. The theory is that neither is to intrude on the other. Yet, research shows there is a constant tendency for the union to discuss matters with management that are not grievances within the strict meaning of the term. It is almost impossible to separate the two completely.

There are at least two reasons for this. In small- and medium-sized companies there are only a limited number of employees whose personalities make them potential candidates for union office. Individuals who do have adequate personalities to handle successfully both members and managers are not likely to draw a hard and fast line between the subjects under discussion. In terms of their relationships with a manager, there is little difference between working for a better method of handling materials and a looser incentive rate. The limited number of such individuals cannot be divided between union functions.

Impact on Management

If anything, the adjustment management must make to cooperative relationships is more difficult than that of the union. Within the union, important decisions are usually subject to extensive discussion, and union officers are accustomed to objections from members. On the company side, one-man decisions are typical. Ironically, union-management cooperation, in many instances, may be introduced without consulting middle or lower management, resulting in feelings of antagonism on these levels. Yet, if this new system of cooperation is to be successful, middle and lower managers must adjust to radically new patterns of interaction with subordinates. These patterns involve both the ability to ask for necessary comments and criticisms before introducing changes ("consultation") and to accept frequent suggestions for improvements from employees.

Supervisors are accustomed to criticism from above. Now, however, subordinates may question their decisions, and the adjustment is often difficult. Although the usual grievance procedure is limited to a relatively small range of management activity, the acceptance of union cooperation in management decisions brings the whole range of company decision-making under union scrutiny. The individual who wants to be a union leader because it gives him the opportunity to use his powers of dominance and argument usually takes an active part in union-management cooperative activities for the same reasons. He enjoys the opportunity of talking down a company official whom he has caught making a blunder. While managers give efficiency an important place in their scale of values, how frequently do they appreciate the alert insider who provides a running critique of their activities?

Take the foreman as an example. His attitude is decisive in what will happen. An antagonistic foreman can easily cut off the flow of potentially good suggestions.[12] Suggestions can, in fact, easily threaten his own position.[13] Others call attention to his inefficiencies or bring forth ideas that he should have thought of himself. He may have adjusted to union grievances against his personnel policies, but it requires considerably more adjustment to accept criticism of how he handles the production end of his job.

Furthermore, an active union-management cooperation system makes it possible for the union to go above him and expose his shortcomings to top management. Even if the suggestions imply no failure on the foreman's part, this by-passing nevertheless takes away his decision-making power and threatens his established relationship with his superiors.

From two directions, then, the supervisor is "caught in the middle" and his position worsened. Subordinates may come to him more often and give him a sense of pressure and tension as do actions initiated by a staff department. Secondly, his subordinates may fail to contact him with their normal frequency and seek instead to gain a response from his superiors. This can be equally stressful and threatening to his leadership position. How stressful, of course, depends upon his personality.

Whyte's analysis here is very perceptive and expands substantially on these same conclusions. Note also his proposals for improving the supervisor's position:

Here we see that it is possible to work out a harmonious relationship at top levels in such a manner that the foremen feel themselves under increasing pressure from above as well as from the union. For a complete understanding of this situation, we should consider the pressure of staff organizations, for in recent years the foreman's freedom of action has been seriously curtailed by the development of staff activities in engineering departments, in industrial relations staffs, and so on. The foreman's situation today often means that while the union is originating action for him, the very presence of the union limits his freedom to originate action for his subordinates. Moreover, the presence of the union may also lead to

[12] Harold Dreyer, *The Scanlon Plan: An Analysis and a Case Study,* Unpublished Ph.D. thesis, Massachusetts Institute of Technology, 1953.

[13] George P. Schultz, "Worker Participation in Production Problems," *Personnel,* vol. 28, no. 3, November, 1951, pp. 201–211.

increasing pressures on the foreman from the top down. We often find top management regarding the foreman as something of a scapegoat. As union-management frictions chiefly crop up at this point, some top management people regard the whole problem as one of foreman training and, therefore, they seek to devise more elaborate methods of telling the foreman what to do. With all these pressures converging upon him, the foreman finds himself limited in his opportunities to compensate for them, consequently it is not unusual to find him complaining that he has become a bumping-post between labor and management, and expressing in many ways the feeling that he is what we have described as "The Man in the Middle."[14]

. . . It is not suggested that an organization of foremen is the only method by which they can reestablish their equilibrium in management's system of relationships . . . [There are] possibilities of adjustment in three directions: Foremen may be encouraged to increase the frequency with which they originate action upon their superiors. The origination of action from superiors to foremen may be decreased. The foreman may be encouraged to originate action for the union steward. . . . The foremen should also consult with the union stewards before taking action on discipline and other problems involving the union within their department. In general, we find that where a situation giving scope to these adjustments prevails, the foremen have high morale and express favorable sentiments toward both management and the union.[15]

Traditionally, of course, management has used such staff activities as accounting, quality control, safety inspections, etc., to find out what is happening on the worker-foreman level. Yet, over a period of time, lower management has developed informal techniques to prevent bad news from being communicated upward, thus avoiding stressful contacts with superiors, i.e., disciplinary sessions. With the acceptance of union cooperation in management, the foreman must make similar new arrangements to protect himself. As in the case of grievances, informal agreements can be expected between the foreman and the union leader or an active member to prevent his troubles from being exposed, i.e., keeping interaction on their level. (After all, those who criticize the foreman also receive their work assignments from him.)

Top managers, too, must adjust. They must consult with the union on a much broader range of subjects. Probably a majority of suggestions include matters that would not normally be taken up at their level,[16] and conse-

[14] Burleigh Gardner and William F. Whyte, "The Man in the Middle: Position and Problems of the Foreman," *Applied Anthropology*, special issue, vol. 4, no. 2, Spring, 1945.

See also, F. Roethlisberger, "The Foreman: Master and Victim of Double Talk," *Harvard Business Review*, vol. 23, no. 3, Spring, 1945, pp. 283–298.

[15] William F. Whyte, "Patterns of Interaction in Union-Management Relations," *Human Organization*, vol. 8, no. 4, Fall, 1949, pp. 16–18.

[16] Dreyer's thesis, which includes a complete listing of the suggestions offered in the plant he studied, confirms this point.

quently, their own decisions are questioned less often. In fact, they may find they are provided with information that thcy might not otherwise obtain. And, being top management, they do not fear the union will report their errrors.

Staff (particularly production control) and middle management are probably most threatened. They are subject to the same embarrassment as the foremen and can easily become the scapegoats for everyone's troubles in the joint discussions on production problems.

If union-management cooperation is to be successful, top management must constantly be alert to the danger that lower levels of supervision may feel excluded and believe top management listens and responds more attentively to the union than to them. The authors discovered many incidents in which foremen induced workers to file grievances or suggestions for improvements that they were unable to obtain themselves through normal channels.

Unless morale of management is to decline disastrously, the establishment of effective two-way initiations between workers and management must be accompanied by equal improvements within the management hierarchy.

Impact on Intergroup Relations

The authors also predict that union-management cooperation might bring greater interdepartmental antagonism,[17] because it will no longer be possible to unite all departments against the common enemy, management. It is always easy to pass the blame for poor production and other failures to another work group.

Just as in the study of seniority and unionization, the authors can predict with some measure of confidence that the greater the number of areas for which the union takes responsibility, the greater the internal union strife.[18] Each increase in area increases the likelihood that a union leader will have to reject or respond negatively to an action initiated by a member. He cannot do otherwise because the request from the member conflicts with the interests of another member or group of members. The more frequently a union leader must reject member initiations, the greater the likelihood that the system of a compensatory channel will be destroyed.

[17] The situation at La Pointe (the best-known of the Scanlon Plans of union-management cooperation) where some draftsmen and designers tried to break away from the Steelworkers Union to join the American Federation of Technical Engineers and remained with the Steelworkers only after considerable pressure was exerted by management is still to be investigated.

La Pointe Machine Tool Company, 109 NLRB 514, 1954; 113 NLRB 171, 1955.

[18] Leonard R. Sayles, "Seniority: An Internal Union Problem," *Harvard Business Review,* vol. XXX, no. 1, 1952, pp. 55–61.

Of course, the larger the plant, the greater the possibilities for dissension, and the more difficult it becomes to maintain consistent support for plant-wide, as distinct from department or group, objectives. Indeed, it is doubtful whether support for a plant-wide goal can ever be maintained for long periods in larger plants. The pressure-group activities described in Chapter V make unified agreement on a plan of cooperation unlikely because the leaders are under too much divergent member pressure that tears them in several directions at the same time.

In fact, in their studies on work groups the authors found that plants in which union-management cooperation flourished were very different technologically from those in which there had been no history of harmonious union-management relations. The plants in which one was likely to find cooperation were those in which there were few if any strong, occupationally oriented groups. Here the union leader could frequently be more independent of rank-and-file control.[19] On the other hand, if work groups are well organized internally, they are constantly contacting the leader and demanding appropriate responses to their demands and grievances. (Of course, management may derive a different kind of benefit here. If a number of groups actively make demands on their leadership, it is unlikely that a union can run rampant and irresponsibly create strife and threaten the job security of all.)

A union-management cooperation plan may help to eliminate the problems of intergroup rivalry in incentive plans through the establishment of plant-wide incentives. A disadvantage of traditional incentive plans is that they engender ill-feeling between groups. As relationships of earnings shift from one group to another, so does the pattern of interaction both within and outside of the plant. A group that was formerly near the bottom of the wage ladder begins to act superior to those who were earlier above them. The mutual recriminations involved, both between the employees themselves and also between union members and their leaders over which group has "looser" rates, are a continual source of disequilibrium.[20]

A plant-wide incentive means that each individual's earnings depend upon the efforts of the entire plant. Harder work by any one individual will bring him only slightly higher monetary return. Hopefully, self-satisfaction, a desire for praise from fellow workers, and interest in the group as a whole will be sufficient to elicit high productivity, but this requires a high degree

[19] This point is discussed in greater detail in L. R. Sayles, *Behavior of Industrial Work Groups*, John Wiley & Sons, Inc., New York, 1958, pp. 113–115.

[20] Leonard R. Sayles, "The Impact of Incentives on Inter-Group Work Relations," *Personnel*, vol. 28, no. 6, May, 1952, pp. 483–490.

of cohesion and identification with both the entire plant and the individual department.

The likelihood of this occurring depends on a number of factors, including the size, homogeneity, and history of the work force. Plant-wide incentives would probably be more successful if workers are tied closely together by the flow of work.[21] If there are sharp technological boundaries between departments and the work of one is relatively independent of the others, less feeling of plant-wide unity can be expected. At the other extreme, if the plant is technologically a single unit, such as in assembly-line production and certain chemical processes, the efficiency of a single department is hard to measure. Consequently, the identification of sources of trouble is difficult, and the plan may suffer. This suggests that systems involving plant-wide incentives would be most successful within a narrow range of technologies. One matter is certain: there are bound to be some rivalries between groups, and constant skill in human relations is necessary to prevent them from becoming more serious. All of the evidence suggests that loyalty is greater to the face-to-face group than to the plant as a whole. It is too much to expect that traditional differences between the office and the shop and also among the various departments in the plant will disappear as soon as cooperation begins. In one situation studied, there was considerable antagonism expressed against the office group. The production men said, "Why should they get a bonus when we are doing all the extra work? They come late to work and no one cares." In another situation, Department X complained, "Why should we work hard when Department Y has fallen so far behind?"

Impact within the Department

Good relations within the department are crucial to the success of union-management cooperation. Although good relations between top union and top management officials are imperative to create the conditions necessary for cooperation and high productivity, there must also be a change in the interaction and behavior on the shop level. The patterns of interaction of the union representative, the shop foreman, and the workers are essential for this. The union must make an active effort to involve workers in suggestion-making processes and encourage group discussions of production problems. If relations are good, the foremen may take part in these discussions.

Consider the union leader who is responsible for making production-improving suggestions. If he is to do a good job, he must do more than sit

[21] Note that these same organizations are also more susceptible to work-flow problems because interruptions spread quickly, causing frictions and tensions. This may explain why there are so few examples of such systems of cooperation.

in on periodic meetings; he must make an active effort to get others to participate in the suggestion-making process and make regular rounds to collect suggestions. If the plan fails, many workers pass the blame to this man and complaints may arise such as, "We certainly have a lousy representative; there are dozens of possible suggestions he never noticed."

The role of the foreman has already been discussed. If he is unresponsive, workers may feel the system is entirely useless. Suggestions may become group demands because individuals are afraid to make them individually. Under such circumstances, the purpose of suggestions is to bring out evidences of inefficiency that can be brought to the attention of top-level union and management, to the embarrassment of lower levels. In fact, some workers might by-pass their representatives and foremen altogether and give suggestions, or more properly complaints, directly to the suggestion committee or to the membership meeting.

On the other hand, the foreman can take the initiative and present problems on which he needs help directly to the union representative in charge of suggestions and his men. Conceivably some decisions could be made the basis of group discussions, with the foreman functioning primarily as a discussion leader. Workers would bring their problems directly to the foreman or whichever person is in a position to implement a suggestion.[22] The foreman would ask the advice of the group whenever he encounters difficulties. Thus, communication would be two-way, as would originations of action. Obviously such a relationship requires that foremen and union representatives make considerable adjustments in their traditional behavior.

Further research is needed to discover the administrative skills used by leaders on both sides in the plants where such plans have been most successful.

In the study of grievances the authors found that as relations became more friendly and mature, a smaller proportion of grievances were put in writing. The same thing might be expected with suggestions. If relations are good, suggestions will be discussed informally between the foremen and workers. They will be put in writing only if the suggestion requires approval of higher management and even then problems can be handled informally.

The number of written suggestions cannot be considered as a measure of the success of union-management cooperation or of the relative interest

[22] Apparently it was quite common at La Pointe to bring problems directly to the staff department concerned.

George P. Shultz and Robert Crisara, "The La Pointe Machine Tool Company and the United Steelworkers of America," *Causes of Industrial Peace Under Collective Bargaining, Case Study no. 10,* p. 57, National Planning Association, Washington, 1952.

in various departments any more than the number of grievances are an indication of poor union-management relations. In fact, because grievances and suggestions seem to converge, it is curious that, although a large number of suggestions are considered evidence of good relations, the reverse is supposed to be true of grievances.

As other research has indicated, good ideas or suggestions are frequently not the product of a single individual. In the industrial plant at least, and probably in the laboratory as well, they are in part a function of the freedom and willingness to interact with one another, to express ideas freely and discuss them back and forth, with each individual introducing modifications and suggestions.

Organization Specifications for Successful Cooperation Programs

From analysis, the authors can arrive at some tentative ideas as to the major requisites for implementing union-management cooperation programs.

1. Interaction must be balanced and include all segments of the plant community. Cooperation will fail if the union uses it exclusively to vent its complaints, or if management looks upon it as a means to make the workers docile enough to accept increased production rates. Similarly, cooperation will not be effective if important groups of workers do not participate.

For a fuller explanation of this requirement, Whyte's observations are cited again:

> There must be frequent opportunities for union officers, at all levels, to originate for their opposite numbers in management. This includes the handling of grievances, of course, but it must also involve the encouragement of a union-management flow of suggestions.
>
> Management must originate activity for the union at various levels of the organization. Here it is unrealistic to draw a line separating potential grievances from potential suggestions. Management presents problems—sometimes complex problems—to the union. These union-management discussions, backed up by discussions within management and between workers and union officers, develop the suggestions that lead to both greater efficiency and higher morale. In some . . . cases we have seen instances of problems that could not be solved through suggestions until management had taken the initiative in posing these problems to union representatives . . .
>
> The cooperative relationship depends upon maintaining reciprocity in the origination of activity within management, within the union, and between union and management. Cooperation requires a regular and continuing pattern of interaction. The pattern cannot be interrupted and then resumed after a space of time as if nothing had happened—for something will have happened.[23]

[23] Whyte, *op. cit.*, pp. 238–239.

2. Unless the union members are to think their officers have "sold out," to management, there must be considerably more communication between the leadership and the members. The local meeting is one form of communication, but informal contacts and departmental meetings may be even more effective. It may be better not to separate union collective bargaining functions completely from the cooperation system.

3. Within management, more communication is also required. Special efforts are required to prevent middle management and staff from feeling left out. Management in general must become more tolerant of criticism and willing to look to the union for advice. If cooperation is regarded simply as a means for reducing worker-management conflicts, it is bound to fail. Rather, it is a method of bringing such differences into the open and perhaps resolving them.

4. Particularly in larger, more diversified plants, there is a difficult problem of preventing passing the blame between rival interest groups and maintaining their involvement in the over-all goal. As the size of the unit increases, however, the difficulties in maintaining involvement and interaction will probably increase even more rapidly. This may explain why such programs as the Scanlon Plan have been adopted so far chiefly in smaller companies.

5. Cooperation can be confined within the top union-management level too easily. There must be more cohesion and greater communication within the face-to-face work groups and between these groups and the foremen.

6. The whole method of supervision of the foremen must be changed. They must ask the group for suggestions, coordinate their replies, and possibly even lead them to group decisions to raise production levels. Many supervisors are unlikely to have personalities that permit the full use of such techniques.

Conclusion

The need for designing the manager's job in terms of the various work flows in which he participates was presented in an earlier chapter. Using the same interactional terms, it was shown how the work process itself can best be organized and managed by isolating the unit flows and placing them under the jurisdiction of a single manager.

This same concept of work flow, both the number and the type of interactions necessary to complete a job, a system, or a procedure, can also be applied to other aspects of the organization. Collective bargaining is essentially a work-flow process because it consists of patterned sequences of interaction involving employees, various members of management, and union officials. Collective bargaining does not take place at one instant in time nor does it usually involve only one or two people. Thus, it can be analyzed in terms of work flow just as any other organization activity. The authors believe nearly all programmed decision-making sequences, i.e., the members of the organization who interact in predictable patterns to deal with specific problems, are comparable to the manufacturing or clerical flows discussed earlier.

As an example, here is a typical work-flow sequence for grievances concerning incentive rates in the XYZ Company. If Bill Jones is assigned a job with a "tight" piece rate, he takes it to the department steward. The steward talks with him to get all the pertinent information and then goes to see Jones's supervisor. This second contact, however, is a short, formal one because the supervisor, considering his own organization position and knowledge of industrial engineering techniques, nearly always takes a safe position by giving a negative answer to the grievance. The steward then transmits the grievance to the chief steward, who, in turn, telephones the labor relations director for an appointment to discuss the problem. The director contacts the industrial engineering office before meeting the chief steward and reviews all available data from previous studies, relative earnings over a period of time in the department, etc. Usually the industrial engineer and the labor relations director discuss the issue and the former frequently advises a course of action. Finally, the chief steward and the labor relations director meet and negotiate a settlement. In nine out of ten cases, this pattern is repeated almost exactly. The exceptions involve very difficult or very easy problems that go through another sequence of contacts.

And, as before, the critical question posed for the manager is what interactional patterns or what work-flow arrangements are most effective? Collective bargaining "work flows" are not expected to produce a product or service in the usual meaning of those terms. However, from the point of view of management, the redress system is supposed to contribute to the maintenance of organizational stability by providing necessary resiliency. Management actions, even the behavior of fellow employees, impose pressures and tensions that are frequently focused at the level of the hourly workers.

The development of a systematic, organizational method to handle these actions without producing disruptive, emotion-laden outbursts such as stoppages and slowing down of work is a crucial test of executive skills. The most farsighted of all the methods tried have been the efforts to relate these redress procedures to the production system by union-management cooperation. The many difficulties that handicap such a development, particularly the need for a delicate balance in the interactional components at every level of both union and management structures, should not discourage efforts to attain this challenging objective.

Collective bargaining, and especially the cooperative systems described in this chapter, is not a simple pattern of give and take. The union is not an entity pitted against a rival, management. The process involves a whole series of interconnected relationships, some of which extend outside the company. The results of this process can only be understood by analyzing the interactional variables: "who does what with whom, when, where, and how often?"

CHAPTER XI

ALTERNATIVE APPROACHES to ORGANIZATIONAL CHANGE

It has been emphasized repeatedly that although human relations are important in the design and operation of an organization, they should not be regarded as something apart from the process of getting work accomplished. The authors' criticism of much of what has been done in the field of human relations, as their comments on aspects of the management movement, have not been intended to further the cause of those who argue, "Let's get back to the good old days when the businessman was only interested in making another dollar, and let people take care of themselves." Unfortunately, the problems of maintaining coordination and efficiency in anything but the smallest company are not that simple. Furthermore, it would be a great waste of resources to ignore the knowledge that has been accumulated about the behavior of people in organizations.

However, this knowledge is not to be confused with the usual principles and stock phrases about what makes a good organization. No one personality pattern can be exclusively identified with good leadership or executive capabilities. Almost every managerial position is distinctive, and the combination of personality characteristics that are successful in one such job may not be suited to another, even though the titles may sound alike! Similarly, there are no magic numbers that establish the number of subordinates than can be adequately supervised by a manager; it depends upon the types of organizational controls that can be developed and the frequency with which stress-producing incidents requiring administrative action occur. Rather than using arbitrary assessments of these, it is necessary to observe and measure each particular executive job.

Just as there is no perfect leader type, so there are no all-purpose, all-potent supervisory styles to guarantee job success, such as "group decision" or multidirectional "communication." The range and variety of the supervisory techniques or administrative behavior patterns that are required in a given organizational position are determined by the layout and flow of work, the controls, and the personalities of the subordinates, superiors, staff members, and colleagues with whom the supervisor must interact.

Similarly, it has been shown that concerted group action and grievances, and even the results of union-management relations, are predictable and explainable in terms of the impact of given patterns of interaction in the organization.

Throughout this volume one point has been emphasized. The researcher or executive who wants to understand and control the organization must look at the behavior of people in the context of time. Put in another way, there must be a shift away from the concern with feeling and intentions to the same kind of objective measurement that has characterized the physical sciences.

Another means of summarizing the position taken in this book and the differences between its approach and that of some of the other studies mentioned is to study the matter of introducing change. This will also give the reader the opportunity to obtain historical perspective on the subject by tracing its evolution from the time of the now well-known Western Electric studies.

In fact, the question most often asked is, "How do you change people?" based on the assumption that when a change is made, there must be some sort of magic formula to get the people concerned to act in a different way. The consultant, the staff expert, and the professor are constantly asked, "How do we get people to accept this change?" These two questions are really the same because "accepting a change," whether it is new equipment, new methods, new processes, new people, or new organization, actually means changing one's behavior to adjust to the new situation.

Whatever conclusions are reached in this analysis of industrial organization, the test of the success of the formulations is how well one can predict what will happen when change is introduced. The change might involve a new method of manufacture, a new procedure or set of controls, or it could be limited to a change in the individuals who make up the organization. On the other hand, it might be as far-reaching as the development of relationships with a union or with subsidiary companies after a merger. Much of the present concern with skills in human relations, in one form or another, is organized around the question of the "proper" method of introducing change, that is, knowing that what is done will have predictable effects.

Because changes are constantly occurring, either planned or otherwise, it is no wonder so many efforts and remedies have been developed to deal with them.

This chapter will contrast two very different approaches to the solution of the problem of change. The approach that has received perhaps the greatest attention in the United States in recent years from both the scientists and businessmen emphasizes changing people through efforts to modify their attitudes, values, and feelings, that is, by "working on their personalities." The other point of view, to which this volume has been devoted, is that individual personalities can be changed only with the greatest difficulty, if at all. The authors believe that, with rare exception that would necessitate continuous psychotherapy, the most efficient way of accomplishing change is to modify the organization itself: the technology, systems and procedures, layout, controls, and the positioning of individual personalities within the organizational structure. Subject to these changes, the attitudes will naturally follow in due course.

Now to look more closely at the alternatives the manager faces.

Change by Conversion

In recent years, enormous sums of money have been invested by private industry, governmental agencies, and foundations on the assumption that one can remake the individual, which, for business, usually means the supervisor and executive. The basic assumption of nearly all current management development and training programs is that a large share of any organizational problem is due to the managers' ineptness in handling people. Given the proper training, it is assumed that poor managers can become effective. In a recent summary and endorsement of this approach, Chris Argyris provides the basic principles of the conversionists:

> The "training" experience offered the executive should focus on helping him understand himself . . . The objective should be to help the individual have greater feelings of tolerance for himself. This will lead naturally to greater tolerance of others, for the way we evaluate others, we have seen, is based on our own self concept . . .
>
> Basic to these requirements, the individual must develop a philosophy of life and of leadership which is thought through to the point where it can be used to guide him in his behavior under varying conditions . . .
>
> One reason why this requirement is difficult to fulfill is that most such learning requires individuals who are willing not only to learn but also to express their true feelings and to respond to others' feelings with a minimum of defensiveness. Katz defines the conditions necessary for learning as follows:
>
> *a.* The man must sincerely *want* to improve his human relations skill.

b. He must be willing to face up squarely to his own inadequacies, without rationalizing or minimizing them.

c. He must be provided with a permissive atmosphere which shields out censure or ridicule when he exposes his weaknesses.

d. He must have someone whom he trusts, who is interested in helping him improve his performance, and who is himself sufficiently skilled that he is *able* to help without imposing his values on the trainee.

e. He must be provided with direct experiences in working with others, where he can learn and practice the new skills he acquires.[1]

We understand ourselves primarily through others and we understand others primarily through ourselves. Understanding does not exist unless the result is an acceptance of and a deep emotional respect for ourselves (or others).

No one starts from scratch in human relations training. All of us have our own feelings, values, needs, and prejudices which greatly influence our behavior. Therefore, the emphasis in human relations training should really be on re-education or redevelopment of executives. This is not simply a play on words. Re-education points up the important fact that the first step in self-development is *not* the acquisition of new ideas, new attitudes, and new skills. Rather it begins with a careful examination of the presently held ideas, attitudes, and skills in order that the individual may gain insight into *why* he believes what he does, he feels and behaves as he does. Re-education emphasizes that the "old" must be "unfrozen" before the "new" can be acquired.[2]

In the above quotation, that can be duplicated from many other students of human relations, the reader can see how much emphasis is placed on the basic reorientation of the personality. In looking back at the emphasis of the conversion school, observe how much faith is placed on the ability of people to change their behavior through insight, self-discipline, and gentle treatment. Note these intangibles:

. . . understanding himself . . . and tolerance for himself . . .

. . . to express their true feelings and to respond to others' feelings with a minimum of defensiveness . . .

. . . sincerely want to improve . . .

. . . face up squarely to his own inadequacies . . .

. . . a permissive atmosphere . . . when he exposes his weakness . . .

. . . someone whom he trusts . . .

. . . insight into why he believes what he does, he feels . . .

Considering the formidable difficulties experienced in the educational system and by psychiatry with this kind of endeavor, it does not seem wise to expect that many managers will change significantly.

[1] Robert L. Katz, "Human Relations Skills *Can* Be Sharpened," *Harvard Business Review*, vol. 34, no. 4, July–August, 1956, pp. 70–71.

[2] Chris Argyris, *Personality and Organization*, Harper & Brothers, New York, 1957, pp. 216, 218–220.

UNDERSTANDING IS NOT ENOUGH

Yet, a firmly held belief of many in the field of human relations states that people can only put knowledge to work if administrators, in either government or business, gain understanding, insight, or a new frame of reference. Understanding usually means a conversion to the point of view of the human scientists or a re-education to the acceptance of the significance of the human equation in daily administrative practice.

Most of the theories of human relations experts to accomplish change can be summarized in these principles: [3]

1. One should try to persuade, not force changes on people.
2. One should get the other person's point of view and allow him to feel that he is contributing to the change.
3. If you know why the individual is resisting change, you can change him, particularly if he also understands your point of view.

Although this may not be an exact translation of a large share of the conversionist literature, it comes close to expressing much of what is said regarding management training and development, that is, "sensitizing" managers to the existence of real people. This viewpoint has been bolstered by the great emphasis on a clinical approach to organization. It is argued that efforts to introduce change should be concentrated on speaking the doctrine and teaching appreciation of the human relations approach to the responsible administrator, who, if he is sensitive enough to the uniqueness of each situation, will be able to find fruitful solutions to his human problems.

This whole approach fails to recognize that experience suggests it is possible only in rare instances and by subtle and refined human relations methods to maneuver the busy administrator to accept statements on the value of human relations as more than articles of faith. They are something to believe in but not to act upon.

The factors that make most administrators successful involve at least an intellectual capacity to understand and use business or political logic better than most people. There is no question that the successful administrator has to be skillful in handling people, but that skill is more a matter of his personality and the absence of stress-inducing organizational pressure. Only rarely is it linked to or correlated with the traits of reflectiveness and self-analysis that could be the basis for "understanding" or conversion. The

[3] Cf. Keith Davis, *Human Relations in Business,* McGraw-Hill Book Company, Inc., New York, 1957, p. 160.

typical merchant, production man, financier, or bureau chief is driven by interests than other primary concern with human relations—many will argue that this is appropriate in our type of economic system.

This need not cause despair. The development of modern technology did not depend upon the businessman or government administrator acquiring the point of view and knowledge of the physicist, the metallurgist, or even the engineer. Rather, and this is the crucial point, the administrator found by experience that technological processes could solve practical problems of improving output, quality, costs, etc. The decision to accept or reject a given method or innovation was appraised in terms of the administrative logic of the profit and loss system.

The same must hold true for changing the behavior of people in the organization. The same kind of tested principles that engineers use in designing a machine is needed. One does not know or care whether the engineer has "empathy" with his drawings or the finished product. He is expected to be able to predict from his technical and scientific background what will happen under certain conditions and to formulate a means of testing out and verifying these predictions, whether they involve the way a machine will operate or the characteristics of a chemical process in a specific type of plant.

For progress to take place in the field of human relations in industry, what has been called "organizational behavior" throughout the book, emphasis must be shifted to seek generalizations that are testable. The apparent resistance of management to many of the teachings of human relations, often attributed to recalcitrance and "old-line" thinking may actually be something much stronger: disbelief. Although an executive may find it difficult to avoid giving lip service to the importance of human relations, he may remain convinced there are surer ways to run the company.

The result is that management often represents a split personality, the "do-good" alternating with the "do-work" approaches to operating the organization. It is necessary to realize these are spurious problems, resulting from failure to integrate the relationship problems of the work process into the total organization, to make real progress and to gain firmness in what is now euphemistically referred to as a "soft" field of knowledge. Management can only deal with sciences or technologies based on measurement and predictability. These can be fitted into its administrative logic, but "understanding" and "conversion" are far outside its limits of competence and responsibility. Students of organizational behavior need to realize and accept the limitations of human beings in organizations.

The History of the Conversion Approach

For reasons that can probably best be assessed by tracing the history of ideas, the emphasis on conversion developed from research whose major results were inconsistent with this method of introducing change. The now well-known Western Electric studies had as one of their major conclusions the recognition that organizational change comes about by structural changes, not by "conversion." But this highly important result was lost in the gradual evolution of the studies. Although Henry Landsberger in his excellent book, *Hawthorne Revisited*, has already helped to set the record straight,[4] it is interesting to review the Western Electric studies from the point of view of this volume.

When the Committee on Industrial Physiology was set up at Harvard University through grants from the Rockefeller Foundation as a committee of the several schools (business, medicine, public health, law, and arts and sciences) its initial interest was in the study of fatigue among industrial workers. Elton Mayo, one of its principal members, was an Australian psychiatrist and a friend of the illustrious anthropologists Malinowski and Radcliffe-Brown. As a psychiatrist, Mayo was primarily a follower of the psychologist Janet rather than Freud. His interest was in the influence (which, with R. H. Tawney, the English economic historian, he considered to be deleterious in contrast to that of peasant or primitive cultures) of modern industrial society on the production of psychiatric disorders. He believed much of what was classified as "fatigue" or "feelings of fatigue" among workers in modern industry was not physiological in origin but was the result of what he called "obsessive thinking." He had performed some successful experiments in a textile mill in Philadelphia where there had been a high labor turnover and he had treated "fatigue" by allowing workers to talk freely to a nurse.[5] The establishment of the Relay Assembly Test Room at the Hawthorne Works by the Western Electric Company, in collaboration with the Harvard group, was intended to test on an experimental basis the effects on fatigue of various physical changes, such as intensity of illumination, humidity, temperature, rest periods during the day, food intake, and so forth. As has been so well described, the results of the experiment were completely contrary to engineering, medical, and economic expecta-

[4] Henry A. Landsberger, *Hawthorne Revisited,* Cornell University Press, Ithaca, N.Y., 1958.

[5] Elton Mayo, *The Human Problems of an Industrial Civilization,* The Macmillan Company, New York, 1933.

tion. Whether the changes imposed on the girls were, in terms of management logic, for better or for worse, productivity in this group consistently increased. Detailed examination of the evidence clearly indicated that changes in organizational factors were primarily responsible for this sustained increase in output.[6]

The analysis of these relationships further indicated that the interaction patterns of the individuals in this group, both within and outside the plant, had resulted in the formation of a tightly knit group. Its output increased as the members spent more and more time with one another in free give-and-take while they were working, a situation made possible by the unusual relationships that they had with supervisory authority. Because of the nation-wide as well as company-wide interest in the study, the girls had frequent opportunities to take the initiative in going to their supervisor and to control the interpersonal conditions of their work.

This new pattern of subordinate-superior relationship was in sharp contrast with the prevailing one in which the boss can act freely on the subordinate, but not the reverse.

Discovery of "Informal" Relationships

This discovery of the overriding importance of human relations factors marked a turning point in the history of the Western Electric studies. Mayo brought W. Lloyd Warner, who had recently come to the department of anthropology at Harvard, in as a consultant. Warner, a student of Radcliffe-Brown, Malinowski, and Robert Lowie, had just returned from a field trip in northern Australia among the Murngin. As a result of his influence and Mayo's own interest in anthropology, there was a marked change in the research. In what was called the "Bank Wiring Observation Room," a segment of a working department in a "natural" industrial situation was physically set off from the rest of the department. The relationships of these workers were described and analyzed in terms of the concepts of the "functional" school of anthropology.

An observer, seated in the back of the room, made daily records of what he heard and saw, and an interviewer worked with each man on a regular basis. For the first time, a systematic description of the social organization of an industrial working group was obtained. It clearly demonstrated the significance of cultural processes and techniques in determining that what

[6] T. N. Whitehead, *The Industrial Worker: A Statistical Study of Human Relations in a Group of Manual Workers,* Harvard University Press, Cambridge, Mass., 1938.

F. J. Roethlisberger and W. J. Dickson, *Management and the Worker: An Account of a Research Program Conducted by the Western Electric Company, Hawthorne Works, Chicago,* Harvard University Press, Cambridge, Mass., 1939.

the investigators called the "informal" organization of the group, that is, the division of labor, the work flow, and work layout which were all determined by management and the engineers, had a major influence on the pattern of relationships that evolved to get the work done. The investigators saw that the minute-by-minute interactions of wiremen, soldermen, and inspectors were not simply chance vagaries or functions of personality differences, although these were important. They were predictable from the work methods and technology. These clique and teamwork patterns among individuals were opposed to the "formal" organization or the hierarchical departmental groupings on the organization chart.

This artificial distinction between "formal" and "informal" structure, symbolized by the organization chart, tended to obscure the significance of this part of the Western Electric investigation. The fact that workers have "informal" relations fundamental in determining their attitudes was so emphasized that the overriding importance of the technological work procedures of the Bank Wiring Observation Room in determining these relations, and in rendering useless the semantic dichotomy, was neglected. These factors included specific techniques performed by the workers; the interdependence of one operation and one operator upon another through the ordering of the flow of the work; the influence of the spatial differentiation of the room; and the way in which these factors, operating upon individuals with different personalities, produced an effective and working system of relations with well-defined equilibrium characteristics that was represented both in the limitation of output and also in the behavior of the individuals toward one another.

Many of the incidents reported clearly show how changes in personnel or in cultural process or technique directly affect or disturb the system of relations.

As readers are already aware, the investigators observed systematic restriction of output, pressure on employees to hold back production, and widespread violation of company rules. Many human relations commentators, aware of this reduced productivity, have sought to provide remedies for management through improvements—the development of new leadership techniques. They have even argued that the Western Electric supervisors could have been changed or converted into better leaders. However, as Landsberger cogently points out:

> The authors [Roethlisberger and Dickson] quite specifically argue against the theory that this situation [in the Bank Wiring Room] would be capable of improvement through mere changes in interpersonal relations at the first-line supervisory level. They state explicitly that supervisory training could not solve the

problem (p. 537—*Management and the Worker*) since little can be done "by sheer force of personality" (p. 536). For years we have been accustomed to tracing the rationale of supervisory training back to the "lessons" of the Hawthorne Studies. Yet the authors foreshadowed the failure of attempting to dispel conflict through improved face-to-face practices some seventeen years before actual studies of the effects of supervisory training caught up with them.[7]

Emergence of Sociological and Psychiatric Approaches

It is interesting to find that the significance of the Hawthorne experiments was little realized even by the investigators themselves. To a considerable extent, this derives from what might be called the "interview bias" of the researchers and their inability to describe the behavior of people objectively. In the texts and in the observations and interviews themselves, shorthand sociological and psychiatric concepts are repeatedly substituted for actual first-order abstractions: the who does what to whom, when, and where, of the anthropological field method. Such terms as "antagonism," "social distance," "interests," "sentiments," and "obsessions" interfered with the descriptive account.

The bias referred to above, however, was far more important in its effects on the future direction of industrial research. In part, it resulted from the heavy psychiatric preoccupations of the principal investigators. At the time the Bank Wiring Observation Room was set up, a plant-wide interviewing program was also underway to ascertain the attitudes of the workers toward their work situations. The findings of this program indicated that such interviewing had a marked cathartic effect, and the interviewing in the Bank Wire Observation Room seemed to substantiate this. As a result, both Mayo and the Western Electric Company concluded that the installation of an interviewing program on a permanent basis would be of major therapeutic value and would have the palliative effects on personnel relations that they hoped to obtain.

The efforts of the group then became directed toward the institution of a counseling program, using a nondirective type interview that was comparable to, but apparently developed independently from the technique associated with Carl Rogers.[8] At the beginning, the counseling was intended to provide both an organized system of plant psychotherapy and a means of communication up the line through which information relating to emotional and working problems would be channeled to top management through a staff personnel unit. Counselors were assigned to the floor, the

[7] Landsberger, *op. cit.*, p. 66.

[8] C. R. Rogers, *Counseling and Psychotherapy,* Houghton Mifflin Company, Boston, 1942.

interviews analyzed, and reports and general recommendations made to management without violating personal anonymity.

Gradually this communication function became less and less important, and, for reasons connected with the organizational stresses within the company as the program went on, greater and greater weight was laid on the counselor-client relationship itself. It, therefore, set out upon a course exactly parallel to that of Rogers with the basic emphasis on the client-oriented interview and working on the assumption that for industrial purposes it was sufficient to help the individual reorganize his concepts and attitudes to adapt him better to the external environment.

The results of this change in the emphasis of the Western Electric work to the psychiatric or clinical-psychological approach in industrial relations had considerable influence in retarding the application of direct observation techniques in industry. Counseling programs, both within the American Telephone & Telegraph Company, of which the Western Electric Company is a subsidiary, and also in industry generally, became widespread. Except for a few investigators who continued along the line suggested by the Bank Wiring Observation Room, most of the effort in industry was devoted to establishing counseling systems and finding, after a shorter or longer period, that they were of only minor benefit in the over-all personnel picture.[9] The significance and the potentialities of a new approach to organization problems were only dimly perceived in management circles. As for counseling, the rise of industrial unionism provided employees with a far more powerful and direct method by which communication could be conducted up the line.

Group Dynamics

The counseling technique of the Western Electric Company has been extended to the group with enormous popularity. The objective again is the conversion or changing of "hostile, uncooperative, aggressive" members of an organization into a harmonious team by the use of conference techniques: consultative or participative management, as it is sometimes called. Members of the same department or employees drawn from a number of groups or even various levels meet in a conference designed to work out their mutual suspicions and dislocations.[10] The function of the leader is to make sure that a "permissive" atmosphere exists and the individuals are free to talk and formulate their problems and attitudes toward one another explicitly. In Great Britain, Elliott Jaques described the use of group meet-

[9] Jeanne L. and Harold L. Wilensky, "Personnel Counseling: The Hawthorne Case," *American Journal of Sociology*, vol. LVII, November, 1951, pp. 265–282.

[10] Cf. Chris Argyris and Graham Taylor, "The Member-centered Conference as a Research Method, II," *Human Organization*, vol. X, no. 1, 1951, pp. 22–27.

ings for self-understanding and mutual problem-solving throughout a small metal working plant, and in this country, Norman Maier is one of the best-known exponents of democratic conferences as a means of introducing change.[11]

From the authors' point of view, however, these studies, although extremely suggestive, are self-limiting as they are presently carried out. Because the aim of science is to predict, the question yet unanswered is, "Under what specific organizational conditions is a given social technique, such as the free-expression conference, indicated?"

Through the unusual skills of Alex Bavelas, a group of women factory workers after experiencing changed work methods were induced to improve their production performance at a much faster rate than other groups not exposed to Bavelas.[12] However, attempts by others to reproduce the striking results of this study have not been successful. Dr. Harold Wilensky, a careful and methodical social scientist, recently reviewed the research literature covering the use of subordinate participation and group techniques to accomplish organizational change. He finds the effects have been "positive and neutral or negative" depending upon the type of situation in which these methods were introduced.[13]

The problem not dealt with is the precise description of the conditions that can lead to the prediction that organizational situation Z requires a sequence of interactions by given individuals of type X. In other words, it is necessary to advance from the intuitive formulations of the clinician to the objective and abstract method of the scientist or engineer.

Importance of Technological Factors

This lack of systematic examination of organizational structure seems to have been produced by two factors. First, many of the investigators have been unwilling to follow through analytically the implications of the tight controls imposed by work-flow processes and the technical systems on individuals of given personalities. Although intuitively they may have been well aware of the importance of organizational factors, by failing to describe them systematically and abstractly, they have not grasped the potentialities

[11] Elliott Jaques, *The Changing Culture of a Factory*, The Dryden Press, Inc., New York, 1952.

Norman R. F. Maier, *Principles of Human Relations*, John Wiley & Sons, Inc., New York, 1952.

[12] L. Coch and J. R. P. French, "Overcoming Resistance to Change," *Human Relations*, vol. 1, 1948, pp. 512–532.

[13] Harold L. Wilensky, "Human Relations in the Workplace: An Appraisal of Some Recent Research," *Research in Industrial Human Relations*, (ed. C. Arensberg et al.), Harper & Brothers, New York, 1957, p. 23.

of producing change by altering these factors. Second, as in the case of the Mayo group, they have, in effect, gambled on the conversion process, and, by so doing, have accentuated their unwillingness to define and to utilize to the maximum the analysis of interaction patterns within their cultural contexts. Thus, they have ignored the troublesome fact that susceptibility to conversion is rare in the general population and, in any case, for success it requires a kind of human relations skill on the part of the practitioner that is also found infrequently.

There is no question that some people actually do achieve a better adjustment to those with whom they have to work, whether as supervisors or as members of a working team, by intensive therapy. On the other hand, if the science of organizational change is to depend upon this as its primary weapon, it is faced with failure both as a science and as a discipline of social utility. Conversion, or the achievement of "insight" or "understanding," by itself is not enough. It may merely create a more sophisticated state of frustration for the individual.

This, for example, seems to be one of the conclusions that can be drawn from the studies of those few courageous researchers who have attempted to validate human relations training programs in industry. These not only indicate that "sensitization" programs for supervisors fail to improve organizational performance, but in some cases, the situation after training is worse than before! [14]

Unless the structure changes, the change in attitude has little lasting impact, and structural changes involve systematic alteration of the human organization through its controlling techniques and routines. A science of organization, if it is to be truly scientific, must be able to secure its successes without reliance on the emotional sophistication of the members of any given institution.

Changing the Organization

The basic assumption in the approach to human relations in industry outlined in this volume is that attitudes and emotional reactions, as well as productivity, are functions of the interactional situation, and this interactional situation represents the interplay of personality, methods, systems, and technology. Consequently, unlike the approach of the conversion school, facilitation of change should be primarily brought about by changing the inter-

[14] E. A. Fleishmann, E. F. Harris, and H. E. Burtt, *Leadership and Supervision in Industry: An Evaluation of a Supervisory Training Program,* Monograph no. 33, Bureau of Education Research, The Ohio State University, Columbus, Ohio, 1955.

actional system through changing the technological patterns, meaning the structure, the work flow and control system and, secondarily, by the transfer of personalities to situations within which their interactional patterns make it possible for them to adjust. Much research has been done to illustrate the subtle dependence of human relations systems on environmental and technological patterns and the ways in which entire social organizations change as a result of changes in one of these patterns.

Because it becomes possible not merely to place people in the organizational position for which their personalities fit them but also to define each organizational position in the same quantitative terms as the personality, one can define and prescribe a given type of personality for a particular organizational position. This means the organizational structure can be reinforced by an individual who is capable of carrying out the interactions needed to make it effective. By appraising the individuals in connection with the analysis of the organizational structure, through statistical techniques, one can determine whether a given problem situation is created by technical and structural stresses or by the personality limitations of a given individual.

In industry, by determining the areas of stress and the processes and techniques that control the relationships undergoing stress, it is possible to bring about substantial and significant changes in the relationships of people in the organization. Moreover, this can be done without requiring the conversion or master-minding of the individual to fit an investigator's understanding of human relations. No pressures for like-mindedness are generated. By changing layout, changing material handling, changing methods of keeping records, or changing a hundred and one things that are built into an industrial organization, a reorganization and re-formation of relationships can be achieved naturally and inevitably.

As observed before, the prescriptions of the management consultant, as the sermons of the boss who implores for more loyalty to the over-all goals of the organization, nearly always dissipate themselves. To obtain lasting change one does not try to change people, but rather to change the organizational constraints that operate upon them. If supervisor A has a tantrum whenever situation X occurs, his job can be changed so the behavior that is difficult for him is not required. It is unlikely that he will ever learn to tolerate situation X. Coordination breakdowns are constantly occurring between two departments. One can restructure department lines and shift the control system to eliminate this break in the work flow. It is unlikely, however, that stern warnings and pleas to the supervisor involved to "cooperate or else" will have really lasting effects. Similarly, committees will not resolve organizational faults. Appeals to managers to work harder cannot compensate for inadequately apportioned work loads or misplaced personalities. Malfunctioning compensatory channels can cause recurring crises that no amount of increased wages and fringe benefits will change.

Needless to say, to make such changes effective, one has to develop techniques to make sure the old patterns do not re-emerge through the natural tendency of systems of human relations to return to a previous state of equilibrium.

One recent field study provides a hopeful sign that this point of view is beginning to gain wider acceptance. Paul R. Lawrence, the author, studied the efforts of a grocery store chain to develop a changed organization structure:

> The principal organizational changes the top management group wished to make were in the overt behavior between superiors and subordinates at certain key spots in the organization. To succeed in effecting these changes, they had to get the members of their supervisory forces to actually change their interaction patterns—their customary conversational practices with their subordinates. Top management could not be content with gaining a mere intellectual understanding of what they wanted, nor would it be enough to secure merely verbal agreement with their plans . . . The on-the-job, moment-to-moment, verbal behavior of people had to change or the new organizational model would not become a reality. Because this overt behavior was the true test of the success of the change . . .[15]

Conclusion

The great advantage of this approach, of course, is that it does not seek miracles. More important, it begins to utilize scientifically the ways in which organizational changes have always been brought about. Whether it was the introduction of the loom or the use of steam as a source of power, the technique forced the individuals using it to reform their customary relationships; the only other choice would have been not to use the technique at all.

The study of history also shows that lasting changes in civilizations have come about primarily as a consequence of man's need to adapt to a changing environment or technology. This does not mean there is always a one-to-one correlation. Rather, it indicates that if the technological change necessitates a change in interaction, the organization of the society will change with it. Mere substitution of one object or one technique for another that does not modify the interaction of individuals will have no discernible effects.

Personalities cannot be thought of as mere ciphers in the changing structure of organizations. The technique, the process, or the procedure, whatever

[15] Paul R. Lawrence, *The Changing of Organizational Behavior Patterns,* Harvard University, Graduate School of Business Administration, Cambridge, Mass., 1958, p. 130.

is included in technology taken in its broadest sense, sets up potentialities for interaction. Too often a new method or control fails to work because the personalities who must operate it are unable to carry on the required interaction patterns. Moreover, personalities in their turn must have available techniques to obtain full expression of their needs for interaction within their job, and frequently, the presence of such personalities makes possible the acceptance of the technological innovation. Thus, personalities and the patterns of work flow that complement them are both necessary to achieve a permanent change in organization.

Too often the great leader or outstanding executive is considered without concern for what he does within the framework of the organization that makes him "great." Such people rise and fall, but unless there are changes in jobs and work-flow systems, the organization returns to its state of equilibrium no matter how much appearances suggest that a new state has been achieved.

The point of view taken in this book leads inevitably to the bringing about of change through organizational means. In fact, the cases and analyses cited strongly support the position that no method of conversion can overcome the continuous impact of the organizational system on the individual. The triumphs claimed for training in sensitization are the results of uncontrolled experiments. They ignore the organizational situation existing at the time and the way the individual's personality and temperament factors are utilized within it.

This does not mean the authors consider training in administrative skills, including interaction patterns, of no value to the individual. On the contrary, they are teachable within the individual's personality limitations, just as anyone can be taught to play baseball or hit a golf ball with a fair degree of accuracy. No one, however, would be so deluded as to think he can turn each individual into a professional, and, in the same way, the authors think the advocates of conversion have confused "self-concepts" with the learning of skills. Instead of worrying the novice ball player with the "right point of view," he should be taught the mechanics of the game and the various alternative patterns of behavior that different situations in the game require. If he learns the skills by arduous practice, it then becomes the manager's task to fit him into a team with eight other players.

But no matter how well schooled the players are, their organization is based on the technology. To change it, following the lesson of history and the authors' point of view, it must be attacked at its base. This provides a great practical advantage in securing change because the logic of technology has a much sounder foundation than the logic of conversion. Although everyone can become emotionally involved in "his" solutions to technical problems, at least this method has the external possibilities of proof by which a disagreement can usually be resolved. Changing techniques is, therefore, less threatening than the indictment of an individual for lack of "understanding." It is also more powerful.

In fact, the introduction of change in an organization is accomplished best by varying two of the three basic factors that are determinants of the total system. Most commonly, the techniques can be altered to solve a business problem. Realizing that each such technique sets up constraints on the interaction of the responsible individuals, the layout, the methods, and the procedures should be examined to see what quantitative differences in relationships will ensue. There are direct effects on the individuals immediately concerned; what changes in their interaction patterns will do to other people with whom they also interact must also be considered. If the redistribution of the resulting interaction creates no major displacements for the individuals through lack of satisfactory outlets and at the same time does not create greater pressures for people who are temperamentally incompatible, it is possible to proceed. If displacements and increased pressures might result, the plan must be examined to see if it can be modified to eliminate those difficulties or if a calculated risk must be taken because of the severity of the problem.

Alternatively, the natural process of change in every organization makes possible a new positioning of individuals within the same organizational framework. Deaths, retirements, resignations, and growth of the enterprise enable transfers to be made. These position changes involve personality shifts within the technological system of the organization. By careful choice of individuals for transfers, relationships within the company can be shifted, and thus the work flows in which they play a part can also change.

Through either means, or both, the organization begins to change, bringing about changes in the formal structure of authority. Changes in the latter are usually secondary, because the personalities and what they do determine the real power structure that is inaccurately represented by the charts and job descriptions.

The science of change, in a systematic sense, awaits the future. The cases available and the evidence at hand suggest that the understanding of business organizations can lead not only to a comparative study of corporate enterprise, but more broadly and significantly to a comparative science of institutions, national and international, in every existing society. Using the tools of interaction measurement, the accidental can be isolated from the essential, and in the future a means of developing organizations can be established that fits the needs of the people involved, rather than, as at present, creating an organizational strait jacket that makes it difficult to use people's abilities to their full capacity. Perhaps the authors have been too harsh on the advocates of conversion. It is because, like many others, they are unconscious advocates of the theory that man is made for and to be made over for organization. Surely the time has come when organization should be designed for man.

CHAPTER XII

NEW RESPONSIBILITIES for EXECUTIVES[1]

Custom and convenience dictate that the last chapter of a book make some efforts in the direction of summarization. This place is often also reserved for prophecy and the broader questions of values and propriety ignored in earlier chapters. This chapter endeavors in small measure to do these things while concentrating on the responsibilities of the executive toward his organization and the individuals who comprise its membership.

THE NEW PROFESSIONAL MANAGER: SPECIALIST OR GENERALIST?

Along with the shift in power from owner-entrepreneurs to professional managers, the job of manager has changed immeasurably from the days of the robber barons. Most of the great enterprises of the past were built primarily on finance. Manufacturing, selling, technological development, even the managing of people, were secondary to the art of trading.

Each merchant prince's organization had managers on the lower levels, men who ran the factories or the branch banks, supervised the mines, captained the vessels, or kept the books. But success came from capacity to make a shrewd deal, not from competence in these areas. Whether the businessman loaned his money out at 260 per cent or financed a conquest by some princeling to get monopolies on all the major commodities of the conquered kingdom, his predominant skill was in how to make money.

Today success as a manager is both different and more difficult. Not that return on investment is no longer a primary consideration, but the means of achieving it are changing and probably permanently. The countervailing power to "free exploitation" that built the business empires of the past has been the growth of governmental controls, given political effectiveness by

[1] An expanded version of the material in this chapter first appeared in *Nation's Business*, vol. 47, no. 5, p. 58 ff. Copyright, 1959, by *Nation's Business.*

the multiple interests of the "public" as consumer, producer, and investor. In a consumer economy, each enterprise becomes vulnerable to the shifts in popular attitude and demand.

As a consequence, specialists and specialties have grown in numbers and importance only within this century. The pre-eminence of finance has not been lost. It is only that other aspects of management, formerly subordinate, have gained equal rank. Manufacturing, sales, advertising, law, industrial relations, and personnel are the prime contenders, but, in the new technology, other specialties are making their way to the front. Controls and data-processing, marketing, public relations, engineering, and that catch-all phrase, research, are moving up to prominence, with sound reasons for inclusion of each in the managerial armory.

As specialization grows, top management jobs are increasingly being filled by specialists. Sometimes the specialist is chosen because the major problem of the corporation is in a particular area: a financial man with the necessary skills to manage complex relations with banks, insurance companies, and underwriters in a growth company; a salesman, if top management has to sell its products to the top managements of its customers. More often, though, the mastery of a specialty brings with it habits of mind that can be applied to other fields.

This trend to specialization conflicts with the long-held belief that the successful manager must be a generalist. If this be taken to mean that the higher up one goes, the greater the number of specialties he must know, the statement is self-evident. A successful manager must thoroughly understand the various components of the business.

But today, it is sometimes held that a manager no longer needs this kind of knowledge, but only an acquaintance with or a smattering of information about every subject. In business schools, where the debate is pressed most actively, there are attempts to provide an understanding of the generalization, but they differ radically on whether a series of specialties should be thoroughly taught or whether this aim should be subordinate to instilling in the incipient manager a "feeling for the broad approach."

Whatever the outcome of the debate in universities, the nature of professionalism means that in practice a manager has to master the fundamentals of the various specialties. He must be able to examine the premises of each because no one can make effective decisions on data if he does not understand their limitations.

Cross-cutting these specialties, and in some instances intermingled with them, is another set that makes the manager what he is, the arts concerned with organization and administration. It is worth emphasizing that these are arts, because, contrary to belief, little effort has been made and little support given to research that might put them on a scientific basis. Most people are content to take the folk knowledge of the practitioners at face value. They talk of line and staff, the span of control, committee management, decentralization and outline rules by which the manager delegates, communicates, and coordinates as if the statements were based on scientific laws.

Just as medicine is both scientific and clinical, so is management. In medicine, however, concentration on basic research which is supported by foundations and industry is bringing more and more diseases under scientific control. The sole dependence on clinical experience that characterized the physicians of the past is thereby steadily reduced. In organization and administration, the clinician reigns almost undisputed. Yet who shall say that the diseases of government and business institutions—bureaucracy, inflexibility, monopoly of capital, gigantism—are not a greater threat to civilization?

The professionals argue, if thermonuclear intervention does not make the question academic, that scientific investigation will someday be fostered. Without it, control over institutions and preservation of their stability can never be attained, because human personality within an organizational frame, contrary to some, can too easily become an explosive, injuring itself and all its fellows. Hopefully, then, a manager in A.D. 2061 will have at hand the technical skills now emerging.

Look at his job today. Whether he is chief accountant, foreman, training director, district sales manager, or president, he has to have, in addition to the technical know-how of the traditional specialties, a mastery of a series of administrative techniques, the patterns of behavior by which he manages his relations to others to get things done. Considerable attention is paid in the literature to some of these, but almost entirely on the clinical level. Executives have to supervise, a term that covers a multitude of subsidiary patterns such as delegate, issue orders, discipline, run meetings, etc.; but also, during the working day, they may have to negotiate, interview, train, sell, advise or consult, pass on information, or make a speech. The list is by no means inclusive, and the phrases are only intended to be suggestive.

Not one of these administrative patterns of behavior is confined to a single specialty such as finance, personnel, or sales. Interviewing is done in a variety of styles for quite different purposes by foremen, controllers, engineers, the general manager, or the various members of the personnel department. And so with others. Each style or subtype can be accurately and objectively defined, but little systematic research has been carried out.

The manager of the future, then, will have been trained in the administrative specialties, have a repertory of each and a solid grounding by which he can recognize the situations in which they should be applied. And this latter knowledge, because situations are necessarily organizational in the proper sense, will be based on a science of organization and, in the sense the term was used by Henry Dennison, Mary Follet, and other pioneers in the field, on the professional practice of organizational engineering.

The Meaning of Organization: A Summary

In recent times, organization has become a much-abused and misunderstood term, largely because too often it is associated only with charts, procedures, and job descriptions. Since Elton Mayo started to write about industry, it has been fashionable to oppose "formal" with "informal" organization, the chart being defeated by the personality. This is, of course, a meaningless kind of controversy. One cannot, as Mary Follet insisted long ago, "divorce the person from the situation."

To make the situation more confusing, Mayo and his followers made the "informal" a catch-all for everything not on the organization chart. The flows of work determined by the technical process, the procedures that order the flow of paper, and the physical layout of plant and office were tumbled together into the same category with the individual's personality. Of the entire technological framework, only who reports to whom and the resulting departmental groupings were left. In such an artificial division, the organization could not be treated as a system.

What is organization? In essence, it is a group of people whose relationships are mutually dependent, and thus it is a system. This basically means that what one individual does affects the other. Watching the give-and-take of individuals, and the interaction that goes on between them, the ways in which each personality acts and reacts can be seen. Each represents a force with varying interactional needs that must be taken into consideration.

When people come together in an organization, the contacts in which they interact do not occur at random. For what has to be done on the job orders the relationships, sets up the sequence, and specifies the time and place. These orders of events make up the work flows and, remembering that the term includes the systems and procedures as well as the movement of material through production, work flows are the arrangement of tubes, beakers, and piping that control the rates at which the processes of human interactional chemistry occur. Change the arrangement but keep the same compounds (people), and a new organization or a new experiment is underway.

Time provides the measure of the interaction. Whether the work flows involve materials, paper, or people, timing is a consequence of the technical or procedural orders. The work flows specify who is to be seen, when, and where, and they necessarily state how often the particular action must be taken. The accounting calendar and the administrative controls outline a framework of interaction and activity for each day, week, month, quarter, and year. Thus, there is a regularity in relationships, varied to some degree by how long each contact lasts and how many contacts are needed to keep the work flow moving.

Here, the administrative patterns are the controlling factor, varied by the differences in personalities. The weekly report on variance requires checking the reasons for deviation with two foremen; renewing the lease on Building 10 at the end of the year involves negotiations with the owner and his attorney; reviewing the performance of subordinates semiannually means a long interview to get agreement on how they will improve their performance. When a crisis occurs or is anticipated, administrative behavior is used again to restore the balance. What is done and how long it lasts depends on individual skills and whether the personalities involved have been upset themselves and are reacting temperamentally.

Beyond the crises such as machine breakdowns, late delivery, errors in control reports, or absenteeism, changes are also taking place. New methods, new procedures, or new personalities require readjustments and often reorganization of relationships. When these occur, the manager must use his skills to re-establish a smoothly working organization and reduce disturbance to a minimum.

Externally, there are similar processes. Crises occur in relationships to other organizations with which the company is interdependent, such as customers, financial institutions, suppliers, unions, stockholders, governmental agencies, and the community. Because of these, there may be systematic changes in the pattern of adaptation that require internal reorganization to compensate for what has taken place.

The manager, consequently, is concerned with maintaining the stability of his organization, restoring it to its former working system after a crisis, or assisting it to adapt to change. He has the technical and administrative means at hand. Assuming there is no major technical weakness in quality or acceptability of product, his primary emphasis is on the management of the interaction of the people who have to do the job.

The science of organization that the manager of the future will possess will enable him to predict what effects he can anticipate on the people and their relationships to one another when change is introduced. From the data he will have available, he will know what steps to take to produce the most effective organization and the maximum productivity from his people. The technological system and the interactional requirements of the individuals operating it will be jointly engineered. Organizations will no longer, as at present, provide a Procrustean bed for personalities.

THE MORAL PROBLEMS OF THE EXECUTIVE

The growth of such a science will facilitate a major shift of emphasis in society. Even today there are signs of a beginning, but as the professional manager consolidates his position, he will have to face openly the moral character of his job. Decisions, of course, will be based on objective evidence, but as an organization engineer, the problem of choice and the moral responsibility for choice will become more evident. The manager will have to calculate the chances of success and weigh the alternatives on the basis of his evidence.

In the past the businessman as owner was primarily concerned with the acquisition of wealth. The codes of ethics available to guide him dealt with his personal relations to his fellows and were completely unrelated to any organizational situation. Whether he followed moral precepts or not, the choices in what he did or authorized were fairly clear.

The managers who worked for him took his orders and had no responsibility of their own. Now, the moral situation has altered fundamentally. The religious codes that deal with personal behavior and personal indulgence touch only the periphery of the professional manager's job today.

Chester Barnard, former President of the New Jersey Bell Telephone Company and the Rockefeller Foundation, raised the whole question of organizational and administrative morality in his essay, "Elementary Conditions of Business Morals." [2] He mentions by way of introduction that from his own experience as a manager, "Judeo-Christian ethics . . . seem to have . . . little application or relevance to the moral problems of the world of affairs." He quotes Alfred North Whitehead as saying, "a sense of responsibility for the continuance of a social system is basic to any morality. Now this form of responsibility is almost entirely absent from Christianity." Whitehead went on to explain that because the "Hebrews had no inde-

[2] Chester I. Barnard, *Elementary Conditions of Business Morals,* Committee on the Barbara Weinstock Lectures, University of California, Berkeley, 1957.

pendent state to govern" and, it could be added, no large enterprises of any sort to manage, "a man cannot be blamed for failing in his period to consider what there was in his period no occasion for considering."[3]

Barnard comments on attending a conference held by the Federal Council of Churches of Christ that was trying to deal with this and related problems: "I observed that whenever the discussion related to public or business affairs, the assumptions as to the nature of such affairs seemed to me quite unrealistic. Whenever an attempt was made to apply a moral precept, it seemed to me to be substantially irrelevant; and what seemed to me the essential moral dilemmas of business and public affairs were evidently not contemplated at all. Why? Because, I thought, the facts of business life were not available."

Barnard then points out that "adherence to organizational interest, to correct procedure" is moral because the decisions that have to be made are governed by feelings of right and wrong. When problems of responsibility come up—whether they are technical, as in the case of an engineer deciding on the "proper" limits of safety, or administrative, as when a manager comes in on a Saturday because people are working on a special assignment—there are moral issues. People talk about "loyalty to the company," about the "duties" of the job or "obligations" to others without perhaps fully realizing that they are talking about morality. Barnard emphasizes that business managers too frequently are at a loss when such matters are discussed, because they have no explicit guides to which to appeal.

Yet, numerous moral decisions have to be made every day. A department head has been with the company thirty-five years and only has five more to go before retirement at his full pension. He is a major obstacle in modernizing the department even though he works hard and faithfully. Stubborn and difficult, he persists in doing things his way and fights the introduction of changes that are competitively necessary. What should be done?

The mechanical engineering department of a company, as a matter of procedure and technical pride, insists on producing a completely detailed set of engineering drawings and blueprints for a prototype machine. Both the project engineer and the client company for whom it is being made are violently opposed to this, pointing out to the head of mechanical engineering that they are sure substantial changes will have to be made before manufacturing can proceed.

The management of a large company has been secretly acquiring the stock of a smaller rival, yet, both the chairman of the board and the president

[3] *Dialogues of Alfred North Whitehead* (as recorded by Lucien Price), Little, Brown & Company, Boston, 1954.

are well known in business circles for their impassioned speeches in favor of free enterprise.

Are these in conflict?

These examples by no means cover the wide variety of moral problems that managers encounter, but they illustrate that morality is not simply a question of the personal ethics of the Ten Commandments. Managers must accept moral responsibilities. They will be aided immensely by the development of the science of organization and administration because with its aid the issues on which moral and professional decisions are based can be formulated.

The manager of the future may thus become a leader in the development of a new morality. As a professional, there is no way he can avoid doing so. Society will never return to the ancient pastoral and agricultural technology that conditioned the outlines of the existing system of religious ethics. And the corporate revolution will not be reversed.

Therefore, a beginning must be made now. Moral decisions have to be made every day. Managers cannot continue to be largely unaware of the body of moral principles they practice intuitively, but which differ for each as their organizational positions differ. This does not mean the traditional morality of personal relations learned in childhood should be neglected. However, it should be supplemented and made part of a working ethics for a corporate civilization that will be useful in every action in life.

Like it or not, the professional manager will be the means by which this transformation takes place. Because he will learn to take moral responsibility for his actions as a manager knowingly, by the nature of his organizational position he will assume a similar responsibility for the society in which he lives. This must extend beyond national borders. Because organizationally all societies are now interdependent, the technology which others take from us must be accompanied by a living morality to implement it for all the peoples of the world.

INDEX

Accounting techniques, 69–72
Activity, level of, 138
Activity periods, 118–119
Administrative orders, 3
Administrative patterns, 52–54, 55, 57–59, 61, 64, 67, 79, 209, 211
duration of, 57–61
frequency of, 56–61
Anomie, 11
Anthropology; *see* functional school of anthropology
Apathetic groups, 86–87, 92, 96, 97
supervision of, 95
Arensberg, C. M., 162, 163*n*, 200*n*
Argyris, Chris, 4, 5*n*, 10, 191, 192*n*, 199*n*
Assembly lines; *see* crews and assembly lines; long assembly lines
Attitude questionnaires, 153

Bard, P., 156*n*
Barnard, Chester, 13, 212–213
Bavelas, Alex, 200
Brayfield, Arthur H., 153*n*
Burtt, H. E., 201*n*

Calkins, Robert D., 1, 13, 14*n*
Cannon, W. B., 156*n*
Carroll, V., 149*n*
Chapple, Eliot D., 9*n*, 55*n*, 118*n*, 120*n*, 150*n*, 173*n*
Chart of Accounts, 70, 77
Coch, L., 200*n*
Collective bargaining, 85, 171, 172, 178, 186, 187, 188
Committees, 167
Compensatory behavior, 156, 174
Compensatory mechanisms, 164–167
Compensatory reactions, 158, 160, 161, 162, 163, 165, 166, 168
Comprehensive medicine, 150
Concentration; *see* functional concentration
Conservative groups, 85–86, 87, 96, 170
supervision of, 96
Consultative management, 199
Controller, 71–72
Controls, 41–43
see also organization controls
Conversion, 191–192, 193, 195–196, 201
Coon, Carleton S., 9*n*
Counseling, 104–105
Crews and assembly lines, 90–91
see also homogeneous crews; long assembly lines
Crisara, Robert, 184*n*
Crockett, Walter H., 153*n*

Dalton, Melville, 146*n*
Davis, Keith, 193*n*
Decentralization, 66
limited by personality, 102–104
Delegation, 55, 66
Dennison, Henry, 210
Dickson, W. J., 154*n*, 165*n*, 196*n*, 197
Direct costing, 78
Disequilibrium, 164, 168, 182
Dollar component, 76–77
Dominance, 121–126, 138
Dreyer, Harold, 179*n*, 180*n*
Drucker, Peter F., 7, 8*n*
Durkheim, Émile, 11

Emotional reactions, 149
Emotionality, pathological, 147
Employee health, 142–151
Environment, 19
Equilibrium, 155–159, 160, 161, 162, 163, 164, 165, 166, 168, 172
see also disequilibrium; morale
Erratic groups, 83–84, 87, 89, 96, 97
supervision of, 94
Exception principle, 44
Executive neuroses, 142

Executive work flow, 48–55
 see also work flow

Fatigue, 195
Faunce, William A., 81*n*
Financial statements, 70–71
Fisher, Lloyd H., 8*n*
Fleishmann, E. A., 201*n*
Flexibility, 139
Follett, Mary Parker, 67, 210
Forecasting, 78
Formal organization, 197, 210
 see also organization theory
French, J. R. P., 200*n*
Freud, Sigmund, 195
Friedman, M., 149
Functional concentration, 20–21
Functional school of anthropology, 196

Gardner, Burleigh, 180*n*
Ginzberg, Eli, 147*n*
Grievances, 84, 85, 86, 92, 93, 173, 175, 176, 180, 181, 182, 184, 185, 190
Group decision, 189
Group dynamics, 199–200
Group formation; *see* technology and group formation
Guest, Robert, 38, 39, 91, 108*n*

Harris, E. F., 201*n*
Hawthorne Revisited (Landsberger), 195
Hawthorne Studies, 195–199
Health problems; *see* employee health
Hesitancy, 139
Hinkle, L. E. Jr., 143*n*
Homans, George, 81
Homogeneous crews, 89–90
 see also crews and assembly lines
Human relations
 conflict of, 6–8
 emergence of, 3–6
 and manager's job, 66–67
 and organization, 189

Incentive plans, 182, 183
Indispensability, 92–93
Industrial relations, 80
Informal groups, 82
Informal leader, 87–88
Informal organization, 40, 197, 210
 see also organization theory
Informal relationships, 196–198
Initiative, 127–128, 138
Interaction, 19, 37, 38, 39, 44, 45, 48, 51, 54, 55, 56, 57–59, 62, 64, 66, 67, 75, 77, 81, 83, 89, 90, 97, 99, 122, 125, 132, 133, 136, 150, 158, 159, 160, 164, 165, 171, 185, 186, 197, 200, 204, 211
Interaction patterns, 100, 105, 106–108, 111, 120, 126, 129, 134, 145, 147, 155, 158, 160, 161, 162, 168, 174, 183, 187, 190, 196, 201–202, 205
Interactional dimensions, 101
Interactional psychiatry, 150
Intergroup relations; *see* union-management cooperation

Janet, P. M. F., 195
Jaques, Elliott, 199, 200*n*
Job description, 44, 67, 75–76, 98, 102, 112
 see also superintendent's job description
Job redefinition, 108–110
Job requirements, 101–102
Jobs, diversified, 110–112
Jones, Bassett, 153*n*

Kahn, Robert L., 4*n*
Katz, Daniel, 4*n*
Katz, Robert L., 192*n*
Kerr, Clark, 8*n*
Komarovsky, Mirra, 8*n*
Kuhn, James, 92–93

Landsberger, Henry, 195, 197, 198*n*
Lawrence, Paul R., 203
Lesieur, Frederick, 172*n*
Listening ability, 138
Long assembly lines, 91–92
 see also crews and assembly lines
Long-range planning, 78
Lowie, Robert, 196

MacGregor, D., 162, 163*n*
McMurray, Robert N., 7*n*
McNair, Malcolm, 6, 7*n*
Maier, Norman, 200
Malinowski, B. K., 195, 196
Management; *see* union-management co-operation
Manager, professional, 207–210
 moral problems of, 212–214
Management accounting, 42*n*, 72, 77
Managerial jobs, production standards for, 46–68
Matarazzo, J. D., 120*n*, 137*n*
Matarazzo, Ruth G., 137*n*
Mayo, Elton, 4, 5, 11, 81, 195, 196, 198, 210
Mead, Margaret, 6
Melman, Seymour, 46*n*, 47
Mental health, 142, 143
Metcalf, H. C., 67*n*

Morale, 152–169
effect of outside organizations on, 163–164
and equilibrium, 155–159
a management responsibility, 168–169
an operational concept of, 159–160
traditional concepts of, 152–155
Multidirectional communication, 189
Murchison, C., 156*n*

Nonresponse situations, 126–127
Nyman, R. C., 167

Obsessive thinking, 195
Organization
in action, 100–102
defined, 99–100
and employee health, 142–151
health problems in, 148–149
meaning of, 210–212
Organization behavior, 1–17, 194
Organization charts, 3, 98
Organization controls, 69–78
real meaning of, 72–74
responsibility for, 112
see also controls
Organization design, 8–9
and work flow, 18–45
Organization man, 10–16
Organization Man, The (Whyte), 10
Organization, science of, 19–21
Organization theory
formal, 2, 9
informal, 9–10
see also formal organization; informal organization
Organizational change, approaches to, 189–206
Overhead, 46–48
Overeagerness, 139

Parkinson, C. Northcote, 47*n*, 65
Parkinson's Law (Parkinson), 47
Participative management; *see* consultative management
Permissive atmosphere, 121, 199
Persistence, 139
Personality, 61–62, 102–104
evaluation of, 114–141
management check list for appraising of, 137–141
observation of, 117–118
Personality and Organization (Argyris), 10
Personality problems, 114, 142, 148
Personality traits, 137, 138–139
Ponder, Quentin, 108*n*
Pressure groups, 170
Production standards; *see* managerial jobs
Productivity; *see* union-management cooperation
Professionalism, 208
Psychiatry, use of in business, 142–145, 147–149, 150–151
limitations of, 143–145
Psychological tests, limitations of, 114–117

Quality control, 74–75
Quantitative criteria, 16–17, 41, 44
Quickness, 127–128, 139

Radcliffe-Brown, A. R., 195, 196
Reactibility, 147
Resonance factor, 80
Responsibility accounting, 78
Roethlisberger, F. J., 4, 154*n*, 165*n*, 180*n*, 196*n*, 197
Rogers, Carl, 198, 199
Rosenman, R. H., 149
Routines, 13–14, 160

Saslow, G., 120*n*, 137*n*
Sayles, Leonard R., 83*n*, 93*n*, 170*n*, 176*n*, 177*n*, 181*n*, 182*n*
Scanlon, Joseph, 172*n*, 177
Scanlon Plan, 172, 186
Schoen, Ronald, 7*n*
Schultz, George P., 179*n*, 184*n*
Scott, W. H., 174*n*
Sensitization, 201, 204
Slichter, Sumner H., 173*n*, 176*n*
Smith, E. D., 167
Social cohesiveness, 81–82
Specialists, 43, 65, 73, 208
Specialization, 208
Spontaneous activity, 119*n*
Stabilization, 79
Staff-line relationships, 40–44
Statistical quality control, 74–75, 76
Stier, T. J. B., 120*n*
Strategic groups, 84–85, 87, 89, 96, 97, 170
supervision of, 95–96
Strauss, George, 31*n*, 146, 170*n*, 176*n*, 177*n*
Stress
definition of, 133–136
of dominance, 122–126, 141
and equilibrium, 155–162
at first meeting, 132–135, 140
of nonresponsive situations, 126–127, 140
sources of, in organization, 37–40, 105–106, 145–147, 162
Stress analysis, 135–136

Superintendent's job description, 49–50
  by patterns of activity, 52–54
  see also job description
Supervision
  selection and development of, 94–96
  and training and counseling, 104–105
Synchronization, 120–121, 126, 133, 134

Tawney, R. H., 195
Taylor, Frederick, 2
Taylor, Graham, 199*n*
Technology; *see* work flow
Technology and group formation, 88
Temperament characteristics, 148
Temperament traits, 137
Temperamental reactions, 140–141
Time dimension, 55–61, 63–64
Time, use of, 118–133
Training, 104–105

Union-management cooperation, 172–188
  impact of, on intergroup relations, 181–183
  impact of, on management, 178–181
  impact of, within the department, 183–185
Unions, 82, 84, 86, 87, 95
  as compensatory channels, 166–167, 170, 172, 176, 181
Unit work flow, 34–37, 41, 42, 43, 70, 73, 77
Urwick, L., 67*n*

Variable budgets, 78

Walker, Charles R., 91, 108*n*
Wallace, S. Rains, 116*n*
Warner, W. Lloyd, 196
Whitehead, A. N., 212
Whitehead, T. N., 163, 164*n*, 196*n*
Whyte, William F., 12*n*, 39*n*, 41*n*, 171, 175, 177, 179, 180*n*, 185
Whyte, William H., Jr., 10
Wilensky, H. L., 200
Wilensky, J. L. and H. L., 199*n*
Wolff, Harold, 143*n*
Work flow, 73, 75, 77, 78, 92, 183, 186, 187, 204, 211
  as basis for organization design, 18–45
  see also executive work flow
Work group, as redress channel, 82
Work-group behavior, 79–97
Work-load determination, 64–66
  manager's, 79–80
Worker satisfaction, 81–82
Worthy, James, 40*n*, 41, 70, 71*n*

Zaleznik, A., 91